How To Behave So
Your Dog Behaves
2nd Edition

Dr. Sophia Yin, DVM
with illustrations by Mark Deamer

How To Behave So Your Dog Behaves

Project Team
Editor: Heather Russell-Revesz
Indexer: Dianne L. Schneider
Design: Mary Ann Kahn

TFH Publications
President/CEO: Glen S. Axelrod
Executive Vice President: Mark E. Johnson
Publisher: Christopher T. Reggio
Production Manager: Kathy Bontz

TFH Publications, Inc.
One TFH Plaza
Third and Union Avenues
Neptune City, NJ 07753

Printed and bound in China
11 12 13 14 15   3 5 7 9 8 6 4 2

The Library of Congress has cataloged the hardcover edition as follows:
Library of Congress Cataloging-in-Publication Data
Yin, Sophia A.
How to behave so your dog behaves / Sophia Yin.
p. cm.
ISBN 0-7938-0543-0 (alk. paper)
1. Dogs-Training. 2. Dogs-Behavior. 3. Human-animal communication. I. Title.
SF431.Y56 2004
636.7'0887--dc22
2003025857

This book has been published with the intent to provide accurate and authoritative information in regard to the subject matter within. While every reasonable precaution has been taken in preparation of this book, the author and publisher expressly disclaim responsibility for any errors, omissions, or adverse effects arising from the use or application of the information contained herein. The techniques and suggestions are used at the reader's discretion and are not to be considered a substitute for veterinary care. If you suspect a medical problem consult your veterinarian.

The Leader in Responsible Animal Care for Over 50 Years!®
www.tfh.com

Praise for the first edition of

How To Behave So Your Dog Behaves

"Do not let the canine-oriented title fool the potential reader; this book should be of great help to novice animal trainers, or anyone wanting an introduction to the world of operant or 'scientific' animal training."

—Bob Bailey, co-founder of operant conditioning workshops in Hot Springs, AR and former general manager of Animal Behavior Enterprises, the first company to apply the principles of science to train animals

"The book is full of practical everyday and entertaining explanations of the scientific principles of dog behavior and learning. Some of them…are not only an accurate presentation of an important scientific learning principle, but had me laughing out loud; the information [is] accessible and memorable as well as informative."

—Dr. Janice Willard, DVM, MS, columnist for *Knight Ridder Tribune*

"It is often said that the only thing two dog trainers can agree on is what a third dog trainer is doing wrong. Not so! Now we can all agree that Sophia Yin's *How To Behave So Your Dog Behaves* offers much worth considering. Because she provides the rationale behind her techniques [the book] provides a framework people can use to examine their dog's behavioral issues. For those who have tried and failed to fix their dog's behavior problems the first two sections especially…are worth their weight in gold."

—Sergeant Steve White, police K9 trainer and consultant

"Dr. Yin combines her extensive scientific knowledge in veterinary science and animal training to present a practical, readable and scientifically sound text. [She] ensures that training is fun and that good science can be simple. Experienced or novice, you will learn something from this text."

—Dr. Daniel S. Mills, RCVS, Recognized Specialist in Veterinary Behavioral Medicine, University of Lincoln, UK

"There are books that emphasize normal behavior and learning theory, and there are books that teach your dog to obey obedience commands, but this book includes both in a logical and easy-to-read fashion—AND tells you what to do to correct things if your training program isn't going exactly as planned—AND gives you real-life situations where knowing and using that particular command would be helpful. That is rare. Dr. Yin knows how—and why—to train, and how to convey the finer points to the average dog owner who wants a better relationship with their dogs."

—Dr. Leslie Larson Cooper, DVM, Diplomate, American College of Veterinary Behaviorists

"Any student of canine behavior will be pleased to read about Dr. Yin's perspectives on living with and training a pet dog. It is delightfully well-written; meaning it has substance while being easy to read and remember."

—William E. Campbell, author of *Behavior Problems in Dogs, 3rd ed.*,
The New Better Behavior in Dogs, and *Dog Behavior Problems:*
The Counselor's Handbook

"Looking at your dog is to some extent like looking into a mirror. Dr. Yin's book is not only about dogs, but perhaps just as equally about us. Well-behaved dogs need good teachers, but are we? Dr. Yin describes the step-by-step methods needed in order to become a good teacher, and perhaps more importantly a good learner."

—Dr. Adam Miklosi, ethologist specializing in canine ethology and
dog-human communication, Eötvös University, Hungary

"Sophia Yin's approach to dog training is a perfect meshing of the scientific theory and practical application. What is most important is her introduction to trainers of the significance of the person's behavior and its effect on the dog's learning ability. Sophia has done this better than anyone else, emphasizing in a very readable fashion the lasting effects of people's actions on their dog's behaviors. This is an important book for anyone who wants to maximize correct interactions with the pet."

—Dr. Raymond Coppinger, PhD, Professor of Biology, Hampshire College,
author of *Dogs, A New Understanding Of Canine Origin,*
Behavior and Evolution

"Dr. Yin's book includes just about all you need to know to get the most enjoyment from your pet and to discourage it from developing bad habits."

—Dr. Edward Price, Professor Emeritus of Animal Science, University of
California, Davis, author of Animal Domestication and Behavior

"In a humorous and insightful manner, Dr. Yin presents a tremendously useful approach to understanding and changing dog behavior. Lively descriptions are given of a slew of powerful techniques to supply even the most naïve of pet owners with the armament needed to tame the most willful beast. Dr. Yin focuses on the positives: Her equation for success is: positive behavior + positive consequences = positive progress!"

—Dr. Marcie Desrochers, PhD, BCBA, Professor of Applied Arts in
Behavioral Psychology, St. Lawrence College, Kingston, Ontario

"*How To Behave So Your Dog Behaves* is directed towards the responsible dog owner who wants a good, well-behaved companion. Of the many good dog books on the market this one ranks among the best.

—Erich Klinghammer, PhD, Eckhard H. Hess Institute of
Ethology, Wolf Park, IN

Contents

Foreword

Your mission, should you accept: train two chickens to perform four tasks. You have five days.

Task 1—The bread pan pull—the chicken must grasp a loop tied to a bread pan, and with one continuous tug drag the pan two feet.

Task 2—The ping-pong peck—the chicken must peck a tethered ping-pong ball one time hard enough to sent it flying in a circle up and over its support post.

Task 3—The bowling pin strike out—the chicken must sequentially knock down a blue bowling pin and a yellow bowling pin in a specified order.

Task 4—The vertical dot spot—the chicken must peck a vertical 1-centimeter black dot on cue and only on cue three times in 15 seconds. The cue is a red laser dot.

Either bird can learn the tasks, but each must learn at least one task and one must perform three tasks in sequence. Time is of the essence.

Sounds like a joke, but this is serious business. It's the intermediate operant conditioning workshop, a.k.a. chicken training camp, taught by Bob Bailey and psychologist Marian Breland-Bailey. And trainers flock from all over the world to participate.

To be fair, we don't attend just for the opportunity to train a chicken, rather, we're here to learn the intricacies of a universal mechanism of learning called operant conditioning. Elucidated in the early 1900s by psychologist B.F. Skinner, this theory says that if you reinforce a behavior, it's more likely to occur again. If you don't reinforce it, it's less likely to occur. It's a simple idea, almost intuitive, but it is easy to bungle.

Our chickens have already been trained that a click from a toy clicker means food is coming, so we can use the sound to bridge the gap between the behavior we want and the food reinforcement. This bridging stimulus allows us to tell the chicken precisely when it's doing something right. Unfortunately for us, even a fraction of a second error in timing can give the chicken the wrong idea. We soon have chickens that peck our laser cue instead of our black dot, shake the loop tied to the pan instead of pulling it, and grasp the ping-pong ball rather than giving strong pecks.

An onlooker might attribute the incorrect behaviors to the dimwitted chicken, but the student trainers know better. As the Baileys constantly remind us, "You get the behavior you reinforce." We're familiar with these words. We've spoken them to our own students. "Your dog won't come when you call because he's getting better reinforcement from his puppy playmates." Or "Your horse keeps dragging you around because he gets to eat grass once he gets you to where he wants to go."

Now it's our turn to heed out own words. We desperately search for our mistakes and try to correct them. The clock is ticking.

You're probably wondering, why chickens? For one, their speed means that our timing must be impeccable. But in addition, say the instructors, "No matter how you slice it, the chicken is the best teaching tool for training animals. It offers more behaviors and more repetitions in the shortest amount of time." And they have the experience and records to prove it. Together the Baileys have trained over 140 species of animals and represent 103 years of animal training.

A hundred-plus years seems like a long time, but Marian and her now-deceased first husband, Keller, learned these techniques directly from the source. Among B.F. Skinner's first graduate students, they learned to gradually shape behaviors using positive reinforcement, and as scientists they learned to do something that most animal trainers omit—keep rigorous records.

We try to follow their example. During every training session, we take notes. How many times have we reinforced the correct behavior? What percentage of the time does it offer the correct behavior? By keeping these records, we can make better decisions on when to expect more from our bird and easily discover when we've messed up. We also record the number of times we reinforced at the wrong time. A few of these and we're back to square one. It's an uphill battle for us, but a few make it to the top.

On day five, it's time to show our bird's stuff. My bird has a weak chain of two behaviors that it can perform. In a sort of abbreviated mission, I set her down on the table for all to see and then hold my breath. She makes a beeline for the blue bowling pin and beaks it off the table. Then, like poultry with a purpose, she heads over to the yellow. Ponk! It's off the table. She turns to me expectantly. No treat yet. She searches for the second task, then sees it—a little white ball hanging a foot high. She struts over, cocks her head and bam! It flings over its post.

Click. Treat. Mission accomplished.

Chicken camp is where I first fully understood the power of positive reinforcement. It's where I learned that even simple animals could learn incredible tasks through trial-and-error learning, and where I observed that simple animals unmistakably make a conscious effort to solve problems. Since then, I have taken numerous classes in psychology, behavioral ecology, and comparative animal behavior. I have taught university (UC Davis) courses in domestic animal behavior for 5 years as well as lecturing internationally, supervised college students in research and training projects, attended a wide assortment of workshops dealing with behavior and training, and have trained many animals, ranging from rats, cats, goats, and dogs, to horses, ostriches, and giraffes. Because the principles that guide learning and behavior are universal across species, each new experience adds a new dimension to my understanding and makes me a better trainer, teacher, and researcher.

Few people have the opportunity to attend a chicken training camp to learn the finer points of animal training, or to take off and travel in a quest to study with the most knowledgeable teachers. On the other hand, everyone does have the opportunity to learn how to observe, understand, and modify behavior in their pets. They can see the universality of the principles guiding behavior, and apply those principles, all the while building better relationships between humans and their pets.

In this book, I hope to help you see the world of your pets differently, and to provide you the tools necessary to effect amazing behavioral change. This book is divided into four sections. While the ideal approach would be to read the book from cover to cover, each section also stands alone.

Section 1, called "Understanding Dogs," presents information on natural history, domestication, communication, and motivation that are essential to understanding how dogs behave, and helps you see your dog's point of view. It also includes exercises to help you observe your dog and come to your own conclusions about his behavior.

Section 2, "The Science of Learning: How to Modify Behavior in Your Dog, (or Cat, Horse, Rat…)," presents the practical aspects of learning theory. It includes examples spanning many species, both wild and domesticated, and includes exercises to help you apply the information to everyday life. It also includes a section on problem solving and provides a systematic way for dealing with unwanted behaviors in any species of animal, and converting them into acceptable behaviors.

Section 3, "The Five-Minute Guide to Basic Good Dog Behavior," goes over specific training exercises for dogs, as well as games you can play based on each exercise. There are a total of nine exercises; however, if you learn four really well—say please by sitting, watch-me, pay attention on walks, and come when called—you will have the tools to solve most problems that might arise with your dog.

Section 4, "The Five-Minute Guide to Common Canine Challenges," puts it all together by showing how you'd incorporate the information from Sections 1 to 3 when handing specific behavior problems, including barking, aggression to other dogs, chasing cats, barking at intruders, etc.

The Appendix includes a treat for advanced trainers and behavior enthusiasts—two landmark psychology papers that helped shape the field of applied animal psychology, as well as an interview with Marian and Bob Bailey, two key players in the early scientific revolution.

Lastly, while I hope to have provided a book that's clear, concise, and filled with interesting and entertaining examples, it can be extremely helpful to actually see behaviors change and have someone help you make those changes. For those who would like to see behaviors being modified and watch the training exercises from the book, please visit my behavior website at www.drsophiayin.com. It contains many free downloadable Quicktime videos, which illustrate various aspects of training and behavior. The site also contains additional questions and answers to help develop your training skills. I periodically update this website based on visitor questions.

Additionally, many of the exercises are shown in great detail in the instructional DVD that accompanies the MannersMinder Remote Reward Dog Training System. (More information is available on www.mannersminder.net.) The system includes a remote-controlled, automated food reward device, along with an extensive and carefully explained protocol on teaching dogs to target, lie down, go to place, stay in a down-stay with distractions, and ultimately behave better for you and for visitors who come to your house. It is the first dog training product or system that has ever undergone extensive peer-reviewer research prior to product release. It makes training otherwise boring exercises (such as down-stay), into a fun game for your dog.

I hope you enjoy the book and the games as much as my dogs and I have, and I hope you come out with a better understanding of and relationship with your dog.

Section 1

Understanding Dogs

Sometimes in life, solutions are simple. If you want to learn about vocal communication in squirrels, you go outside and find some squirrels. If you want to study mating signals in chickens, you observe male and female chickens. If you wonder how sparrows in different regions learn their songs, you study sparrows in different regions. This idea seems straightforward, but for some reason, when we want to know more about behavior in dogs, we suddenly look to wolves. "In a pack, wolves do this!" or "When wolves are exerting their authority, they do that."

One reason we turn to wolves is because we know relatively little about behavior in the domestic dog. While researchers have studied behavior in chimpanzees, chickens, squirrels, and many other animals in depth, domesticated dogs have received only a cursory look in most cases. Much of what we think we know is either extrapolated from wolves or is a product of personal impressions. Nevertheless, because even wolf packs behave differently under different ecological conditions, and because dogs have undergone changes due to domestication, if we want to understand dogs, we have to study dogs.

Chapter 1

Domestication and Behavior

Whenever someone tells me wolves are smarter, more athletic, and generally superior to domestic dogs, I look at my parents' Scottie, with her stubs for legs and her oversized cartoon-like head, and I see what they mean. We've turned out an odd assortment of dogs in the domestication process, ranging from teacup-sized door yappers and four-legged, floppy-eared low-riders to dogs who look like they are wearing coats that are three sizes too big. These are dogs who would have no business out in the wild.

Surprisingly, though, differences in behavioral tendencies and athletic abilities between dogs and wolves, as well as the inability to survive free of human provision, don't mean that domesticated dogs are inferior, degenerate, or mentally dim. If it did, then dogs would be on the endangered list and wolves would be overpopulating villages and cities in developing countries, instead of the other way around. To understand why dogs are as respectable a species as wolves, we first have to look at the process of domestication.

Definition of Domesticated and Tame

Domestication is the process occurring over many generations by which a population or species of animals becomes adapted to living with humans in the captive environment. During these many generations, the genetic composition of the population changes in order to make the adaptation possible. Domestic dogs are well adapted to living with humans; wolves, on the other hand, are adapted to living on expanses of land vast enough to support enough prey for them to eat. With habitat destruction, the number-one cause of extinction in animals today, many wild animal species, including wolves, are dwindling in numbers, and some are close to extinction. Species such as dogs that have adapted to living around humans are the ones most likely to survive.

While domestication is a process that takes many generations, **tameness** is a process that occurs within an individual's lifetime. In science circles, tameness describes an animal's willingness to approach humans, and is measured by the animal's flight distance. Tame animals have zero flight distance. That means you can walk right up to the animal and he won't flee. For instance, a 10-foot (3-m) flight distance is one where you can walk up to 11 feet (3.5 m), but when you hit 10 feet (3 m), the animal runs away. It is also important to note that animals can be domesticated but not tame, or they can be tame but not domesticated. For instance, dogs and cats that grow up in the wild or with little human handling when young are still domesticated, but because people can't get close to them, they are not tame. Birds such as the blue-footed booby of the Galapagos Islands, where animals have evolved free of predators, are not afraid of humans, and thus are tame but not domesticated. Animals can also be tame but aggressive. For instance, many dogs who are aggressive when you try to trim their toenails or clean their ears or who bark ferociously when pedestrians pass by the house, have a zero flight distance from humans—so they're tame, but in some situations they may bite.

How Dogs Were Domesticated

Dogs were domesticated from wolf-like ancestors somewhere between 14,000 and 15,000 years ago. A common idea is that humans purposefully domesticated dogs by stealing wolf pups from dens and then selectively breeding the ones they liked. For anyone who's raised wolf puppies, this probably seems like an impossible, labor-intensive task for man in ancient times. Studies at Wolf Park in Indiana—where wolves are bred in captivity, managed in naturalistic conditions, and studied scientifically—reveal that even pups born from tame wolves and raised in captivity become extremely fearful of humans starting around eight weeks of age. These puppies have to be hand-reared away from the pack well before 14 days of age. Additionally, after puberty, these now-adult wolves living in mixed-family packs become more aggressive due to their drive to be at the top. And, unlike domesticated dogs, who show signs of tension when vying for position, signs of imminent attack in wolves are often more subtle or even absent, because status is frequently gained more through opportunistic aggression. For instance, a wolf that is lowest on the totem pole one year may find a chance opportunity to topple the alpha wolf at any time. This ruthless system for climbing the hierarchal ladder dictates that all wolf interactions, including play, are chances for wolves to test each other for weaknesses. Consequently, play can suddenly break out into serious fights. Even when wolves are playing with humans who are sick or show

signs of injury, and even if they have known and liked these humans for years, the wolves may attack without warning.

An alternate hypothesis to the labor-intensive and potentially hazardous method of plucking wolf pups from the den and then hand-raising them is the model of self-domestication supported by Darcy Morey, as well as Ray and Lorna Coppinger. This hypothesis says that as humans moved into permanent settlements, they also developed trash sites that some wolves were able to exploit for food. Those that were the tamest or least fearful and best able to scavenge in this environment survived and reproduced better. Their pups inherited this degree of tameness and, in turn, survived better than their peers. In time, such populations of "village wolves" arose in many different settlements around the world. Due to the decreased fear in these village wolves, humans were able to interact with them easily. At first, they started playing favorites by tossing food to those individuals they liked best, with no specific goals for long-term artificial breeding programs. Then, at a more recent point in time, humans started to systematically select dogs for specific traits, which led to the development of many different dog breeds.

This method of self-domestication is supported by findings in other animals, as well as in the current state of the world's dogs. Three quarters of the world's dog populations live in developing nations as village dogs. Like the model of the village wolf, they scavenge from human discards and are considered pests rather than pets.

How Domestication and Tameness Go Hand in Hand

While domestication is a process that occurs over many generations and tameness occurs within an individual's lifetime, the two processes go hand in hand. In order to adapt to captivity, domesticated animals must be easier to tame than their ancestral counterparts. In other words, during domestication, humans purposely or inadvertently select animals that were easier to tame than their wild counterparts. This process of domestication was recreated in a long study performed by Dimitri Belyaev and his colleagues. Starting with commercial farm foxes, they bred and selected foxes solely for tameness over many generations to see if they could get a population that was as tame as the domesticated dog. The first generation of foxes was tamer than the wild relatives, but the foxes were still extremely fearful and dangerous to handle. In each generation, the researchers raised all of the pups the same way, and at seven to eight months, they scored them for tameness. In each generation, the ones that scored the highest were bred.

In this study, which spanned over 40 years and involved over 10,000 foxes, Belyaev and his colleagues found that tameness is clearly a hereditary trait. By the sixth generation of breeding for tameness, some foxes were eager to establish human contact. They whimpered to attract attention and sniffed and licked the experimenters like dogs. By the 20th generation, 35 percent were this tame. By the 30th to 35th generation, 70 to 80 percent of the population was docile, eager to please, and unmistakably domesticated. When tested in group enclosures, they competed for attention by snarling fiercely at each other. Even ones that escaped for several days eventually returned on their own.

In addition to the overall tameness that selection for the trait brought, this population of fox puppies developed an expanded window for forming social bonds. During the **sensitive period for socialization,** which occurs during the first days to months of life, animals learn which objects and animals are safe. Those objects and animals they don't contact extensively during this period tend to elicit a strong fear response down the road. After the sensitive period for socialization, the default setting in animals is to be fearful of new things, which is why wild animals don't come walking out of the woods to greet us like in an animated movie. When dogs and other domestic animals don't get enough positive exposure to humans and common everyday objects (such as people and their cars, hats, and umbrellas) enough to generalize their learning to similar things, then as they mature they may act as fearful as wild animals. Having an expanded window for forming social bonds provides more time for humans to assimilate into a dog's life, to form bonds with dogs, and to expose dogs to the many odd objects associated with human civilization. In the domesticated foxes, this window was nine weeks, compared to six in their unselected counterpart. This expansion was due primarily to a delay in development of the fear response that follows the **sensitive period for socialization.**

The changes in tameness level and timing of the fear period in Belyaev's foxes correlated with differences in hormonal and neurotransmitter levels. The delay in the development of the fear response was linked to lower levels in corticosteroids, which are stress hormones. The levels rose later and remained at a lower level in the farm foxes, so that by the 30th generation, the levels were approximately one-fourth that of the wild animal. Additionally, the adrenal glands, which produce corticosteroids, released fewer corticosteroids when these farm foxes were subjected to emotional stress. Serotonin, a neurotransmitter in the brain that inhibits aggressive behavior, was higher in the domesticated foxes than the wild ones.

Overall, the selection for tameness resulted in a fox that was tamer, less aggressive, and less reactive to stressful stimuli, as well as a fox that went through an expanded sensitive period for socialization. Consequently, domestication imparted a number of changes that allowed these foxes to adapt to living with humans.

What Does Domestication do to Individual Traits?

The big question is: Did domestication lead to loss of important traits or development of abnormal traits in our dogs? In general, domestication doesn't lead to new behaviors, abnormal behaviors, or loss of behaviors. Instead, it changes the stimulus threshold for the behaviors. That is, some behaviors exhibited in the wild ancestral counterpart require a different level of stimulation in order for the domestic counterpart to exhibit them.

For instance, both wolves and dogs have a prey drive, but the drive is more dangerous in the wolf. Thus, while tripping and squealing in the presence of a wolf could trigger an attack resulting in a fatal bite, the same reaction in the presence of most dogs just leads to a startled dog. Dogs generally need a relatively strong stimulus for prey attack, such as a fleeing rabbit or cat. Additionally, while some dogs chase cats and squealing kids, virtually all wolves hone in on infants and children, whether crying or still. They show this interest with a tail wag and a play face that fools observers into thinking they're friendly with children. Dogs, on the other hand, have had their prey drive adapted to human needs. Their drive has been directed to herding sheep, hunting with humans, or bringing back toys. And while some dogs, due to poor management, direct their prey drive toward passing bikes, joggers, and kids, in general, when trained and socialized properly, most dogs can be dependable in the presence of these stimuli.

Like wolves, dogs are also social animals with a hierarchy, but wolves have a heightened need to be on top. While dogs can exhibit dominance aggression toward humans, this behavior is relatively tempered and usually very predictable. It occurs in specific situations and in dogs who've been gradually showing escalating signs. As stated earlier, the behavior in wolves is more severe and opportunistic and consequently it is more dangerous and less predictable to those who are not experts in wolf behavior. As a result, in places such as Wolf Park that deal with tame, hand-raised wolves on a daily basis, caretakers that enter the wolf pens must enter in teams of two, and no one can enter if he or she is injured or sick.

Both dogs and wolves are territorial, possibly to the same extent, except that wolves tend to kill intruders if given the chance. To humans, dogs may seem more territorial than wolves, because dogs bark frequently. The difference here is that dogs have smaller territories, more frequent intruders, and a much higher tendency to bark overall. This means they actually have more need as well as opportunity to practice their territorial defense as well as a higher motivation to bark.

In short, domestication has converted dogs into animals that coexist well with man. Thousands of years of natural and artificial selection have molded their behaviors and made them, in general, easier to tame. They haven't lost their ancestral traits; instead, these traits have been modified to fit our needs. So, overall, while wolves are superior at living in the wild, when it comes to living with humans, clearly dogs come out on top.

Chapter 2

Dog-Dog Social Skills

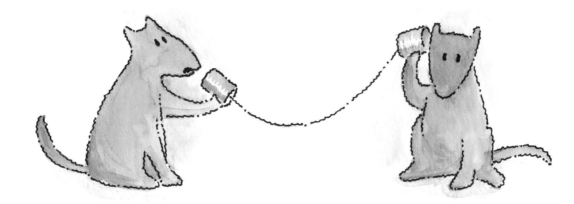

While dog parks are nice playgrounds for Rovers to romp and Spots to socialize, without proper supervision, squabbles can break out faster than pimples on a teenager. Luckily, physical injury is relatively rare, but sometimes the damage delves deeper than skin. A few bad experiences for an impressionable pup can progress to a lifelong fear of other Fidos.

So why do supposedly friendly Fidos fight with their own kind? Are they menaces in disguise, or are they good dogs who are just misunderstood?

It turns out that these dogs may indeed be friendly, but they are certainly not polite.

The Importance of Socialization Skills

Unbeknownst to some, dogs don't instinctively know how to behave in groups any more than people automatically know how to behave at posh dinner parties. Dogs learn their code of conduct through interactions with other dogs, and the most influential interactions occur when they're young. During the **sensitive period for socialization** and continuing afterward, dogs learn how to interact with others appropriately. In these early days, between 3 to 12 weeks in general (which probably varies across different breeds), they learn which animals and species are their friends; if they have enough positive experiences with other unfamiliar dogs, then they learn that dogs in general are friendly. If they miss out on this socialization they may instead fear unfamiliar dogs later on. They also learn the basics of being in groups. They practice with their littermates, as well as related adults. This is where they first discover that a bow and a bounce means the other individual wants to horse around, but get too rough or hurt your friend and suddenly all play comes crashing to an end.

Unfortunately, some pups cut out on classes early on by leaving the litter before about seven or eight weeks of age and moving into an environment with little dog contact for months. Down the road, when other dogs their age know when a look means to back off, these naïve newbies think everything is fair game. They tail terriers who want their own space and harass hounds by getting in their face—or when they see new dogs, they charge into the dog's personal space.

A good puppy socialization class starting as close to 8 weeks in age as possible (well before the puppy vaccination series is complete) would have done most of these dogs some good—assuming the class is well supervised and only appropriate play is allowed. These dogs would have learned that a yelp, a stare, or a lift of the lip all mean the same thing—"Go away." But even with puppy class and plenty of prolonged interaction in the litter, social skills may not be complete. Some pups still learn to be bullies by bossing around their peers, while others just never learn the proper way to greet others.

Like polite humans who casually shake hands the first time they meet, etiquette-trained dogs are relaxed when they greet others (Figure 2.1). Their head is somewhat level and eyes are averted slightly to the side. Their tail waves slowly at half mast back and forth or in a circle or arc. On the other hand, a head held high, accompanied by a direct stare, indicates an individual is aroused or excited. This stance is amplified by a tail fluttering high like a flag in the wind, which (surprising to some) is also an indicator of high arousal and does not necessarily mean that the "wagger" wants to make friends (Figure 2.2). If both dogs meet in this charged position and neither has the social smarts to back down, an explosion of barks, growls, and even bites

Figure 2.1

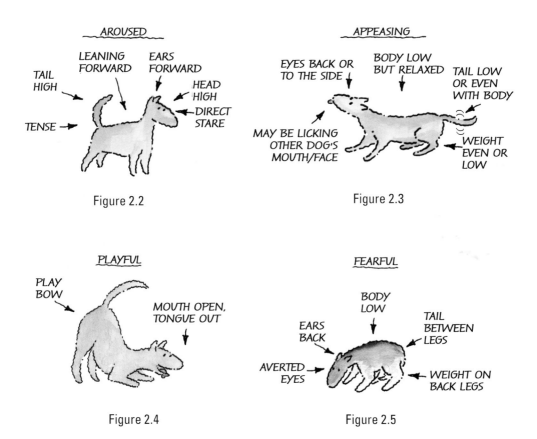

AROUSED

TAIL HIGH

LEANING FORWARD

EARS FORWARD

HEAD HIGH

DIRECT STARE

TENSE

Figure 2.2

APPEASING

EYES BACK OR TO THE SIDE

BODY LOW BUT RELAXED

TAIL LOW OR EVEN WITH BODY

MAY BE LICKING OTHER DOG'S MOUTH/FACE

WEIGHT EVEN OR LOW

Figure 2.3

PLAYFUL

PLAY BOW

MOUTH OPEN, TONGUE OUT

Figure 2.4

FEARFUL

BODY LOW

EARS BACK

TAIL BETWEEN LEGS

AVERTED EYES

WEIGHT ON BACK LEGS

Figure 2.5

may break out. But if the second dog remains relaxed or shows appeasing and submissive gestures—such as licking the other dog's lips, avoiding eye contact, lowering his body, and making himself small—he can telegraph his friendly intent and turn off a potential fight (Figure 2.3). In fact, the definition of submissive gestures is gestures designed to turn off aggression.

Some puppies are clearly friendly, but still create trouble because they think that all dogs want to play and everyone is happy to see them. Their forceful "hello" is a huge etiquette faux pas. A shy dog or one not used to such outward displays may take the loud greeting as a threat. He may run if he can, or make himself small and freeze in a fearful posture. Note that a fearful posture and an appeasing or submissive posture are not necessarily synonymous. When the dog is fearful he's more likely to be tense, hold his tail between his legs, and freeze or move in slow motion (Figure 2.5). Alternatively, the fearful dog may learn to growl and lunge to try to chase the bumbling Bowser away. Even a confident, mature dog who wants his peace can lose his cool.

This might still seem odd at first, but just imagine you're walking down the block and a stranger runs up and gives you a bear hug. At minimum, you'd be startled, but you might also yell and try to hit him. Then the next time you were walking and someone else approached in the same way, you might respond sooner to get him to back off. Similarly, dogs with one or two bad greeting experiences may be tense and nervous when new dogs come to greet them. When in doubt, they may elect to just keep these unfamiliar dogs at a distance.

This defensive barking and aggression is worse for dogs tied up or on leash, and here's why. If you were walking and saw a potential bad greeter, you could cross the street to avoid him. But if you were tied to a pole even on a long 20-foot (6-m) leash, you would know you couldn't get away. You might put on an aggressive display in hopes that he'll take

AGONISTIC PUCKER

FEAR GRIMACE

SIDES OF MOUTH PULLED BACK

Figure 2.6

a wide berth. Similarly, dogs on leashes are less secure. When they're not sure what will happen next, they may elect to practice their offense. Sometimes you can tell they're barking out of fear, because their body's leaning backward, and their snarl looks like a maniacal grin from ear to ear. But other times they learn that acting tough works well, so they lunge toward the other dog and growl with their lips forward in an **agonistic pucker** (Figure 2.6).

Preventing Greeting and Interaction Problems

Good puppy classes can prevent these greeting and interaction problems. These classes let the puppies play with appropriately matched playmates, but insert interruptions every few minutes by having owners call their pups and having them sit or lie down and focus on them until they are calm. This way the puppies learn to control themselves, and play doesn't get out of hand. Once the puppies respond to their owners and can remain focused on their owners, they can return to play as their reward. This game teaches puppies that interruptions and controlled play are good. Follow-up practice at the park or on walks is important as well, but make sure you and the other owner practice on a 6-foot (2-m) or longer leash at first so you can control the situation. The leashes should hang loosely at all times so that the dogs do not feel restricted or defensive. The dogs should greet offset or side to side, so that they don't lock gazes and start a fight. If they get overly excited or tense, separate them before trouble ensues by calling your dog and initiating a game of chase, in which your dog runs after you and gets a reward once he reaches you. In other words, you're redirecting your Rover's attention to a fun race.

Owners should also realize that they may need some one-on-one coaching in addition to the puppy classes, or may need practice with play partners who are appropriate for their puppy's size, energy, and social etiquette needs. For instance, some rambunctious pups may need to interact with larger, confident, relaxed adult dogs. Well-chosen adult playmates can make it clear to the puppy that pushy behaviors are not tolerated and that warning signals should be heeded; these types of adult dogs can do so without hurting the puppy or becoming overly irritated themselves.

Even after your pooch develops good etiquette, make sure you supervise all greeting and play the way you would supervise young children at the park. Toss a ball or keep walking if that's what you need to do to keep Rover out of trouble, and keep your eyes open so you can intervene before scuffles break out. By paying attention to the dogs and understanding their body language, the dog park and your walks will be a much more peaceful place to play.

Chapter 3

Dog-Human Communication

People frequently debate over which foreign language is the most difficult to learn, but based on a 2001 study by Nicola Rooney at the Anthrozoology Institute in Southhampton, UK, the answer is clear. The language humans have the most difficulty understanding and using is "dog." In this research, featuring 21 owner-dog pairs, the scientists videotaped the owners engaged in play with their pooches. In what surely would have been billed as a comedy, owners patted the floor, barked, bowed, shuffled their feet, slapped their thighs, crawled on all fours—anything to get their Rovers to romp with them.

The researchers identified common actions owners used to elicit play and then tested them to see which signals actually worked. As a result, they discovered that bowing or lunging while verbally encouraging your dog usually elicits play. Tickling Fido like he's a human infant or stamping your feet like you're dislodging a weeks worth of dried mud is likely to just get odd looks. Even patting the floor and clapping were less than 50 percent successful. And while barking at, kissing, or picking little Fido up may bring on some laughs from passersby, the dog usually fails to find these actions amusing.

The Real Lesson

Like all good plots, though, the real lesson was in the secondary message. The researchers found that although some actions tended to instill silent stares and others instigated play, the frequency with which the owners used the signals was unrelated to their success. In other words, owners tended to use unsuccessful gestures as frequently as successful ones. This means that we're oblivious to whether our dog is responding to us and whether our actions create the appropriate response. Instead, we babble and gesture blindly like actors practicing in front of the mirror for the next cattle call. If this were only about how we solicited play, it would provide a good laugh; but it also is about how we greet dogs on the street and how our bungling ways can get us bitten.

For instance, a dog owner once wrote to me:

"Our five-year-old Soft Coated Wheaten Terrier seems a furry, loveable, and inviting dog while he sits waiting outside the café for me to finish my morning latte. Trouble is, he's taken to growling and barking at some well-meaning types, especially those who come on too enthusiastically. This behavior is slowly starting to accelerate. What would be the best approach short of hanging a sign on him saying, "Beware, looks can be deceiving"?"

The safest approach involves going way beyond a sign warning people to stay away. Because you can never control how humans will act when they're unsupervised, a barricade keeping people out of your pooch's personal space, or simply keeping him with you and not tying him up at all would be the safest solutions. All would be well if humans heeded the two golden rules—*never pet a dog without the owner's permission, and always let the dog make first contact.* Instead, well-wishers approach him too quickly, crowd him too closely, or loom over him like a thunderstorm (Figure 3.1). Under this pressure, some dogs will freeze or shrink, pretending it's all a bad dream. Others take action—usually a reflex bark or low-level growl. A few successes and the message is loud and clear: When strangers approach, growl and bark to keep them away. Pretty soon, your sweet, slightly insecure dog has turned into a mass of defensive rumbling.

Approaching a Dog

Many humans can't understand why Fido would be afraid of them when they're obviously making friendly human gestures. Turn the tables, though, and the picture becomes clear.

Figure 3.1

How To Behave So Your Dog Behaves

Figure 3.2

Imagine you're afraid of spiders, and your friend shoves her humongous hairy tarantula in your face (Figure 3.2). If she simultaneously reassures you, "She's a friendly tarantula. See her amicable expression?" or "She can't cause harm, she's just an innocent baby," would you suddenly feel safe?

No—in fact, the only way you could get used to the spider is if you greeted it at your own pace. That means it would have to be on a table or in some other location where you could control your distance from it. Then, when you were ready, you could gradually approach for a closer look and even touch it. The same goes for dogs. All dogs are not outgoing or used to meeting many types of strangers, especially if they were already shy when you adopted them as a puppy or if they received poor socialization before and after you got them from the breeder. If you walk into a dog's personal space or even stand and reach out to touch him, he may feel threatened or be unsure of your intentions.

If, however, you stand straight up or crouch down on one knee while looking slightly away, then he can approach and sniff you at his own pace (Figure 3.3). Once he's relaxed, you can calmly pet him under the chin and neck or on the side of the front half of his body. Offering treats that the shy Fido can choose to take out of your hand while you avert your eyes (or look the other way) will speed the friendship process and will teach the dog to associate unfamiliar people with good things.

Often, people manage to get through the initial greeting with Fido okay, but then they make a quick or inappropriate move that scares him into snapping or running away. This is similar again to the situation with the giant spider. When you're finally comfortable enough to examine

Figure 3.3

and touch the tarantula, if it suddenly moves its mouthparts or waves one of its legs in the air, you might jump away out of fright. To you, these movements may conjure images of the tarantula leaping at you and taking a bite, whereas to the tarantula, the movements may just be a subconscious change in position or even a signal that it's your friend. The trick to ensuring that you don't frighten Fido even after the initial greeting is to gradually get him used to you in different positions. Avoid leaning or reaching over his head or grabbing and hugging him so he feels confined. Instead, move slowly and smoothly in order to give him a chance to back away. Most importantly, always be aware of the signals he's sending you with his body language. Is he tense and fearful, with eyes darting back and forth, or is he looking away while cringing submissively? Or is he yawning, flickering his tongue in and out of the front of his mouth, or panting with his lips drawn way back to the sides? These are signs of conflict or anxiety. In all of these cases, make sure you give him his space.

If his pupils are hugely dilated or pinpoint, and he's suddenly stiff with mouth closed and completely motionless or giving you a hard stare, it's a little late, because he's probably about to bite. But if you still have time, you can calmly avert your gaze and back away out of reach.

The body language you'd like to see when greeting a dog is one that says this whole business is ho-hum. The dog should remain relaxed, with his muscles loose rather than tense and stiff. His gaze should be steady and soft. His tail should either wag or hang loosely down, and he should never suddenly freeze.

Q&A: DOG COMMUNICATION
Can you answer these questions?

Q: How do you know when your dog wants to be petted?

A: He approaches you with a relaxed body posture. He may rub or lean against you. When you pet him, he stays relaxed and wags his tail, or he raises his head so that it meets your hand. When you stop, he may rub against you again to solicit petting or push his head against your hand.

Q: How do you know when your dog doesn't want to be petted?

A: He either doesn't respond to your petting, stiffens his body, walks away, or gives a body posture indicating fear. If these postures have no effect, he may growl or snap.

Q: Children who own friendly dogs are probably more likely to be bitten by their friends' dogs or unfamiliar dogs than those who don't own dogs. Do you know why?

A: Like the puppies in the last section who thought everyone was glad to see them, these children think all dogs are happy to see people. They treat other dogs the way they treat their familiar dog at home, instead of greeting the dog politely and respecting his space.

Q: Young boys are by far the most likely group of people to be bitten by dogs. Based on what you know about dogs, and about boys in this age group, can you guess why?

A: As a group, these young boys are loud, move quickly, and tend to ignore the dog's signals that he doesn't want to be bothered. Often, these kids also play games that trigger the dog to bite, such as rough-housing or jumping toward and away from dogs who are tied up. This is how you'd specifically train a protection dog to bite.

Chapter 4

Learning to Understand and Read "Dog"

Even though dogs are considered "man's best friend," and many of us have lived with dogs all of our lives, we really know relatively little about communication in dogs compared to what scientists know about other animals, such as vervet monkeys, brown-headed cowbirds, and even chickens. On the other hand, many of us have strong ideas about what different visual signals mean, and many of our ideas conflict. For instance, some might say a slow, circular tail wag means a dog is friendly, while others say it means he is about to attack. Or some state that dogs with ears that naturally stand up or those that are cropped are more likely to be "read" by other dogs as overly assertive, and consequently get into more fights. So who is right? What are the visual cues that indicate that attack is imminent? Are ears the most important signal of intention upon greeting, or are other signals equally (or more) important? Do dogs with tails that curl over their backs look more aggressive to other dogs and thus get into more spats? What do tail positions really mean?

Unless we systematically observe dogs, we'll never have the true answers, nor will we appreciate the wide range of canid body signals. Once we start looking closely at our own dogs, we will probably find that postures are more complex than we think. Maybe we'll find that signals vary predictably by breed and individual, or that dogs with certain features communicate better with other dogs and people.

Recording Behavior

For those who want to learn more about canine communication, you need not wait until scientists work it all out. The best way to learn to read "dog" is to observe and study behavior the same way a scientist would. That is, observe your dog's behavior, then describe and record what you see in a systematic manner.

Behaviors can be described in several ways. We can describe the behavior in terms of **motor patterns** (empirical description), which means we describe how each specific body part is moving; or we can provide a **functional description**, where we describe the behavior in terms of its function. For instance, if we say a dog greets in a dominant posture, this is a functional description. It indicates that we know the intention of the posture is to send the message that the dog wants to be higher ranked so he can have priority access to resources—and will use aggression to attain this. If we were instead describing the motor pattern, we would say the dogs has an upright body posture, head and tail held high, and ears erect.

When you're just learning about a species or you want to know more about a specific aspect of visual communication, it's best to use motor pattern descriptions, because there's no interpretation involved. Consequently you aren't likely to attribute the incorrect motivation. For instance, while people tend to call the posture where a dog has an upright body and holds his head and tail high a *dominant posture*, dogs may also exhibit this posture when they see a squirrel they want to chase, a ball that's out of reach, or an unidentified object in the distance. Thus a more appropriate name for this posture would be an *aroused posture*.

Once you're familiar with the motor patterns in different situations, then you can work on determining the function of the postures. The function of the posture is generally determined by the recipient animal's response. For instance, a play bow is called a "play bow" because most of the time it elicits play in the animal the bow is directed to.

Ethograms

In this section we start with a simplified ethogram—a catalogue of the dog's typical behavior patterns—and record the contexts in which these postures and body movements occur. If we can correlate certain body positions with specific types of contexts, then we can determine that body position's function. For instance, if we find that a particular dog wags his tail in a circle primarily upon greetings that end up with no fighting, but when his tail wags quickly and side-to-side he does fight, then we may conclude that tails wagging in a circle correlates more predictably with friendly behavior in this dog. In this manner, we can systematically learn to interpret our own dog's signals. The following is a list of motor patterns that you can observe in different situations and use for the exercises included at the end of this section. Each motor pattern is followed by a letter or abbreviation, which you can insert in the behavior chart. Alternatively, you can make up your own abbreviations.

MOTOR PATTERNS FOR ETHOGRAMS

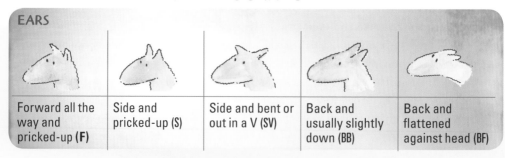

EARS				
Forward all the way and pricked-up **(F)**	Side and pricked-up (S)	Side and bent or out in a V (SV)	Back and usually slightly down (BB)	Back and flattened against head (BF)

How To Behave So Your Dog Behaves

EYE–GAZE

Staring or looking straight ahead (S)	Averting gaze (A)	Eyes darting from side to side (D)

EYE-SIZE

Eyes open as wide as they can go. Often you see more of the whites of the eyes than usual (VW)	Open wide (W)	Squinting or half-closed (HC)	Closed (C)

MOUTH

Closed (C)	Licking lips (LL)	Agonistic pucker or submissive grin, where lips are raised and puckered so only the front incisors and canine teeth show* (AP)	Fear grin or grimace, where lips raised and sides drawn back, revealing premolars and molars (FG)	Pant (P)	Yawn (Y)

*NOTE that both lip positions look the same, but the rest of the dog's body posture determines whether the dog is being agonistic or submissive.

HEAD

Held above body (AB)	At body level (B)	Below the body (BB)

TAIL POSITION

Sky high, as high as it will go (SH)	Above the level of the back (AB)	Level with or slightly below the back (LB)	Hangs down towards floor (H)	Between the hind legs (BL)

TAIL MOVEMENT

Motionless (M)	Wagging in circles (C)	Wagging in a slow, wide sweep (S)	Short fast flutter (F)	Accompanied by the whole rear end wagging (R)

OVERALL BODY WEIGHT DISTRIBUTION

Leaning forward, weight more on front end (LF)	Leaning back, weight towards the rear (LB)	Evenly balanced but tense (EBT)	Evenly balanced with muscles relaxed (EBR)	Crouched (C)

Exercises

The following exercises will give you practice observing your dog methodically so that you can be aware of what he is communicating to you and to other dogs. Once you have completed one or two, you'll be more in tune to observing your pet, and when you've completed them all, you'll be an expert in reading your dog. We'll start with looking at single features one by one, then put them all together to develop a complete picture. You may be surprised. For instance, you may find that while you think your dog wants to play with other dogs at the park, what he's actually telling them through his body posture is that he's overly aroused, tense, or socially uncomfortable. Or, if you have two dogs, you may find out that one has more facial expressions than the other.

Exercise 1: One Minute Observations

Observe your dog for one or more full minutes while he's engaged in different activities, and concentrate on one body part. That is, for one minute observe ear position, for another minute observe head position, for another minute observe tail position, etc. During that time period, note every time the position changes. Alternatively, record the position every five or ten seconds for the whole minute. This exercise gives you an idea of the range of postures that occur within a short period, and will make you more aware of the possibilities for signaling.

Exercise 2: Activity Observations

Each day, observe your dog in his daily activities. One day pay attention to ears; on a separate day pay attention to the mouth; on yet another day watch the eyes, and so on, until you've gone through all of the activities and signal systems. Make sure you note interesting responses, such as responses of other dogs to your dog, in these situations. Compile your results for all body parts and positions to get a big picture of Fido's body language during different events. For example, note his posture when he greets another dog right before play, versus when he greets a dog and then gets in a fight; or when he scans the ground by sniffing versus when he actually finds something significant (such as a morsel of food).

Exercise 3: Predicting Postures

Using the chart on pages 36-37, see if you can predict the postures you will see in both familiar and new situations. What will be the postures when he goes to the vet or visits the pet store? What posture will Rover take up when he sees a friend versus someone on his territory who he doesn't know?

Exercise 4: Greeting Other Dogs

Go to the dog park and watch how your dog greets other dogs. Each time he greets someone, pay attention to one detail (i.e., tail height, etc.). Concentrate on one characteristic each day. Note the outcome of the greeting, such as fight or play, and whether the dogs are on leash.

Exercise 5: Greeting People

Go to the dog park and see how your dog greets people. Observe whether your dog shows the same postures when meeting an unfamiliar person who approaches and reaches for him versus one who lets the dog make first contact. Based on what you know about postures from previous chapters, you should be able to determine whether your dog is confident or non-threatening, or whether he's fearful or pushy.

POSTURES CHART (EXERCISE 3)

Sleeping							
Eating meal (no other animals near)							
Chewing a bone or long-lasting toy or treat							
Standing around the house or yard, not interacting with anything or anybody							
Waiting to be fed a meal							
Waiting to be fed a treat (begging)							
Soliciting petting from owner							
Sniffing in the yard for a place to urinate or poop							

On walks when energy is high								
On walks when tired (at end)								
When greeting owner								
When greeting unfamiliar people								
When greeting friends								
When the doorbell rings								
When locked outside and wants to come in								
Greets familiar dog playmates								
Greets unfamiliar dogs off leash								
Greets unfamiliar dogs on leash								

Section 2

The Science of Learning:
How to Modify Behavior
in Your Dog
(or Cat, Horse, Rat...)

Whether or not we're aware of it, every time we interact with an animal, we're learning something, and the animal is learning something, too. In essence, each interaction is a training session. However, whether the animal is learning something we want him to learn is another story. For instance, if you walk your dog and he drags you down the street, barks obscenities to passing pooches, and stops on a whim to water the plants, he's learning that it's okay to do those things. In other words, each time you let him perform those behaviors, you're training him to do those things, and he's training you to let him do those things.

If you want Fido to walk politely, you have to modify your own behavior in order to modify his behavior. You can do this most efficiently if you understand how dogs think and learn. In this section, I focus on the two main types of learning—*classical conditioning* (learning by association) and *operant conditioning* (learning by trial and error), which guide learning in all animals, ranging from hummingbirds to horses to humans. To illustrate the universality of these principles, I use examples and present practice problems involving a wide variety of species. Consequently, once you read this section and work your way through the practice problems, you'll have the tools for modifying behavior in your dog—and even a cat, hamster, horse, or your human housemates.

Chapter 5

Classical Conditioning:
Learning by Association

In the early 1900s, a Russian physician and researcher named Ivan Pavlov was studying digestion in dogs. He was giving meat powder to dogs and then measuring salivation. At first, everything went well. He'd give the meat powder, and the dogs would start to salivate. However, as he repeated the trials, he noticed that the dogs started their reflex salivation early. They would start drooling when they saw the food or heard the footsteps of the feeders.

This early salivation messed up his experiment; however, instead of scrapping the project, Pavlov decided to study this new phenomenon. He took dogs and paired feedings with the sound of a stimulus that previously had no meaning. He chose a bell because animals don't normally have an innate response to bells. He would ring the bell and then immediately present the food. After doing this many times, he tested the dogs with the bell alone. When the dogs heard the bell, they immediately started drooling. Thus by presenting the bell with feeding, the two stimuli became associated. The bell elicited all of the same internal responses as the food and essentially took on the same meaning as the food.

Classical conditioning generally follows this pattern, involving two stimuli and one response. In Pavlov's experiment, dogs reflexively drooled while eating. Drooling is an involuntary physiologic response—one that occurs without conditioning or training—and consequently, the food stimulus is called an **unconditioned stimulus** and the drool response is an **unconditioned response**. After pairing the neutral stimulus with the food enough times, the dogs start to drool upon hearing the bell alone. Now the bell elicits an automatic drooling response. The bell starts off as a neutral stimulus, and when paired enough times with the food (i.e., trained long

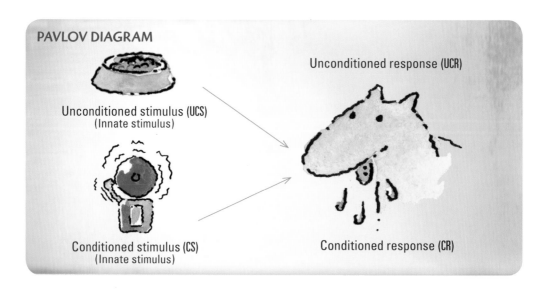

PAVLOV DIAGRAM

Unconditioned stimulus (UCS)
(Innate stimulus)

Unconditioned response (UCR)

Conditioned stimulus (CS)
(Innate stimulus)

Conditioned response (CR)

enough), it takes on the same meaning as the food. It becomes a **conditioned stimulus** and it elicits the drooling, which is now called a **conditioned response**, because the drool response (and its associated changes in internal state) to the bell was trained.

When Does Classical Conditioning Occur in Real Life?

Classical conditioning occurs all the time, every day. For instance, say you have a young puppy that you're taking to the veterinarian for his first shots. You put him in his carrier and take him for his first car ride, which makes him a little nauseous. Then, at the vet hospital, he hears and sees a lot of barking dogs who scare him. Once in the exam room, the vet checks him out and gives him his vaccines. He just sits quietly and doesn't seem to mind. Several weeks later, you go for his second set of vaccines. This time, when you bring his carrier out, he runs and hides. What happened?

The puppy associated his fearful experience with the carrier. In other words, by pairing the carrier with the car ride, which made him nauseous, and the vet hospital waiting room, which was filled with dogs who scared him, you classically conditioned him to fear his carrier.

Of course, if you create a problem, you have to fix it. How could you change the association? You could classically condition another association. You could teach little Fido to associate the carrier with things he likes, such as food (Figure 5.1). This is called **counter-conditioning**, because you're countering the association that was classically conditioned before.

This sounds simple, and it is, but there's often a slight hitch. Often dogs who are afraid of

Figure 5.1

their crates won't even go in, so putting food in the carrier won't work. In these cases, you can place food outside the carrier, far enough away so that Fido will eat it readily. Then gradually, possibly over several days, move the food closer and closer until he's going all the way inside. This gradual step-by-step approach, where we start far away and gradually work closer, is called **systematic desensitization**. Thus, the entire process just described is called **desensitization** and **counter-conditioning**. Generally we use desensitization and counter-conditioning together because together they are much more effective than alone.

Classical Conditioning At Work

Now that you know about classical conditioning, let's see if you can identify the classical conditioning taking place in the following situations. When answering these questions, think of classical conditioning as the emotional associations (e.g., pleasure versus fear) as well as the involuntary physiologic responses that are occurring.

Q&A: CLASSICAL CONDITIONING

Q: How does suckling in lambs and other young animals improve the maternal-offspring bond?

A: Lambs nurse from their mothers throughout the day. This suckling strengthens the mother-offspring bond, because during nursing the lamb learns to associate the mother with food. The presence of the mother elicits internal changes associated with food.

Q: Dairy cows sometimes start releasing their milk on the floor in the milking parlor prior to being hooked up to the milking machine. Why does this happen?

A: Dairy cows get milked two to three times a day. They're herded into the milking parlor, or in some cases they enter at their own leisure, and then are hooked up to milking machines and milked. With some cows, the sight, smell, and sounds of the milking parlor around milking time elicit the hormonal and physiologic changes associated with milking. Thus, as soon as they enter the milking parlor, but often before they're hooked up to the milking machines, they involuntarily start to release their milk and it leaks onto the floor. Dairy managers try to milk these cows first to prevent wasted milk.

Q: Many dogs are energetic and exuberant when they're playing, but as soon as you get them into the obedience ring or into dog training class, they lag behind and provide a lackluster performance. What's the problem and how would you fix it?

A: They associate the obedience ring with unpleasant things. These dogs are being trained with what the dogs consider to be a lot of aversives. (An aversive is anything the dog dislikes or wants to avoid). They may receive praise and other rewards, but they also get yelled at or yanked around, which they find unpleasant. These aversives may seem mild and relatively few and far between to the handler, but they must outweigh the reinforcements to the dog. Alternatively, these dogs may just think the whole training deal is a bore. When these dogs are competing in the obedience ring and the handler is not allowed to yell or correct the dog or to give ample reinforcements during exercises, the dog's true feelings about the situation are revealed. You could counter-condition this association by making training fun for the dog. The dog should not be able to distinguish training from play. In other words, heeling, fetching, and the down-stay should all be games to him.

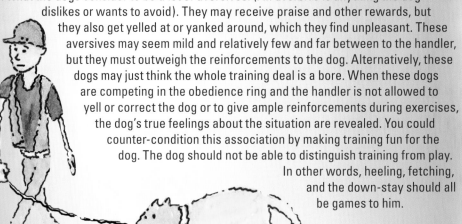

Q: Horseback riding may not be the greatest form of exercise; however, sometimes catching a horse prior to riding is. Horses in pasture are often difficult to catch, even when they appear to really like their owners. Sometimes they'll come right up to their owners, except for the times they see that the owner has a halter. Why would a horse avoid its owner when the owner has a halter? How could you counter-condition the horse?

A: The horse is afraid of the halter or associates the halter with unpleasant tasks or events that generally follow. Usually these events involve saddling, riding them, or some other form of work. Some horses like food, some like grooming, some like socializing with either other horses or with humans, but the one really important motivator that horses like (but that people often omit) is rest. If they always have to work when they're haltered, they will associate the halter with work and unpleasant experiences. You could counter-condition this association by rewarding the horse with treats for coming up to you and then for letting you put the halter on. Once you have the halter on, you can just groom him and give him treats and then release him and walk him around the pasture. You can also take him out of the pasture and let him experience things he likes instead of always haltering him and then riding him. Alternatively, perhaps you need to improve the type of experience he's having when he is ridden.

Now that you know that classical conditioning is occurring all the time, keep your eyes open and see what associations your Fido is forming on a daily basis.

Basics of Operant Conditioning:
Learning by Trial and Error

In classical conditioning, the animal learns an association. That is, when a stimulus such as food is paired many times with a neutral stimulus, such as a bell, the animal eventually associates the bell with the food. The bell elicits all of the automatic internal responses that the food elicits. In operant conditioning, or trial and error learning, the animal learns a behavior. That is, the animal learns to repeat behaviors that work (behaviors that are followed by consequences they like) and to avoid behaviors that don't work (behaviors that are followed by consequences they dislike).

While this phenomenon of repeating behaviors that work and avoiding behaviors that don't work seems simpler than learning your ABCs, the terminology used to describe the phenomenon can confuse both psychology students as well as experienced trainers. It is actually straightforward, though, and somewhat essential for communicating about operant conditioning with others.

Operant Conditioning Terminology
Here are the important terms you should know regarding operant conditioning.

Reinforcement and Punishment
The first two terms we should know are **reinforcement** and **punishment**. Reinforcement is anything that increases the likelihood that a behavior will occur again. For instance, if you call your dog and then give him a treat when he comes, he will be more likely to come the next time you call. Thus, by giving him a treat for coming, you reinforce his behavior of coming when called.

Punishment is anything that decreases the likelihood that a behavior will occur again. For instance, if you call your dog and then yell and scream at him when he comes, he will be less likely to come the next time you call. Thus, by yelling at him you punish his behavior of coming when called. This second scenario may seem an unlikely event, but it happens to people every day. When owners call Rover five or six times before he comes running and then yell at him for taking his time, they are really punishing him for coming when called.

Positive and Negative

The second set of terms is **positive** and **negative**. Positive and negative do not mean good or bad; instead, think of them as a plus sign or a minus sign. Positive means that you're adding something, and negative means you're subtracting something. Positive and negative can be applied to both reinforcement and punishment.

REINFORCEMENT

Reinforcement increases the likelihood that a behavior will occur.

Positive Reinforcement:
By adding something the animal wants, you increase the likelihood that the behavior will occur again.

Negative Reinforcement:
By removing something aversive, you increase the likelihood that the behavior will occur again.

PUNISHMENT

Punishment decreases the likelihood that a behavior will occur.

Positive Punishment:
By adding something aversive, you decrease the likelihood that the behavior will occur again.

Negative Punishment:
By removing something the animal wants, you decrease the likelihood that a behavior will occur again.

Positive and Negative Reinforcement

Positive reinforcement means that by adding something the animal wants, you increase the likelihood that the behavior will occur again. For instance, if you teach your dog to come to you by giving him a treat when he comes, you're using positive reinforcement (Figure 6.1). By giving him food, which he likes, you're increasing the likelihood that he will come to you the next time too.

Negative reinforcement means that by removing something aversive, something Fido dislikes, you increase the likelihood the behavior will occur again. For example, you decide to teach Fido to come by putting him on a leash and choke chain. You pull on his leash until he takes a step forward, and as soon as he comes forward, you release the pressure. That is using negative

Figure 6.1

reinforcement. By removing the pressure as soon as he starts coming, you increase the likelihood that he will come the next time in order to avoid the yanking or pulling.

Another trick for remembering negative reinforcement is to think of it as nagging. When I was a child and my mother wanted me clean my room, she often had to keep telling me until I cleaned it. I would finally clean my room in order to avoid her aversive nagging.

Positive and Negative Punishment

Punishment can also be positive or negative, too. It seems odd, but when we talk about punishment, we're usually talking about positive punishment. **Positive punishment** just means that by adding something aversive, we decrease the likelihood that the behavior will occur again. For instance, your dog raids the garbage can when you're not looking, so you booby-trap the garbage with mousetraps. The next time Spot sticks his nose in search of a snack, he gets a mousetrap surprise, which scares him. This booby trap decreases the likelihood that he will raid the garbage can again; thus, it is positive punishment.

Negative punishment means that by removing something the animal wants, we decrease the likelihood that the behavior will occur again. For instance, when dogs greet us by jumping, their goal is to get our attention. If we remove our attention every time Spot jumps by holding perfectly still and even looking away, eventually he will stop jumping. By removing the attention that he wanted, we decrease the likelihood that he will jump again.

How to Classify Techniques in a Methodical Manner

These terms seem straightforward so far, but often when you start classifying techniques in real life, things suddenly get confusing. The reason for the confusion is that some techniques may fall into more than one category, depending on how you describe the behavior and the technique. In order to avoid confusion, you have to approach this classification in a methodical way.

1 First, define the behavior. For example, if the behavior you want to change is your dog's overexuberant greeting behavior, you may say, "I hate the jumping behavior," or "I prefer he greet by sitting." So in general we usually have two behaviors from which to choose.

2 Next, decide whether you want to increase or decrease that behavior. If you want to increase the behavior, you will, by definition, use reinforcement. If you want to decrease the behavior, you will, by definition, use punishment. For instance, if you dislike the jumping behavior and want to stop it, you'll be using punishment. If you're going to train him to perform the alternate appropriate behavior of sitting, you will be using reinforcement.

Figure 6.2 (Negative Punishment)

3 Lastly, decide whether you're adding something or subtracting something to determine if you're using something positive or negative. If you yank the dog's collar to make him stop jumping, what are you using? You're adding an aversive to decrease the behavior, so you are using **positive punishment** (Figure 6.2). (*Note: I'm not advocating that you yank the dog's collar; I'm just using this as an example.*) If instead you remove the attention that he wants in order to decrease the behavior, what type of punishment are you using? You're using **negative punishment**, because you're removing something he wants in order to decrease his jumping behavior (i.e., you're removing the reward for the undesirable behavior). If you wait until the dog sits and then increase this sitting behavior by giving him a treat that he wants, you are using **positive reinforcement (Figure 6.3)**. If you hook Fido up to a leash and choke chain and step on it so that it tightens until he sits and then release the pressure immediately when he sits, you're using **negative reinforcement.**

Figure 6.3 (Positive Reinforcement)

Can You Classify the Techniques?

See if you can classify the behavior modification techniques yourself. Remember to first define the behavior! Then, to be safe, use the key words "increase" or "decrease/stop" and "add" or "remove." This way, when you're debating the category with friends, you can be sure that you are able to back up your classification. Also, remember that I am not advocating the use of aversives or specific techniques in this section. This section is just an exercise in classifying techniques into appropriate categories so that you can communicate to others using the appropriate terminology.

Example: The Runaway Dog

An owner complains that when she takes her dog, Fluffy, to the park to play with her friend's dog, Paco, her dog ignores her and runs away to play with Paco rather than coming when called. Define the behavior(s) you want to fix and then describe a technique for each category of operant conditioning.

- *Increase*: coming when called (reinforce this behavior)
- *Decrease*: running away to play with Paco (punish this behavior)
- *Positive reinforcement*: Give a treat for coming when called. By giving (adding) the treat that Fluffy likes, you will increase the likelihood that he comes the next time you call.
- *Negative reinforcement*: Shock him with an electronic collar (add shock) until he starts coming and then remove the shock as soon as he starts coming. (Note: I'm not advocating this technique; it's just an example.)
- *Positive punishment*: Shock him with an electronic collar (add shock) when he's running toward Paco in order to decrease the behavior of running to Paco.
- *Negative punishment*: Remove Paco as soon as Fluffy starts running toward him in order to stop or decrease the behavior of Fluffy running toward Paco. (This is not easy to do but it's important to think about this category regularly, as we'll find out in the next chapter.)

By now you're probably noticing something fishy. That is, the technique you use for positive punishment may be similar to the technique you use for negative reinforcement. The difference between the two is how you defined the behavior. If you're using an aversive to increase a behavior, it's negative reinforcement. If you're using an aversive to stop a behavior, it's positive punishment. Additionally, with proper negative reinforcement the aversive must be released immediately as the animal starts to perform the correct behavior. So if you fail to define the behavior, you can be in for a long, pointless argument with others who also fail to define the behavior!

Which One Is the Best?

Although animals learn through all four categories of operant conditioning both in the wild and in specific training sessions, the categories that unequivocally work the best across species for training purposes are positive reinforcement combined with negative punishment.

Consequently, while we tend to solve behavior problems by asking how we can stop the behavior or how we can punish the behavior, we should focus instead on how we can stop reinforcing inappropriate behaviors and start reinforcing alternate appropriate behaviors. For instance, if our dog jumps to greet us, we should ask: how are we accidentally reinforcing that behavior and how can we reinforce sitting nicely during greetings instead?

I'll discuss this more in the following chapters. For now, just know that every time you train a behavior (operant conditioning), the animal is also forming an association (classical conditioning). If you use lots of aversives when training behaviors (operant conditioning), the animal will learn to associate you and the situation with things that he dislikes (classical conditioning). Some animals are more resilient or forgiving when aversives are used; however, many others will never reach their potential or form the strongest possible relationship with the use of many aversives.

There are a few rare situations where certain aversives are useful, but because they should be used very discretely and under the supervision of a trained professional, I will not discuss them here. Instead, we will focus on removing reinforcement for the bad behavior (negative punishment) and reinforcing good behaviors (positive reinforcement). Most behaviors, both desirable and undesirable, can be trained extremely quickly using this combination.

Chapter 7

Putting Your Tools
to Work

Now that you know about operant and classical conditioning, you have the basic tools for solving behavior problems. And it turns out that you can approach most problems in a similar methodical way. All that it requires is a little thinking outside the box. That is, when most people see a behavior they dislike, they automatically ask, "How can I stop that behavior?" In this modification scheme, we will instead ask, "How has the undesirable behavior been reinforced, and what behavior would I reinforce instead?"

Changing Behaviors

Remember that animals perform behaviors because these behaviors are reinforced. Thus, the basic approach to changing bad behavior is to first identify what's reinforcing the bad behavior. Once you identify the possible reinforcer—which may require careful evaluation of the environment and consideration of the animal's individual and natural history—remove the reinforcer. Next, choose an alternate appropriate behavior and reinforce it instead.

For instance, say your parrot screeches continuously from inside his cage every day as soon as you arrive home from work. You yell at him to be quiet, but this seems to make him screech even more. You know he's quiet the rest of the day, because your spouse tells you the screeching doesn't start until you come home. To solve this problem, you first have to figure out what's reinforcing the screeching. You already have two clues: one is that he doesn't screech for your spouse, and the other is that he screeches more when you yell at him. Even if you don't know

FIXING BAD BEHAVIORS
How Would You Fix These Bad Behaviors?

Early Bird Cat: Every morning your cat wakes you up at 5:00 am. He cries and cries and even climbs all over you when you're lying in bed. Sometimes you push him off the bed, but he continues anyway. Usually feeding him finally gets him to shut up. Why does the cat wake you up every morning? How should you fix the problem?

Solution: You're reinforcing his behavior by getting up to feed him and interacting with him when he jumps on the bed. Ignore him completely (e.g., remove your attention) and feed him only after he's quiet, and preferably at the time at which you want to feed him. Note: if you can't stand the noise, lock him in a separate room at night.

Halter-Hating Horse: You own a horse and you give him carrots. He's rude and grabs them out of your back pocket and sometimes grabs them out of your hands. Your friend says "that's why people shouldn't give horses treats." Your other friend says "that's not true, it's how you give the treats that's important." What does she mean? How did you reinforce the wrong behavior and how would you fix it?

Solution: To fix the behavior, hold the treat away from him and only give it to him when he holds his head away from you. That is, make sure he does not get rewarded with a treat when he's nudging you or sniffing your pockets. Only give him the treat when he's holding his head away from you and waiting politely for the treat. Generally, if you break the carrot into small pieces so that you can practice this exercise 20 to 30 times per session, the horse will learn in just a few sessions.

Berserk Barker: Every day when the mail carrier comes, your dog barks at her until she goes away. You remember that when you first moved to the house about a year ago, he only barked a little at the mail carrier, but now he barks a lot and practically goes berserk. You know dogs are territorial and their job is to alert to you to intruders and protect the property. Why might your dog's barking behavior be getting worse? What can you do to fix the behavior? (You can provide a technically correct answer that might be difficult to perform, as well as one that still follows the rules but is more realistic.)

Solution: The behavior is getting worse because every time he barks at the mail carrier, she leaves (after she drops off the mail). Since the purpose of the barking is to protect the property, the barking is reinforced when it serves its purpose of "making" the mail carrier leave.

Instead of reinforcing the barking by leaving when the dog barks, the mail carrier should stick around until the dog is quiet. Realistically, you or the mail carrier would also need to toss a steady stream of treats to the dog, so the dog would associate her with good things. Since most postal workers don't have time to do this (although if all postal workers could do this with young dogs it would solve their bite problems), another option is for the owner to control the environment so that the dog can't see or hear the postal worker. Or the owner could train the dog to come when called instead of running to the door (for a visual aid, view "ZoeUPS" on the "movies" page at www.DrSophiaYin.com). One systematic approach is to use the MannersMinder Remote Controlled Reward Based Training System (Figure 7.1) to reward the dog for running to a rug and lying down (www.MannersMinder.net).

Figure 7.1

what's reinforcing to a bird, you might guess that attention of any kind does the job. Your first line of duty is to remove your attention when you come home and he screeches. Avoid talking to him, looking at him, going close to his cage, and especially avoid yelling at him. Next, reward appropriate behavior. Reward him for being quiet by giving him attention when he's quiet.

Extinction and Spontaneous Recovery

Sometimes when owners decide to fix bad behaviors, the behaviors seem to take a while to disappear, or the bad behaviors still keep cropping up. In fact, sometimes owners get frustrated because at first the behavior may even get worse. That's because whenever a behavior is no longer reinforced, it goes through a process of **extinction** where the behavior gradually disappears. However, behaviors don't just peter out at a constant rate; they may go through an **extinction burst** where they increase in frequency or intensity first.

This may seem surprising, but, for example, if a person attempts to start her car in the morning, and the car won't start, most people wouldn't immediately give up and decide keys no longer work in cars. They would try to start the car at least two or three times. That is, when they don't immediately get rewarded for performing a behavior that's been so successful in the past, they try harder. In fact, if the car has a history of being difficult to start, they will try even harder and longer to start the car. Similarly, if a dog barks annoyingly to be let into the house from the yard and the owner usually eventually caves in, the first time the owner ignores the dog's barking the behavior won't stop right away. The dog will try harder and bark more. How hard he tries depends on how much he's had to bark to get his way in the past. The existence of the extinction burst means that when we address a bad behavior by removing the reward, we have to be ready to endure a temporary worsening of the behavior.

Owners also sometimes wonder in frustration: "When I stop rewarding the bad behavior and train a new behavior, how long will the good behavior last?"—as if the old behavior should be permanently erased from the dog's memory and replaced by the new, more appropriate behavior. Unfortunately for them, information is never erased from an animal's brain. Instead it lurks there, and when inexperienced trainers least expect it, the behavior bursts out. In short, the appropriate behaviors persist as long as we continue reinforcing them and preventing the bad behaviors from being reinforced. If the desirable behaviors are reinforced frequently in a short period of time and the undesirable behaviors are not reinforced at all, then the new behavior may become a habit. But if training is inconsistent and the dog's motivation for the undesirable behavior is extremely high, then the training may need to be lifelong.

Spontaneous Recovery

Spontaneous recovery (or more correctly termed **resurgence** when talking about operant conditioning) is the system of learning where the animal remembers past reinforced behaviors for long periods of time, and a past reinforced behavior suddenly pops up even though it has not been reinforced for a long time. And it's essential for an animal's survival because of their constantly changing environment. For instance, if a food source suddenly dries up, dogs fending for themselves in the wild (as village dogs do on a regular basis) learn to go more frequently to other sources. Or if a dog is no longer getting food reinforcers at garbage can A because the residents of the house moved away, the dog learns to go more frequently to other sites—such as garbage cans B or C—where new owners have just moved and are filling the can with trash on a regular basis. The dog hasn't forgotten about garbage can A; he just learns to visit less frequently because garbage can A no longer provides food reinforcers. If cans B and C suddenly start providing little food, he would go back to searching can A regularly.

Every time we interact with Fido we should keep extinction bursts and spontaneous recovery (resurgence) in mind. If we consistently prevent reinforcement of the bad behavior, the behavior will eventually extinguish. For instance, in the case of the barking dog, the barking will eventually stop. But as stated earlier, the behavior is not erased from the animal's mind. So expect that the next time the dog is locked outside, he will bark again due to spontaneous recovery of the behavior. But this time the extinction burst will be smaller and the extinction time usually shorter.

Chapter 8

Operant Conditioning:
Shaping and Chaining

Teaching a dog to sit is simple, but what about more complex tasks? What if you want your dog to sit for five minutes next to two other dogs while you take his picture, or to heel in a complex pattern in a crowded public place? Complex behavior can be taught through shaping or chaining or a combination of both. We'll discuss shaping first.

Shaping Behaviors

Usually when we're training animals, we can't get the goal behavior in one step. That is, we can't just teach a dog to sit and then expect him to sit nicely for five minutes when the doorbell rings. Rather, we have to start with a behavior that we can train and gradually train behaviors that are closer to our goal behavior. In other words, we **shape the behavior** through incremental steps called **successive approximation**.

For example, if I want to train my dog to do a somersault, I can first teach her to touch a stick or other type of target with her nose. Each time she touches the stick, I give her food as a reinforcement. Once she consistently performs this step well, I can then teach her to touch a stick that's lower than her head. Next I can teach her to touch the stick when it's between her front legs. Eventually, if I continue patiently in this manner and take small, incremental steps, I can gradually teach her to somersault. (To see video, go to www.DrSophiaYin.com, "Shaping a Somersault.")

Where to Start in Your Shaping Plan?

To know where to start, test your pet. Different animals have different personalities, physical abilities, and past experiences that affect their performance. Thus, one animal may immediately be able to touch a target between his legs, while another can only touch at nose level. You just have to try and see.

Recognizing the Intermediary Steps

Most people have an idea of the goal behavior and even the start behavior, but have problems recognizing the intermediate steps to reaching their goal. Because animals go through slightly different intermediary steps, trainers must learn to recognize behaviors that are closer to the goal behavior.

Q&A: SHAPING

In the following examples, decide how you might make the goal task easier and then decide how you would shape the behaviors.

Q: How would you teach a chicken to run up a ramp and then jump through a hoop, land on a second ramp, and run down it?

A: First, make the hoop larger and put the ramps close together. I taught this trick to several of my chickens by first teaching the chicken to run down the ramp. Then I taught them to run up the ramp and jump across a small gap and run down a second ramp. I gradually increased the gap, then I added the hoop. (You can see a video of "Sophia's Trained Chickens" at www.DrSophiaYin.com.)

Q: In order to take group photos of your pets, they have to stay in position for several minutes at a distance of 10 or more feet (3 m) from you. How would you teach your dog to perform a down-stay with several other animals for two minutes at a distance of 10 feet (3 m) from the camera? Assume he already behaves well around the other animals, and they are not afraid of him.

A: You could start with him in a down-stay and walk away one step, but then go back quickly before he gets up. Then gradually increase your distance, making sure that you always get back before he gets up. Once you've built up the distance to 10 feet (3 m) or more, you can continue increasing the time until you reach two minutes. Next you can add in the other pets, but decrease the time and distance. For instance, with the other animals present, repeat the entire process. Gradually add in the time and distance.

When Your Shaping Plan Stalls

Often, shaping plans don't go quite as planned, and you think that shaping doesn't work. When this occurs, rest assured that you've probably just made one of three mistakes:

Mistake #1: Advancing Too Soon

Probably the most common problem is that as a trainer, you're in a rush, and you try to progress to the next step too soon. Just because the animal performs the behavior correctly a few times doesn't mean he knows the behavior really well. In school, getting a few math problems right didn't really mean you had a firm grasp of algebra—when an animal gets the problem right a couple of times, he could just be lucky. As a general rule of thumb, don't advance to the next step in training until you can bet yourself big bucks that your pet will perform the current step correctly the next time you ask. Alternatively, if you're keeping track of successes, you can go on to the next step when your pet has the current step down with about 80 to 90 percent accuracy. If you practice the behavior ten times in a row, the animals should perform it correctly eight or nine times out of ten.

Mistake #2: Skipping Steps

A second common error is expecting too much. We know that even smart humans aren't ready to learn calculus just because they can multiply, add, and subtract. When it comes to animal training, though, it's often difficult to realize that the steps we're asking the animals to take are really more like quantum leaps. For instance, just because a dog can touch a target when it's in front of his nose and at eye level doesn't mean the dog can touch the target when it's 5 feet (1.5 m) away or when it's held near the ground. Similarly, even though an animal can come promptly and consistently when called at home with no distractions, it doesn't mean he will do so when off leash at the dog park. If your pet did well on the previously trained step 80 to 90 percent of the time but can't get this next step (messes up over 40% of the time), try filling the steps in between. Taking many baby steps gets you to the goal faster than trying to make great leaps.

Mistake #3: Staying on the Previous Step Too Long

While most shaping errors are due to our impatience and rush to train too quickly, being overly conservative and cautious, or just not having a plan for what to do next will also bring our shaping plan to a halt.

The Shaping Game

Now that you know intellectually how to shape behavior, see what it's like to shape a real behavior and have someone shape a behavior in you. Get yourself two partners: one person plays the part of the pet being trained, one plays the trainer, and the third person coaches the trainer. The trainer and coach should collude on a plan. They should decide on a behavior to shape and map out the possible steps. This requires that they know what types of steps the "pet/person" might offer that they can reinforce and what steps he may then offer that are closer to the goal behavior. For instance, if the goal is to get the "pet/person" to spin once in a clockwise circle, you might first reinforce when the person looks right. Repeat the reinforcement of this behavior until the "pet/person" does it about five times correctly in a row. Then, when he knows that the behavior earns reinforcements, up the ante by expecting him to turn his head to the right. The next step might be moving the shoulder and head to the right, then turning the hips to the right, turning the right foot a step toward the right, turning the whole body over 90 degrees to the right, then turning the whole body 180 degrees to the right, and so on until the "pet/person" is turning to clockwise a full 360 degrees.

During the game, the trainer should signal with a marker word such as "yes" when the behavior is right and even give a food reward (candy). Then the "pet/person" should come back to the starting location for the next try. The "pet/person" should remember that his goal is only to gain reinforcements, not to figure out the final step.

After you're finished, the participants should get together and discuss how things went and what it felt like to be the animal. Everyone should play the part of the animal before being allowed to train an actual animal.

Chaining Behaviors

Another way to train a complex behavior is to link a bunch of simple behaviors together. Practice the simple behaviors until you have them down perfectly, then gradually link two, three, and then four together. Most people are already familiar with chaining, as some people consciously do it on a daily basis. For instance, golfers and football or basketball players don't just go out and play; they drill on specific individual components of the game. Professional musicians who are preparing to perform a piece don't just repeat it over and over from start to finish; they break it up into measures and phrases, analyzing and practicing it microscopically. Then, once the sections are up to par, they reassemble the piece.

The same steps go for training animals, too. For instance, in obedience competitions, dogs have to heel next to their owners while doing different things—making right and left turns, speeding up, slowing down, and sitting when they halt. The best way to practice is to break the patterns down to component parts such as heeling slowly, heeling quickly, heeling at a regular pace, going from slow to fast, going from fast to slow, making right turns, making a left turn, halting to a sit, and going from a sit to heel. When practicing an element such as the slow-to-fast transition, you should heel at a normal pace and then speed up for several steps. When your dog immediately mirrors your change, you should give him his reward and end the exercise. The purpose of approaching the pattern in this manner is that you gain precision at each step. When the elements are up to spec, you can assemble them into a short chain for two or three behaviors at a time and systematically build the chain.

Back Chaining

Traditionally, when we have a sequence of behaviors or steps to perform in a specific order, we forward chain by learning the first behavior and adding new behaviors onto that. For instance, when learning a dance routine, most people teach the first step, and, after a few practices, go on to teach the second step, then chain the two steps together. At first, this method seems easy enough, but once you start tacking on steps, the last step becomes harder and harder. It may seem easy when you learn it apart from everything else, but when you tack on six or seven steps before it, you often forget the newest step by the time you get to it.

A more effective way to train sequences is to **back chain**. This is where you train the last behavior first, train the second-to-last behavior next, then chain it to the last behavior. You gradually add new behaviors to the chain. Each new behavior is tagged onto the front and is followed by behaviors that you already know. For example, every time you run through the dance routine, you're now starting with the newest move still fresh in your mind and progressing to steps that are more familiar. One reason this works so well is that the behaviors at the end of the chain act to reinforce the newer behaviors at the beginning of the chain.

Q&A: CHAINING
How would you use chaining to train the following behaviors?

Q: How would you train a chicken to play the first three notes of "Three Blind Mice" on the xylophone?

A: I taught this by first teaching my chicken to play the note for "mice." Then I added the note for "blind" until he could play this note well, and back-chained to get "blind mice." Lastly, I trained the first note—"three"—and added it to the chain to make "three blind mice." (For video see "Sophia's Trained Chickens" at www.DrSophiaYin.com.)

Q: How would you teach a dog to run to bed or a special place when the doorbell rings and then sit and stay there?

A: You can train this in two separate exercises. You can first teach the dog to run to bed to get a treat. Next, teach him to run to the bed to get his treat and then turn around and lie down to get a second treat. Once he has this, build up the distance that he starts from. Then, separately work on having the dog stay in bed when you walk away and come back. Gradually walk farther away and add distractions such as knocking on the front door or opening the front door or ringing the doorbell. Then chain these shaped behaviors together.

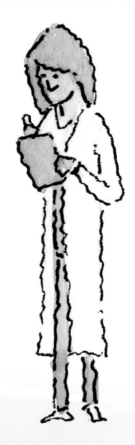

Chapter 9

Training Is a Technical Skill

Now you know the principles of operant conditioning, but in order to implement them successfully you have to practice. While it may look and sound easy, animal training is really a technical skill. That means that there's nothing mystical or psychic about understanding your pet or changing his behavior. You just need to pay attention to both your actions and your pet's responses, especially in the case of dog training, which can involve some running and quick changes of direction and speed.

In order to be successful at training animals and changing behavior, you must:

- have **good timing**
- be **clear and consistent** with your expectations and signals
- provide the **correct rate of reinforcement.**

Mastering these three simple skills will turn even the novice owner into an instant leader. Trainers who gain instant attention from pets, such as horses or dogs, are able to do so because they have these three skills. Animals know that these people are predictable, trustworthy, and reliable. They understand what these trainers want and trust that the trainers can guide them.

Timing Is Everything

Say I'm teaching a chicken to peck a black dot using positive reinforcement. She pecks the white space around the black dot, and then when she finally pecks the black dot, I rush to deliver the treat. Unfortunately, I'm too slow with the food and she pecks the white area again and then grabs the treat.

In this case, I clearly reinforced pecking the white area, not pecking the black dot. As a result, she will be more likely to peck the white area again rather than the black dot I wanted her to recognize.

This example of incorrect timing is clear-cut, but most examples aren't so black and white at first. For this reason, it's important to remember you get the behavior you reinforce—not the behavior you *thought* you reinforced or the behavior you *meant* to reinforce, but the behavior you actually reinforced. That means that if you're not getting the behavior you think you are training, you should first look to see if your timing is on the mark.

Bridging Stimulus

Ideally, you should get the reinforcement to the animal *within a split-second of the correct behavior and before the next significant behavior occurs*. Sometimes animals move too quickly to get the reward to them on time, or, for some other reason, it's difficult to communicate the exact correct behavior. In these cases, we can use a **bridging stimulus** to bridge the gap between the correct behavior and the food reward. In other words, we can pair a novel sound, such as a whistle, bell, or click from a clicker with food until we've classically conditioned the association. Then we can use the novel sound to **mark** the correct behavior, or, as stated earlier, to bridge the gap between the correct behavior and the food reinforcement. While that means that we still follow the sound with the food reinforcement as soon as possible, the bridging stimulus buys us a little time. When the bridging stimulus is a clicker and we use food as the positive reinforcement, the training is called **clicker training**. In other words, clicker training is just positive reinforcement with a clicker as a bridging stimulus.

Games to Test Your Timing

It's best to test your timing before you try it out on a real animal. Here are a few exercises you can try on your own or with some friends.

First, armed with a clicker, a tennis ball, and a friend, have your friend drop the tennis ball and see if you can click right as the tennis ball lands. Try this with a bunch of friends and see if all of you can click simultaneously as the ball lands. For more difficulty, vary the speed at which the ball drops and the interval between sequential dropping of the ball.

Even with a variable-speed tennis ball, this task is much easier than delivering dog treats at exactly the right time when you have a dog, a leash, and treats to handle all at one time. You can increase the difficulty of the timing exercise in several ways. First, follow the click by delivering the treat. Make sure you avoid bending over the pet and that you

Figure 9.1

deliver the treat within a split second. That means you have to get the treat from its holding position to the dog's mouth at superspeed. You can also try hopping on one foot and clicking as the ball bounces. If that's too easy, try walking in a large circle around the person tossing the tennis ball in the middle. Walk at a consistent pace, which the tosser can count out, and during the offbeat (in between each step) pat your head (Figure 9.1). Now, can you keep this syncopated rhythm (step-pat-step-pat-step-pat) and still click when the ball lands? This is the type of timing and concentration that top trainers possess.

Q&A: TIMING
Can you identify the correct timing?

Q: If you're training a dog to perform a long down-stay, where he lies down and you walk away for two to three minutes and then return to let him up, when should you time your reinforcement so that he gets rewarded for the down-stay?

A: Reward him with treats and praise while he's still lying down, rather than waiting until he gets up.

Q: If you tell the same dog to sit and stay and then leave for a minute, and instead of going back, you call him to come to you and give him a reward when he reaches you, which behavior are you reinforcing?

A: You're reinforcing the come when called. You should practice the sit-stay and come when called separately, as well as in a chain, in order to keep both looking sharp.

Define Your Criteria So You Can Be Clear and Consistent

If I'm training my chicken to peck the black dot again, what to reinforce seems straightforward—pecking on the black dot. But what if she sometimes pecks the center of the dot, hits right at the border, or rather than just pecking it, she stabs and grabs it as if she's going to rip it apart? If I reinforce all three of those behaviors, I will get all three of the behaviors. If I only want her to peck nicely at the center, then I have to be careful to reinforce only when she pecks the center of the dot. When training, it's essential that you define exactly what you want to reinforce, or you will confuse the animal and get variable results.

Reinforce at the Correct Rate

When working with chickens, zoo animals, cats, piglets, and other animals off leash, you have

Q&A: DEFINING CRITERIA

The following are some examples that illustrate how important it is to clearly reinforce exactly the behavior you want.

Q: At Safari West, a safari park in Santa Rosa, California, some students and I trained a number of the giraffes to touch a target with their nose. Giraffes are curious and like to examine objects with their nose and then grab the objects with their tongue. When training giraffes to target, which behavior should I reinforce?

A: If you reinforce the grabbing, you will get grabbing as part of your targeting behavior. We only reinforce touching the target with the nose.

Q: Dogs often like to grab targets with an open mouth rather than touching the target with their nose. They also frequently reach their nose close to the target without touching it. Which behavior should you reinforce?

A: If you want the dog to touch the target, you should only reinforce if he touches the target. If you want him to touch only with his nose and not with an open mouth, then only reinforce touching with the nose.

to reinforce the behavior enough to keep the animal interested in the game, or else he will just wander away. With dogs, we use leashes to keep their bodies within our reach; however, they also need a high enough reinforcement rate to stay focused on us and to do what we ask. The leash or halter is just a safety device to keep the dog out of trouble. We should really rely on our good timing, well-defined criteria, and correct rate of reinforcement to keep the animal interested in sticking with us during training.

Which Rate to Use?

When animals (and people) are first learning a behavior, we should reinforce the behavior on a continuous ratio. That is, every time they perform the behavior correctly, we should reward them until they know the behavior well. We should also make the behavior easy enough so that they can get rewarded a lot or they will get confused or bored and give up. Once they know the behavior and you can bet money they will perform it on cue the next time, you can raise the criteria or go to a variable ratio of reinforcement (VR) where the animal doesn't know which time the correct behavior will earn the reward. For the variable reinforcement, you can reinforce the behavior on average every two, three, four, five, or more times (VR 2, VR 3, VR 4, VR 5, VR 5+) depending on your goals and his level.

This means reinforce him on average, but not exactly every second, third, fourth, fifth, etc. time (called a fixed ratio).One way to remember when to reinforce is to decide what schedule you're on and choose a range of numbers lower and higher than that chosen ratio. For instance, if you're on a VR 4 and you're going to practice the behavior of heeling with your dog, you can heel and then reward him at step two, three, four, five, or six. Each time you start heeling, choose a different number within this range. On average, you will reward him at about four steps, but he will never know exactly which number of steps will earn the reinforcement. When using variable ratio reinforcements, start with a low ratio, and if your dog consistently performs well (80-90 percent of the time even when you reinforce on steps higher than the average), then you can go to a higher VR. Variable ratio reinforcements are extremely potent and will make the behaviors very reliable. Casino slot machines rely on variable ratio reinforcements to train gamblers to keep playing.

Q&A: VARIABLE RATIO REINFORCEMENT
Can you identify the variable ratio reinforcement?

Q: At the dog park, most of the dogs don't come consistently when their owners call. Sometimes owners call five to ten times in a row with no success. Why do these owners continue to let Lassie off leash or bother calling her to come?

A: Because sometimes she does come when called. She has the owner on a variable ratio of reinforcement.

Q: Many human couples don't get along. That is, individually, they're nice people, but together they are often miserable. You see them constantly bickering, but they still stick together. Why?

A: Sometimes when they're together, they have a great time. They're always hoping that the next time will be that great time again. They have each other on a variable ratio of reinforcement.

Q: Why do some people love sports so much?

A: Besides the element of competition, sports are fun because you never know how many plays it will take to get a touchdown, number of strokes to finish a hole in golf, or how many points will win the basketball game. The outcome is unpredictable, and the reinforcement is on a variable schedule.

Chapter 10

An Animal Is Not
a Black Box

A dog trainer decided to teach her two Labrador Retrievers to fetch beers off the top shelf of the refrigerator. Each dog could open the refrigerator door using the rope attached to the handle, gently grasp a bottle of beer in his mouth, remove the beer from the refrigerator, close the door with a front paw, and then carry the beer over to the trainer. They both seemed to have mastered this task to perfection, so she decided to test them. She put the beers on the middle shelf and told each dog to fetch. The first dog fetched a bottle of salad dressing off the top shelf. The second dog fetched a bottle of beer off the middle shelf. What did each dog learn? (Told to me by Sue Ailsby.)

While all animals learn through classical and operant conditioning, they aren't like blank slates or black boxes, as researchers in the field once thought. That is, they can't all learn the same tasks equally well, and even when trained in exactly the same manner, they may not learn exactly the same thing. These differences in learning are due in part to differences in past experience and motivation level at the time, but beyond these reasons, there are species-typical traits and individual predispositions. Consequently, to be top-notch trainers or even to understand our pets well, we have to take some species and individual characteristics into consideration.

Natural History and Evolutionary Constraints

Prior to the 1960s, scientists studying learning were looking primarily at pigeons and rats with the assumption that all species were basically the same. Then, in 1961, through their paper The Misbehavior of Organisms, Marian and Keller Breland instigated a change. The Brelands, former graduate students of B.F. Skinner, the founding father of operant conditioning, were the first to extend the use of scientific principles of animal psychology past the research lab into the real world. In doing so, they founded the field of applied animal psychology. They started an animal training business called Animal Behavior Enterprises, where they trained animals en masse for zoos, trade conventions, tourist attractions, and TV commercials. After having trained 38 species, ranging from reindeer and raccoons to rats, and after training over 6,000 individual animals, they identified a pattern of puzzling failures, which they reported in their paper.

In one case, they taught raccoons to pick up coins and deposit them into a metal box. Teaching them to pick a coin up was easy, but as soon as they started shaping the behavior of dropping the coins into the box, odd behaviors appeared. The raccoons would rub the coin up the inside of the container and then pull it out and hold it before finally dropping it into the box to receive a food reinforcement. When the Brelands raised the criteria to two coins, the behavior really deteriorated. The raccoons would rub the coins together, sometimes for minutes, before dropping them into the container.

In a second case, they planned to teach chickens to run to a platform and stand for 12 to 15 seconds, after which the chickens would receive a food reward. Fifty percent of the chickens developed a pattern of scratching the platform repeatedly with their feet. This behavior increased as the time interval grew longer. (The Brelands recouped their training plan by turning this into a dancing chicken exhibit.)

In yet another case, pigs were taught to pick up large wooden coins and to place them into a piggy bank. Teaching pigs to pick up one coin and place it into the piggy bank was easy, as was teaching several coins. However, after months, the behaviors started to deteriorate. Instead of carrying the four coins and depositing them individually as they had originally learned and performed well, they started to repeatedly drop the coins and then root and toss them in the air. It would take a pig up to ten minutes to transport the coins a few feet, even though the pigs were very food motivated.

All of these animals were performing instinctive food-retrieval behaviors in spite of the lack of reinforcement for doing so. Chickens scratch and peck when searching for food, raccoons wash their food in water, and pigs root around. The animals were forming a classically conditioned association between the stimulus (coin, ball, platform) and the food, and consequently performed behaviors associated with finding or procuring food. The Brelands termed this new phenomenon instinctive drift.

Biological Preparedness to Learn
The Brelands also found other species-specific anomalies, such as difficulty teaching cows to

kick and difficulty conditioning vocalization with food reinforcement. Since then, scientists have focused more closely on the idea that animals are biologically prepared to learn certain tasks and make certain associations (Figure 10.1). This has led us to find a variety of learning constraints. For instance, horses kick during aggressive encounters with others, whereas cows engaged in altercations butt heads and then push and shove. Armed with this natural history knowledge, it's not surprising to know that horses can easily be trained to kick on cue, whereas it's more difficult to teach this task to cows. Likewise, goats and sheep are anatomically similar, which you see once a sheep has been sheared, yet goats are much more motivated to climb. It doesn't take an animal behavior expert to predict that it's easier to train goats in climbing tasks.

Knowing the natural history also helps determine how animals will respond when pressed. Animals respond to fearful situations by fighting, fleeing, or freezing. Prey animals such as horses, rabbits, and rodents tend to run, and small predators such as cats follow suit. Larger predatory animals and those higher up on the food chain may also flee, but frequently learn to fight. This explains why dogs who are afraid of other dogs and unfamiliar people can easily learn to bark and lunge as if fearless, whereas horses, cows, or cats have a greater tendency to flee if they have the chance.

It's intuitively easy to see why evolution and natural history require that we take species differences into consideration when training. Perhaps surprisingly, it turns out that we also have

Figure 10.1

to consider the type of reinforcers we use depending on the type of behavior we train. Certain responses naturally belong with certain reinforcers. This concept, termed "**belongingness**," was studied by John Garcia and his coworkers. They found that rats learn to avoid certain foods when the foods are followed by nausea, but did not learn to avoid the foods if the foods were instead followed by a shock. They fed the rats a food or liquid that the rats had never tasted and then exposed them to X-rays, which made them feel nauseous. The rats subsequently refused the novel item that they had eaten or drank before the nausea. If, however, a novel-tasting liquid was paired with a shock to the foot, the rats did not learn that the two were associated, and their drinking did not decrease. Conversely, when a click was sounded several seconds before rats were shocked, the rats were able to learn to take action to avoid the shock after hearing a click. However, they could not learn that a click-sound preceded internal illness.

These findings illustrate that the cue and the consequence have to belong to the same system. Feelings of nausea and the gastrointestinal system go hand-in-hand and are essential for the survival of rats as scavengers. Their strategy for avoiding toxic foods is to sample new foods rather than eating them whole. That way if they get sick, they know which food to avoid in the future. Similarly, shock or stimulation of pain receptors in the skin tell rats which objects and locations to specifically avoid, but has no relation to nausea or eating food.

Another example of belongingness or biological preparedness is that of the three-spined stickleback fish. Males establish territories that they defend ferociously from other males. When a male courts a female and the female responds to that male, she lays eggs in his territory. In 1973, a researcher named Sevenster taught one group of male sticklebacks to bite a rod in order to obtain access to either a female that they could court or a male that they could fight. Because biting is an aggressive behavior for defending territories, the males were able to learn to bite the rod when the reinforcer was a male, but they did not learn to bite the rod when the reinforcer was a female. By contrast, when females were the reinforcer, males could be taught to swim through a ring, but not to bite the rod. The behavior of "biting" belongs with the behavior of fighting other males.

If we think carefully, we can extend this idea to our own animals, too. For instance, when you call a dog out of a dog fight and then reward him with food for coming quickly, you're usually not also reinforcing his bad behavior of fighting. Fighting and aggression belong to a different system than eating food.

Motivation to Perform

Once we've considered the natural history, we're in a prime position to determine which reinforcers are relevant in motivating an animal to perform (Figure 10.2). All animal species are motivated by three things that are essential for survival: food, the need to avoid pain and danger, and the need to reproduce. For general training purposes, opportunities to engage in reproductive acts are not a practical reinforcer, and using aversives that generate fear is fraught with side effects. That leaves food as the common motivator.

In addition to these essential three reinforcers, different species are motivated by other things. Predator species such as dogs like to chase objects and fetch toys, especially ones that squeak like wounded prey. For animals that live in groups, especially those where being in a herd or flock provides safety, social reinforcement is especially strong.

Motivation can vary from animal to animal within a species and even within individuals throughout the day. In order to determine what's motivating in general and which motivator will work, we can refer to the **Premack Principle**, which states that high-probability responses can serve to reinforce low-probability responses. It also states that reinforcers are not necessarily things such as a treat or a bone; instead, a *strong reinforcer is anything the animal would rather do*. For instance, if a dog prefers to play with other dogs rather than eat when out on walks, then play is more reinforcing than food in this situation. Move 10 or 20 feet (3 or 6 m) farther away from the other dogs, and then food may become the stronger of the two. Reinforcer strength changes

Figure 10.2

dynamically based on the animal's state or the contextual status. We can control the strength and type of reinforcer by controlling the animal's situation. We can make sure a cat or dog is hungry by metering his daily food if we're going to use food treats for training. We can reward a dog by letting him play with other dogs at the dog park immediately after coming on cue.

EXERCISE

For the following questions, determine what's reinforcing to your own dog by listing anything your dog would rather do:
- What motivates your dog when he's on walks? (What does he like or prefer to do?)
- What does he want to do when he's at the dog park off leash? Are food treats as reinforcing at the park as playing with other dogs?
- Is dog food a strong enough reinforcer in the home when you're alone versus when you have guests over?

Communication

In order to know which rewards are actually reinforcing to an animal at any instant in time, we can't just memorize a list. Instead, we have to watch the animal and see how he responds. If you praise your dog for fetching and he just stares at the tennis ball in your hand, then it's the toy that he finds rewarding, not all of your talk. If your dog performs a trick on demand and then blows you off when you pet him, but perks up when he sees the food treat, it's the food that he wants, not your petting.

Because humans communicate consciously with spoken words, while our domestic pets use body postures as a primary form of language, our interactions often leave both of us bewildered. We miss all of the messages our pets are sending, and we forget that animals are interpreting

WHAT ARE YOU TELLING YOUR PET AND WHAT IS HE TELLING YOU?

For each of the following questions, think about what body posture or action you should you look for in your pet.
- How do you know when your dog thinks praise is rewarding?
- How do you know if your dog likes being hugged?
- How do you know when a particular treat is rewarding for any of your pets?
- How do you know whether your dog enjoys walks?

our every move. This becomes a particular problem when we fail to notice that our actions are creating fear, or our supposed reinforcers have no effect. For our dog, the situation can become especially confusing when we send mixed messages. When push comes to shove, if there's ambiguity between what we say verbally and what our bodies do, the animal will tend to go based on the visual or tactile signal, even if we didn't know we gave such a cue. In fact, generally animals care more about our actions than our words.

Chapter 11

Four Methods of
Behavior Modification

When working to change behavior, we have four methods at our fingertips: flooding and desensitization, which are forms of habituation; and classical counter-conditioning and operant counter-conditioning, which are types of counter-conditioning.

Habituation

In nature, animals are constantly bombarded with stimuli. A myriad of sounds, smells, sights, and tactile sensations stimulate their nervous systems, and if they attended to each one, they would quickly develop sensory overload. So how do they know which stimuli should incite a startle and which to ignore? One way is through the process of habituation. Habituation is when an animal initially responds to some stimulus, such as the sound of a train or the sight of a car roaring by, but over time, with repeated exposure to the stimulus in the absence of any aversive or pleasurable experience, the response diminishes. In other words, habituation means that the animal "gets used to it."

We're all familiar with habituation, because it happens to us all the time. If you live in a peaceful neighborhood and then move into a neighborhood with train tracks nearby, the sound of the trains keeps you up all night initially. Over time, though, you notice the train less and less, until often you no longer realize when the train goes by. Animals such as dogs commonly develop habituation to loud sounds as well.

Habituation is one of the most common forms of learning, and one of its functions is to teach animals what not to fear. In nature, the default setting for animals is to be fearful of all objects and animals they have not specifically identified as being safe. This is why wild animals don't

IMPORTANT DEFINITIONS

Flooding: You present the stimulus full force until the animal stops reacting to it. The animal learns to ignore the stimulus because the stimulus has no aversive or pleasurable consequence.

Desensitization: You present the stimulus at a low level that the animal does not respond to and gradually increase the strength of the stimulus until the animal learns to ignore the full-force stimulus.

Classical counter-conditioning: You classically condition an association that's opposite to a previously classically conditioned association. With classical counter-conditioning, we're generally changing the underlying emotional and physiologic state that drives the animal to behave in a certain way.

Operant counter-conditioning: You train an alternate behavior that's incompatible with the problem behavior. (Note: Usually, for operant counter-conditioning to work, the animal must associate the alternate behavior with pleasurable consequences.)

just come walking out of the woods to congregate with humans around the campfire like characters in a cartoon. This fear serves as an important survival value. Those that aren't naturally afraid of animals and new objects to which they haven't had time to habituate are most likely to end up on some predator's dinner plate. A prime example is my first rat, Sneakers. When he was young, I handled him frequently and habituated him to many different animals. As a result, when my friend brought her cat to stay for several weeks, Sneakers scampered right up to her and then proceeded to follow her around the house. If Sneakers had instead been living in the wild and walked up to a feral feline, he would have made a filling meal.

Habituation also explains why the local squirrel seems to be teasing your dog by standing in a tree just out of reach and why deer can graze near a road with many passing cars. Initially, the squirrel is afraid of your dog and the deer is afraid of cars, but because both the tree and road regions contain resources such as food, they watch warily and stick around. When nothing bad happens to them, they learn that the barking dog on the ground and the moving cars passing by are not dangerous, or at least can't kill them at that distance. In the case of the dog and squirrel, the squirrel may still give off alarm calls from its safe place on that tree in order to warn other squirrels nearby that the dog is still there.

Habituation is Context-Specific
Often, when our pets habituate to certain stimuli, such as loud noises and new objects, we're

surprised that they still react to the same stimuli in slightly different surroundings or contexts. That is, they don't generalize. The reason they don't generalize right away is that it's important for their habituation to be specific at first. If the squirrel learned that he was safe from the dog when he was in the tree and then also held his position when the dog rushed over barking when he was on the ground, habituation wouldn't have helped him; rather, it would have led to his demise. Similarly, if the deer that learns that moving cars on the road are safe also remains stationary the first time a car pulls to the side of the road, he could possibly end up mounted on a wall. Habituation can generalize, but usually only after the animal has habituated to the specific stimuli under many different contextual variations.

Two Types of Habituation—Flooding and Desensitization

With **flooding**, you expose the animal to the full-force stimulus. Ideally, the animal will gradually get used to the sound. (Figure 11.1) However, one problem with flooding is that if the animal is extremely fearful of the stimulus, flooding can actually **sensitize** him, thus making him more fearful of the same-level stimulus (Figure 11.2).

With **desensitization**, you start far away from the stimulus or somehow weaken the stimulus. As the animal gets used to the low-level stimulus, you gradually increase the strength of the stimulus (Figure 11.3). Ideally, the level would increase systematically enough so that the animal never actually reacts fearfully to the stimulus, or he could become sensitized. If the stimulus level is high enough to cause a significant response in the pet, then the animal is not being desensitized, rather it's being flooded.

Classical Counter-Conditioning

Usually, when you hear the term counter-conditioning, it refers specifically to classical counter-conditioning. With classical counter-conditioning, we classically condition a new association. If a dog is fearful of crates, we teach him that good things happen when he's near the crate (i.e., he gets food when he goes near or into the crate). Or if a dog is fearful of loud noises, we teach him to associate tasty dog treats with the loud sounds (Figure 11.4). That is, we're changing the underlying emotional state the drives him to perform the inappropriate behaviors, such as running away or attacking defensively. We usually combine counter-conditioning with desensitization.

Operant Counter-Conditioning

This is a term coined by Dr. Pamela Reid, a Ph.D. in Psychology and author of *Excel-erated Learning*. **Operant counter-conditioning** is when you train an alternate, incompatible behavior.

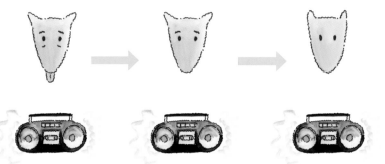

Figure 11.1 (Flooding)

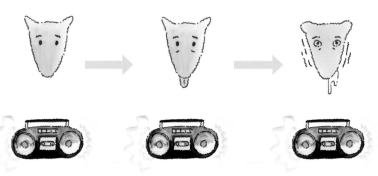

Figure 11.2 (Sensitization)

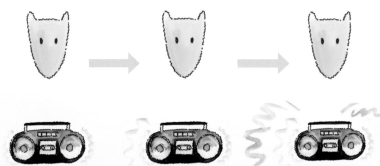

Figure 11.3 (Desensitization)

Figure 11.4 (Classical counter-conditioning)

For instance, if a dog lunges and barks every time he sees other dogs across the street, you can train the aggressive dog to watch you and go through other obedience exercises when he sees dogs. Thus, the new routine changes from "see other dogs and bark like a maniac" to "see other dogs and pay attention to owner" because it's time to do some fun heeling exercises, and he will get treats for good behavior (Figure 11.5). As with classical counter-conditioning, you start at a distance where the stimulus is weak and work closer and closer to the stimulus. It is important to know that for operant counter-conditioning to work in this specific type of case, it's more than just teaching an animal to move his body parts where you want them to be—you have to get the animal to focus on you instead of on the object of his aggression or of his alternate attention. Additionally, usually in cases when the animal is aggressive to another animal or object, you want to make sure that you're using positive reinforcement, because every time you use operant conditioning, classical conditioning is also occurring. Therefore, the animal is learning not only an alternate behavior but is also learning an association. If you use an aversive, the animal may learn to associate the other dog or person with aversives, which could make him more aggressive. We want him to learn an alternate behavior and form a positive impression of the object, person, or animal that scares him.

Using the Four Methods of Modification

Now see if you can come up with plans using each of the four methods (classical conditioning, operant conditioning, flooding, and desensitization). For each problem, list the general behavior modification techniques you could use and then specifically describe how someone might use

Figure 11.5 (Operant counter-conditioning)

each one of these techniques. While a given technique may not be appropriate for your specific case, it's good to know all of the available techniques, because one that you rarely use may be unexpectedly useful.

Case #1: Unfriendly Cats

You own a cat and just adopted a second cat. The cats don't like each other. They growl and hiss when they're in the same room even if they are 10 feet (3 m) apart. You want to fix the behavior. List general behavior modification techniques you could use and then describe how someone might use each one of these techniques.

- **Flooding**: Put the two cats in the same small room until they get used to each other. (*Note, in reality this would be dangerous, so don't try this at home*).
- *Desensitize*: Start with the cats far away, and when they're calm and relaxed, gradually move them closer and closer.
- **Classical counter-conditioning**: Teach them to associate each other with pleasurable things. So when they are in the same room, give them treats or attention. It's best then to only give them food and attention when they are together. Keep them far enough apart so that they only focus on eating and not on each other.

- **Operant counter-conditioning**: Train an alternate/incompatible behavior (that the cats like to perform), such as touching a target. When the cats are together, have them repeatedly touch a target to receive treats so that they are focused on the fun games and not each other.

Case #2: Fear of Strangers

Your dog is afraid of unfamiliar people (he barks at them and backs away), and you want to fix the behavior. List general behavior modification techniques you could use and describe specifically how someone might use them.

- **Flooding**: Put your dog in a room filled with unfamiliar people until your dog gets used to them.
- **Desensitize**: Start with the dog far away, from a stranger, and when he's relaxed, gradually move him closer and closer.
- **Classical counter-conditioning**: Train him to associate unfamiliar people with things he likes, such as food. So when he's around unfamiliar people, give him treats.
- **Operant counter-conditioning**: Train an incompatible behavior (that he likes to perform/ that he associates with good things). For instance, when he's around unfamiliar people have him touch a moving target or practice come when called or play other games that involve him focusing on you instead of the person he's afraid of.

Which Combination of Methods Is Best?

While most people tend to jump right to flooding for the fearful dog and punishment for the aggressive dog (even though aggression is most commonly due to fear), the most effective behavior modification methods for fear and aggression are actually the combination of desensitization and counter-conditioning. We want to change the underlying emotional state that drives the fear and aggression, and once we do this the behaviors associated with fear and aggression will disappear too.

Some people wonder, "Won't you reward fearful or aggressive behavior if you toss food or reward the dog for performing alternate behaviors (such as sitting) after he's just barked or growled or lunged?" It turns out that if we change the underlying emotional state we will diminish the behavior. For instance, if we have a dog who barks at us out of fear, when we toss treats frequently enough to keep him quiet most of the time and systematically move closer or move in ways that are potentially scary to him, then we will teach him to associate us and our movements with good experiences. He will no longer feel threatened and no longer need to bark or perform other aggressive behaviors.

(For a visual example got to www.lowstresshandling.com/dvd/samples/givingtreats.php.)

Chapter 12

Aversives:
The Pitfalls of Punishment

The first dog I owned was a big, bossy Boxer named Max. Hyperactive, humorous, and full of mischief, he was the kind of dog you get as penance for all of your future sins. In our first formal obedience class, which (for reasons beyond my control) began when he was three years of age, our instructor taught us the common method for teaching dogs to heel. As instructed, I hooked his leather leash to the choke chain around his neck, and when he wasn't paying attention, I ran full speed in the other direction. When I reached the end and he was still sniffing around, he got a huge yank meant to hurl a lesser dog off the ground. This quickly got his attention, and by the third yank, he'd learned to catch up and stick by my side. Then the instructor told me to continue practicing when he glanced away, and randomly to test him. Some people think that Boxers are slow learners—not Max. By the sixth yank, he had learned to defensively climb up the leash to growl and snap at me. Thus started a seven-year battle of wills. For the next five years, I searched far and wide for trainers who could help me learn to deal with this and his other aggressive behaviors, and I religiously did whatever they suggested. But it took ten trainers before I finally met one who knew about positive reinforcement, shaping, chaining, and consistency, and thus could start me in the right direction.

After several more years of daily work, Max was finally safe under my supervision, and he even earned an obedience title in three straight shows, with respectable ribbon-earning scores. But

I always knew what could have been. For years I'd searched in the wrong places—becoming an expert in the choke chain, pinch collar, electronic collar, and force techniques where positive reinforcement plus some brainwork on my part would have solved the problem sooner and with more satisfying results.

This doesn't mean I now avoid aversives and force altogether; I just avoid them 90 to 95 percent of the time. I still keep up on the techniques and test new devices, because I see such a wide range of serious and even life-threatening behavior cases and because I deal with such a wide variety of owners with different abilities and needs. However, I study each technique carefully in order to understand in which situations and with which individuals it might work. Because of my experiences with Max and many other animals since then, I only use aversives very discretely, and only after considering the side effects. And realistically, after considering the side effects, the personality of the dog, and evaluating what the owners can do, I generally conclude that most clients will not be able to do even the simpler punishments safely. Here are some of the side effects of aversives you should be aware of, in order to make an effective evaluation.

Punishment Must Be Immediate

Timing is a challenge with all techniques, but it is particularly tough with those that involve punishment. One of the primary problems is that people tend to use punishments long after the behavior has taken place. They come home from work to find that Rover has raided the garbage can or chewed up the couch, and they lose their tempers. While screaming in rage at Rover may make them feel better (positive reinforcement for them), thoughtful evaluation down the road often reveals that their rampage delivered the wrong message.

For instance, if they later notice that Rover now slithers away or stays in bed instead of greeting them at the door even when he hasn't created a mess, then the lesson he learned was that his owners are sometimes angry and out of control when they come home. So Rover waits until all is clear and he's sure that the humans who arrived are in a more stable mood. If Rover slinks off only when there's an accident or overturned trashcan in the house, he still didn't get the message straight. Instead of learning that he shouldn't poop or rummage through the rubbish, he may just have learned that poop is not permitted in the house or that trash on the floor is taboo. You can tell when he has the wrong idea because he'll crouch down fearfully or submissively (a posture meant to turn off aggression in the person or animal it's directed towards), even when he's not the culprit who created the mess. Lastly, even if Rover does know that raiding the rubbish is a "Fido felony," it may still be worth the risk, because often the immediate rewards outweigh the future possibility of punishment.

DR. YIN'S BROWNIE FAT-THIGH THEORY

Sometimes, for dogs and humans, the immediate rewards of doing something "bad" outweigh the future possibility of punishment. I call this the Brownie Fat-Thigh Theory. When we are on a diet, we know to avoid copious amounts of high-calorie foods. However, because they taste so good, we eat them anyway in order to reap the immediate taste rewards. Our reasoning is that we're not absolutely sure these calories will make it to our thighs. Maybe we'll exercise them off, or they are less fattening than we thought. However, if every time we ate brownies our thighs immediately ballooned before our eyes, we would no longer eat high-calorie desserts when on a diet.

Punishment Must Happen Every Time

Another point that's more crucial with punishment than other categories of operant conditioning is that punishment must occur every time the dog performs the undesirable behavior, or on a continuous schedule. The reason seems insidious at first, but once you see it, it's crystal clear. Say your dog raids the garbage can, so you set up a booby trap. You carefully place several armed mousetraps in the can and cover them with a light veil of trash. The next time he investigates the trash, the sudden loud snapping sounds scare him away. This punishment keeps the trashcans safe for a while, but several days later, he tries again. For the second time, the booby trap goes off just as planned. This time, he stays away for several days more. Because this rubbish raiding has been so successful and fun in the past, however, he tries once more several days later. This time the trash is unmanned by mousetraps, so his gamble pays off with a jackpot. While this one reinforcement for pilfering the trash may not seem such a big deal, now Fido is suddenly on a variable ratio of reinforcement, which is stronger than the continuous ratio he was on before.

Punishment Must Be Strong Enough

As you might already suspect, the punishment's success at suppressing behavior is directly related to the strength of the aversive you use. One major mistake that owners make is that they start with a level that's too low. The animal temporarily stops each time the owner uses punishment, but the punishment quickly loses its effect. Then the owner increases the intensity and the animal temporarily stops each time again, but then a few punishments at this level and he's immune once more. When you start with a level that's marginally low, you desensitize the pet to the pain or lose your startle effect. Often, you have to keep escalating the intensity, until suddenly you're at an ultra-high level that's possibly physically dangerous. In many cases, you may never be able to achieve a level high enough to have a lasting effect.

For example, I once tested a remote-controlled citronella collar on a chicken-chasing Great Pyrenees named Charlie. When Charlie ran up to the chicken coop in my yard and stared in, I set off the collar, which squirted a quick jet of stinky citrus-smelling spray past his nose. The first squirt startled him, causing him to shake his head and back off. Several seconds later, he went right back, which earned a second squirt. By the third squirt, the aversiveness was diminishing, and by the fourth or fifth, it no longer had any effect. The problem was that the punishment did not teach the dog what to do instead of the wrong behavior, so all that energy had nowhere to go. When we trained the alternate behavior of having Charlie focus on his owner for treats, Charlie learned within minutes to ignore the chickens, even when they were out of the coop.

Strong Punishment Can Cause Physical or Psychological Injury

You'd think you could avoid having to escalate by going immediately for high intensity and, in fact, this could work. But while an appropriately high intensity or strong enough aversive can suppress behavior for good, it can also lead to side effects, such as physical injury. For instance, yanking a choke chain or pinch collar around the dog's neck can increase intraocular pressure, which is especially problematic in dogs prone to glaucoma. Choke chains can also cause injury to the trachea (especially in dogs with flat muzzles), and to the nerves that travel through the neck. Electronic shock collars used repetitively can cause burns on the neck which sometimes extend to the esophagus.

Punishment can also cause the animal to become overly sensitive or fearful to the aversive or fearful of an object, place or person associated with this aversive, then generalize to similar objects, contexts or people. For instance, when I tested a citronella anti-bark collar on my Australian cattle dog, Zoe, she disliked the aversive so much than when the collar was on another dog and she heard the sound, she ran inside and hid in her crate. She became overly fearful of the sound of the collar even in the absence of the spray. If I'd continued using the collar, she would have learned that it was bad when both she and other dogs near her barked. Another time, I was testing a motion-activated sprinkler system called the Scarecrow, which is designed to keep unwanted animal intruders out of a designated area. When Zoe walked within its range and it gave its characteristic "shwook chuka chuka" sound as it sprayed, she immediately ran inside to her crate and was so disturbed that she refused to go out into the yard even for meals for several days. Then, several months down the road, she heard a similar sound in a different context and became anxious to the point where if she had been off leash, she would have run off and would not have responded to my cues for her to come.

These cases illustrate that to be successful with aversives, you have to first find the right level and mode—which differs for each animal and situation—while taking care not to cause physical injury. As a result, using punishment requires more skill and expertise at evaluating animals. To complicate matters, this evaluation must be based on the individual animal's perceptions, rather than our own. For instance, most people are more likely to believe that prong collars and electric collars are torturous, and citronella collars, spraying with water, or scaring animals with a loud sound is always more humane. But it's the animal that decides which stimulus is more aversive. When I started Zoe back in the old days with the old ways, I used a prong collar and choke chain. She responded like neither was a bother. And when I trained her to come from far away distances off leash using an electronic collar—on a low pager or static level which was turned off as soon as she started to come after being called—she was happy to come running right away. But as stated earlier, when I tried the citronella collar or a seemingly harmless burst of water, she suddenly developed an intense fear of certain sounds.

Any time you use punishment, you're risking potentially serious side effects. You face this chance no matter how mild or physically painless the punishment seems, because in order for the aversive to work, it has to be aversive enough to stop the unwanted behavior. Even if it doesn't do this by generating physical pain, it might have to generate intense fear.

Punishment Can Cause Aggression

Early studies in the 1960s on punishment with rats, cats, monkeys, hamsters, and other animals as subjects revealed another serious side effect of punishment—-punishment can elicit aggression. When researchers applied foot-shock to animals, the animals attacked their cage mates aggressively. This pain-aggression reaction has been shown to occur in a wide variety of animals in response to many different aversive events. The aggression can be redirected toward inanimate objects as well as other animals, including humans, and the punishment need not be physical.

Punishment Can Suppress Warning Signs of Aggression

Some people use punishment to decrease aggression, and it occasionally works. However, it frequently only suppresses a dog's external warning signs, such as a growl or raised lip, without addressing the underlying association or emotional state. The consequence later on may be that instead of giving a warning, your dog breaks out in a bite. In cases where you hear that an elephant or a horse has suddenly gone berserk and attacked out of the blue, or that a dog climbs up his leash and tries to bite when you suddenly run in the opposite direction, a history of punishment may be your clue.

Punishment Suppresses Overall Behavior

Another side effect of punishment and aversives is that they can suppress behaviors besides the one you don't want, which can lead to a bad attitude. You're probably familiar with this in some sense. Remember in grade school when you thought you could draw or sing well, but then a teacher or other adult's critical words told you otherwise? Since then, you've never quite tried being creative in the same way. Or remember when your mother nagged you to clean your room, and to avoid this nagging, you finally cleaned it? You didn't clean it with gusto, but rather with a mild sense of dread. In obedience training, one of the most common examples of this side effect at work is when you reprimand your dog for an exercise, such as going over a jump improperly, or avoiding a jump. Rather than trying harder, he avoids trying altogether, and your training schedule is set back several months.

Behaviors other than the one you're trying to remove can especially be suppressed if punishment is doled out with bad timing. In fact, bad timing can shut the animal down and cause him to give up. This phenomenon, termed "learned helplessness," was first studied in the 1960s, and the model in dogs has provided valuable insights into the physiology and cause of human depression. In the early classic studies, dogs in one group (experimental group) were placed in a harness that prevented them from escaping and were given five-second shocks presented at random times. Twenty-four hours later, these dogs were placed in a shuttle box where they could escape by jumping over the side. On the first trial, they frantically ran around and howled while trying to escape the shock, but then froze and remained silent until the shock was terminated. In contrast, dogs who didn't have prior training in the harness quickly learned to escape.

In a second experiment, two groups of dogs were given prior experience with a shock. Each dog in the control group was paired with a dog in the experimental group. Both groups of dogs were pre-trained in the harness and received random shocks simultaneously; however, the control group dogs could control the escape of the shock by pressing a panel with their head.

This turned the shock off in their own boxes and in the experimental group's boxes. When both groups were then tested in the shuttle box, the control group learned how to escape the shock, whereas the experimental group passively accepted the shock. Taken together, these findings indicate that lack of control of the shock led the dogs to passively accept the shock. This indicates that it's the lack of control of the aversive that leads to what scientists term "learned helplessness." The implications of these findings are that while using rewards incorrectly can lead to a poorly trained pet, using aversives incorrectly can lead to a passive animal that some may describe as depressed.

Punishment Can Lead to a Poor Association

The final pitfall of punishment is something I talked about earlier. Because conditioning is happening all the time, the regular use of aversives will cause your dog to associate you or the specific situation with the aversives and, consequently, your relationship may suffer. This association works both ways. When I used to use force and yelling regularly, I was frequently angry with my Boxer Max. On one hand, I loved him dearly and wanted to be his best friend, but at the same time, I wanted to throttle him. The proper way to use an aversive is to deal it out emotionlessly, and preferably to use some form of remote-controlled aversive so it can be independent of association with you.

Are Aversives Always Bad?

As stated earlier, there are a few occasions where aversives are appropriate for certain individuals; however, most of the time, we can do better without them. If you instead focus on removing the reward for bad behavior, creating an environment where inappropriate behavior is less likely to occur, and then reinforcing alternate appropriate behaviors, you'll form a stronger relationship with your pet.

Chapter 13

Troubleshooting Your Plan

At this point you can approach common behavior problems methodically, and set up training programs that rely on removing reinforcers for bad behavior and instead reward alternate appropriate behaviors. But what if your plan still goes awry? If you've plotted thoughtfully, most likely your plan isn't off base; rather, something's off in your implementation.

Assess Your Plan

One approach to detecting the deviation is to assess every aspect of your plan systematically by asking the following questions.

Timing

Is the timing correct? Are you getting the treat to the animal right after he performs the behavior, or is there some other important behavior that consistently occurs before you give the treat? Do you need a bridging stimulus? Are you taking too long to deliver the treat, even when the animal knows what he did right, so that he gets bored or distracted while he's waiting for you to fumble around?

Criteria

Have you defined your criteria so that you can be consistent and clear? Remember, every interaction is a training session. Are you interacting correctly all the time, or just during times you designate as training sessions? Are others in the house reinforcing the same or different criteria (so that the behaviors generalize to others instead of just being good for you)?

Rate of Reinforcement

Are you reinforcing frequently enough to keep your dog from being bored and allowing him to learn the behavior? Are you reinforcing correct behavior or are you bribing the animal by showing the reward first or luring the animal with the reward? (Read more about bribes in the next section).

Shaping Mistakes

If the behaviors in question require shaping, are you advancing to the next step before the prior step is down pat? If you're unsure, collect data and don't go on to the next step until your dog performs the current step correctly 8 or 9 out of 10 times in a row. Are you making big leaps between steps? Are you staying on earlier steps too long so that the animal has trouble relearning that this isn't the goal behavior?

Chaining Behaviors

Have you broken complex behaviors into their component parts and perfected them individually?

Natural History Considerations and Past Experience

Is the animal biologically prepared and anatomically able to perform the given behavior for the given reinforcement? Will past experience make the goal behavior easier or more difficult to train?

Motivation

Are you using the appropriate reward for the specific environment or situation? Ask yourself, at this moment, what would the dog rather do?

Communication

Are you giving some type of body cue that's "telling" the animal to do something other than what you want him to do? Is the animal's body language conveying an emotional state that indicates he's fearful in this situation or not motivated for the type of reinforcement you're using?

Sample Cases

For each case of a training plan gone awry, come up with reasons that fit into the seven problem-solving steps.

Case #1: Greetings Gone Awry

You're trying to teach your dog to sit when guests come over. You practice with him by giving him treats for sitting and ignoring jumping, and you have had several guests practice this, too, with your supervision. Your family members are supposed to be practicing, too, but you haven't observed them. You've done this for a week, and he's good for you, but he's not good for guests. What might be going wrong?

- **Timing is off:** Family members or guests may have poor timing, so that they don't reward him quickly enough (i.e., he sits a lot but stands up before they have a chance to reward him).
- **Criteria:** Some guests may have reinforced correct behavior, but other guests may not have. Some may reward him only when he remains seated; others reward him for the initial sit, but then let him jump on them. Also, other family members may be reinforcing other jumping instead. Ask them.
- **Rate of reinforcement:** Sitting for guests needs to be reinforced every time until the behavior becomes a habit.
- **Shaping:** Guests are more exciting than you are, so just because he sits well for you doesn't mean he should sit well for guests until he practices with them specifically.

- **Chaining**: None involved here.
- **Natural history/past experience**: His jumping behavior may have been reinforced many times in the past.
- **Communication**: Guests may be exhibiting body language that indicates he should jump on them (e.g., bending over in a human equivalent of a play-bow).
- **Motivation**: He's more motivated for attention and petting, but the reward you are using is food treats. If so, guests should only give attention while he's sitting and remove it when he stands.

Case #2: Unreliable Recall

Owner says Fido frequently comes when called at home, and he is given treats for this behavior. She doesn't understand why he rarely comes when called at the park. Instead, he sniffs the grass or plays with other dogs. What mistakes might she be making?

- **Timing is off**: She doesn't give the treat right when Fido comes. That is, her timing is often too late and he loses interest before she gets the treat to him.
- **Criteria**: She's not consistent about calling him only once or making sure he comes when called (i.e., sometimes it's okay if he doesn't come the first 4 times).
- **Rate of reinforcement**: She needs to reinforce his coming when called every time he does it correctly, both at home and at the park, until he performs the behavior well.
- **Shaping**: The dog doesn't come well when on leash at the park, so he's not ready to come when called when off leash at the park. Or the dog doesn't reliably come when called at home without distractions, so he shouldn't be expected to come reliably at the park. Coming when off leash at home is easy, but he's not ready to come when called when off leash at the park. He needs to first learn to come when on leash at the park, then when on a long leash at the park, and then he can come when off leash at the park.
- **Chaining**: None involved here.
- **Communication**: When she calls him at the park, she's always angry and her tone of voice tells him that he's going to get in trouble.
- **Motivation**: The treats she uses at the park aren't as good as the motivation to play with other dogs. Or at the park she needs to use better treats than the ones she uses at home. Or at the park her tone of voice and body language need to be more energetic in order to make coming to her as (or more) fun than the competing motivations at the park.

Case #3: Kitty on the Couch

Your friend has a cat that gets onto the couch whenever she and her roommates sit on the couch to watch TV. The cat is not allowed on the couch, so they squirt him with water bottle when he jumps up. He jumps up anyway. What mistakes might they be making in their training plan?

- **Timing is off:** They don't squirt him until he's been on the couch for some time, or they do it so slowly that the cat sees the bottle coming out and can easily just wait until he sees the bottle before he gets off the couch.
- **Criteria:** Sometimes they let him on the couch for a few seconds/minutes, or they let him walk across the couch, or sometimes they don't let him get on the couch at all.
- **Rate of reinforcement:** They don't get him every time with the squirt bottle, and sometimes they even reward him with attention when he's on the couch.
- **Shaping:** He may be good about staying on the floor when no one is on the couch, but the owners also have to reward him for staying on the floor when people are sitting on couch.
- **Chaining:** None involved here.
- **Communication:** Their body language tells him to jump on the couch. They don't read his body language well enough to tell when he's going to get onto the couch; therefore, their timing is off.
- **Motivation:** Being on the couch is very rewarding and outweighs the aversiveness of the spray.

Section 3

Five-Minute Guide
to Basic
Good Dog Behavior

This section covers specific techniques for training all kinds of dogs, ranging from tiny to tall to timid to tenacious. In fact, with slight modifications, these techniques, based on sound science, will work with cats, rats, goats, horses, chickens, and other animals, provided you use the right motivation and the animal has the anatomic capabilities.

For each technique, the general steps include:

- Reward the desirable behavior, and remove rewards for undesirable behaviors (and control the environment so these unwanted behaviors are less likely to occur).
- Reward the desirable behavior every time your pooch performs it up to par at first, and practice frequently enough so that it quickly becomes a habit rather than just a trick. Then switch to rewarding at a variable rate.
- Once Fido knows the behavior, add the cue word right before he performs it so he comes to associate the cue with the behavior.
- Use the cue word to get behavior only when the cue word is needed. Instead, rely on your natural body language cues or situational cues (especially for the automatic polite sit behavior).

Chapter 14

Getting Started

Let's cover the basics on how to get started training your dog.

Manage, Don't Micromanage

Managing Fido's every move is a tiring task, one that some humans can't help but attempt. They tell their dog to eat right before they hand him a meal or to sit every time they give him a treat. In this book, we're not going to tell Fido anything at first. In the early silent sessions, we'll wait for the correct behavior, sometimes positioning our body to help him along. When we see what we want, we'll give him a treat. (*Note: when I say treat, ideally you would use his regular kibble except in higher distraction situations*). Then, for some behaviors, such as say "please" by sitting, we'll expect him to offer the behavior in the appropriate situations instead of having to tell him every time.

Make Food More Motivating:
Train Fido to Earn Each Kibble

Good training starts with a reason to learn. Rover's reason or motivator will be a combination of food, praise, petting, play, and anything else he likes or wants at that instant (Figure 14.1). We will ration these currencies carefully. Because food will be our number-one reward, we'll start by teaching Rover that food is no longer free. From here on, he will earn each kibble.

Scheduled Feeding

Rather than leaving his food out all day so that he can snack at his leisure and even demand more costly cuisine at other times, feed him in two meals a day at first. Feed either a measured amount of a commercial dog food that's been through AAFCO feeding trials (as stated on the bag) or use some other balanced diet approved by your veterinarian or veterinary nutritionist.

For dogs that are finicky because they always get what they want, start by putting their food down in a bowl and removing what's left after 10 minutes. Even the dimmest Fido will quickly learn that food only appears at set times determined by you. Anything left disappears for good. After a few days—assuming no one in the house has given in—Fido will be eating his twice-daily dog food like it's a chocolate soufflé.

Use Food to Your Advantage

Now that your food currency has some real value, you can use the kibble for training sessions either at mealtimes, or disperse them randomly throughout the day. In more distracting situations, use more exciting treats. Because training occurs every time you interact with your

ABOUT FOOD REWARDS

In general, treats should make up less than 10% of your dog's daily food allotment, or his diet will become unbalanced or he will gain weight. Consequently it's best if you train Fido to work for his kibble and reserve treats for the more difficult situations. That way you'll get the most bang for your buck. Fido will learn to appreciate what he has instead of expecting you to always provide him with more. (For more information see the "Learn to Earn" section of Chapter 15).

dog, initially you should plan to have rewards available at all times, especially when on walks. If you only have them at set training sessions during the day, then Fido will only learn to behave when he sees the treats and knows he's having a training session. As a result, the good behavior will only be a trick that he performs when he wants treats. If you want him to behave at all times, then you have to be ready to reward him throughout the day, and prevent rewarding undesirable behaviors at the same time.

When Fido is first learning a new exercise, you'll reward him with treats every time he performs the behavior correctly. When he has the behavior down well, you'll reward more with praise, petting, or whatever he wants most, and use food on at an intermittent rate. On days where you have a shorter training session, feed Fido by placing the meal in a special Nylabone treat holder that the dog can roll around, causing a few treats to dispense at a time; or you can

Figure 14.1

freeze it in a stuffable chew to make a dog-food popsicle (such products can be purchased at most pet stores). Both methods ensure that your four-legged friend gets some mental exercise out of his daily meal.

Make Training a Game

Learning to earn doesn't mean life becomes a big boring job. Your goal is to make training into a game. If you are consistent about the rules Fido has to follow and are paying him with food and other rewards appropriately, you'll make his life simpler, clearer, and easier. He'll understand what you want and know he can look to you for leadership. And best of all, playing with and paying attention to you will become his favorite pastime.

Give Reinforcements, Not Bribes

Treats, toys, and praise work well to reinforce good behavior, but turn them into bribes and they can teach Fido to blow you off. When is a treat or toy or even verbal praise a bribe? When you have to show the treat or toy to Fido in order to get the behavior, he's only doing it because you lured him with luxuries (Figure 14.2).

   Luring is sometimes okay at the very start when Fido is just learning the exercise (i.e., the first one or two tries). It can sometime help him understand what you want him to do. But after that you should expect the correct behavior and then give him a reward afterwards. First reward him every time he performs up to par, then either raise your expectation of what you want him to do or switch to a variable ratio, which means maybe you reward him, maybe you don't. The same goes for praise. If you are pleading with him in a praise-like voice in hopes he will perform, then you're bribing him with words rather than reinforcing with praise. Pleading and even repeating commands will tell Fido you don't really know what you're doing and he shouldn't believe that you can guide him.

Figure 14.2

Developing a Habit, Not Teaching a Trick

Your goal is for Rover to behave in real-life situations, not just for 10 minutes a day during a practice session. If you only train in discrete sessions during the day, then Fido quickly learns to behave only during these sessions—and at other times, anything is okay. For instance, if you take treats out and work on heeling front of your house and he heels perfectly, that's great. He knows how to heel in that environment. But if you continue your walk and a half a mile later start letting him pull because you're no longer in training mode, or you've run out of treats/food rewards, now you're training him that pulling is fine, too. In fact, he'll specifically learn to only behave when you have treats or are in front of your house; when you go somewhere else or run out of treats that will be his cue to go back to pulling.

In order to train him to behave all the time, with or without treats, practice in real life—on walks, when guests are over, during everyday life. Have treats ready in the more distracting situations. However, that doesn't mean practicing for hours on end like you are training for a dog-obedience marathon. Just train in short spurts of one to ten minutes throughout the day. Remember that every interaction you have is a training session. End the sessions before Rover loses interest and while he's still hoping for more.

Fix the Communication Gap

Imagine you're walking down the street in a foreign country, and suddenly people start shouting wildly at you. Like a scene out of Hitchcock, you see a crowd of distorting mouths but can't comprehend any words; only the increasingly frantic arm flailing tells you a climax is about to spring.

While you may have never been in such a situation, chances are your dog has. Contrary to popular opinion, dogs aren't born knowing English (Figure 14.3). Furthermore, while they are experts at learning to read human body language, they're no more adept at reading human minds than humans are. That means that half the time when you think your dog knows what you want, he's just feeling his way around.

Figure 14.3

How To Behave So Your Dog Behaves

Teach the Behavior Then Teach the Cue Word

The first step in fixing this communication gap is to teach Fido what's right by simply rewarding the correct behavior. This requires opening your eyes so that you see the correct behavior and closing your mouth so you don't babble all kinds of distracting dialogue.

Once Fido is consistently offering the correct behavior, and you can bet big bucks that he'll offer the behavior when you expect it again, pair the cue word with the correct behavior. That is, using your strengthened skills of observation, say the word once right before he's going to perform the behavior. Make sure you use your normal tone of voice, not the one you used when you were in the military. Then follow through with a treat once he's completed the act. Repeat this pairing many times, and Fido will soon understand that the word is his cue to complete the behavior.

Remember that your dog is learning something every time he interacts with you, but he's not always learning what you want him to learn. Be careful to use the cue word immediately before the behavior when you know he'll perform the behavior. If you use it and he doesn't perform

Figure 14.4

the behavior, he'll learn that the word means nothing. Similarly, if your cue word is really the word repeated over and over, Rover will learn to respond after two or three times (Figure 14.4). If it's repeated a variable number of times prior to the behavior, he may learn to respond after a variable number of repeats.

Once your dog knows the cue word, you'll be tempted to use it all the time. Often, however, it's easiest to teach Fido to perform the behaviors automatically. In the following pages, note carefully the specifics on when cues should be used and when you can save your breath and teach Fido to perform the behavior automatically.

Teach a Unique Word or Sound That Marks the Correct Behavior

The second step is to teach Fido that a unique word or sound means he's doing something right. In this book, we'll use "yes" to mark the correct behavior. In clicker training, trainers use the sound from a toy clicker. First, we have to teach Fido what the sound means. Say the word and immediately give Fido a treat (Figure 14.5). Repeat the procedure in 10 to 20 trial sessions per day. After several days, or even several sessions, Fido should be flying to get his treat when he hears the magic word. Now you have a verbal way to bridge the gap between the correct behavior and the food reward. Your marker word or bridging stimulus marks the correct behavior exactly as it occurs. This buys you a little extra time to get the treat to Fido, although you still want to get thetreat to him as fast as possible.

Figure 14.5

Marker words (bridging stimuli) can be used in several ways. For the purpose of this book, the marker word signals the end of the exercise and should always be followed by a treat, even when you accidentally use it at the wrong time. In the following sections, when you're first learning new exercises, don't use the marker word. Instead, concentrate on getting your timing and body position right in order to get the correct behavior. When you feel comfortable, you can start using the marker word when training new behaviors. For most of the simple exercises, we don't need a marker word, but doing so can increase the speed at which Fido learns what he's done that is right. The marker word is most useful when you can't get the food reinforcement to the dog immediately after the correct behavior. For instance, if you're teaching your dog to run to and touch a pole 10 feet away, you usually can't reward him at the target because you're back at the starting point. You can, however, tell him when he's performed the correct behavior by using the marker word and then following as soon as possible with a reward.

Teach Fido to Respond Consistently to His Name

The third step is to teach Fido to respond to his name every time he hears it. To humans, our name helps define who we are—Conan the Barbarian, Hulk Hogan, Joan of Arc. Dogs, on the other hand, don't necessarily learn that their name is a label that stands just for them. Rather, most dogs learn that when they hear their name, something good, such as petting or playtime, happens to them. For instance, when my dog, Zoe, hears her name, she probably thinks, "Come quick, a treat may appear." When she hears me call my other dog Roodie's name, she probably thinks, "Come faster, before Roodie gets the treat." This works even when I accidentally call Cootie, Tootie, or Fruity, and sometimes even when Roodie isn't even near the house.

One consequence of this phenomenon is that dogs don't learn their name purely through constant repetition; rather, they learn through association with something good. So to teach a dog to respond reliably to his name, use the same procedure you used for teaching the marker word. When Fido is good and hungry, take him to a quiet location where he can't walk off. Armed with treats and standing within Fido's reach, say his name and immediately give him the morsel. That means ASAP, really fast, or at least within one second and before he goes off to do something else.

Figure 14.6

Repeat this procedure a dozen or so times in several sessions a day, and after several days, he should have the hang of it. You can tell because instead of wandering off, he sticks close by, and when you say his name, he immediately looks to you—the direction of entry for the treats.

Once he understands that earning treats is the name of the game, increase the expectation. Say his name and give the treats to him in such a way that he has to look up at your face to receive them. If he's not already looking at your face when you say his name, you can move the treat-holding hand up toward your face before giving the reward 5 to 10 times in a row (Figure 14.6). This way you're consistently delivering the treat from the direction of your face.

Once he's good at this step, the treat no longer has to come from the region of your face. You can now hide it in your pocket or in your hands behind your back and reward only after he looks up at you immediately upon hearing his name. If he's not right 100 percent of the time, then you've either advanced to this step too soon or you're luring him with the treat, which makes him bored, instead of giving it as a reward. In either case, he's now learning to ignore his name instead.

If you've progressed at just the right rate, you can walk around the room, say his name from several feet away when he's not looking, and expect his immediate attention.

When he's 100 percent reliable at this last step, gradually cut down the treats and replace them with praise. Do this by sometimes giving a treat and praising him simultaneously, so that he associates praise with treats. And then you can randomly give him only praise for performing the behavior correctly. Now you have a dog who pays attention to his name and is ready for any cue or command that follows.

As with cue words, once Fido knows his name, we tend to want to repeat it as if we think that each cue needs to be punctuated by his name. We even love the sound so much that we string it together into a mega version "Fidofidofido" so that Fido doesn't really knows his true name (Figure 14.7). Each time we say "Fido" and get a sluggish or non-existent response, we teach the dog to ignore the much-repeated name. To avoid this error, only call Fido's name when you're sure he's going to respond and when there's a question about who's supposed to perform the spoken cue or command. If he's the only dog in the room and he's staring straight at you, he doesn't need to hear his name to know that "stay" refers to him. If you need to get his attention but are unsure if he'll respond, make a smooching sound and reward him when he looks at you. If you want, you can even pair the smooching sound with food a number of times so he learns that it means food may come, but don't be that concerned if he ignores the smooching sound. It's just something to use when we want our dog's attention but aren't sure that one of his cue words will work, and don't want to risk training him to ignore our cue words.

HI! MY NAME'S ROVER ROVER ROVER ROVER, ...WHAT'S YOURS?

Figure 14.7

Get the Proper Supplies

Before you start training, you'll need three things: a nylon or leather flat collar, an inconspicuous bait bag for carrying dog treats, and a 6-foot (2 m) leash. A nice option to a regular leash is a hands-free leash that sits around your waist. This sometimes works better, because as creatures with two arms and dexterous hands, we tend to do odd, distracting things with the leash that end up sending mixed signals. When the leash is tied around our waists, we can concentrate on watching our dogs and delivering the treats. If your dog loves to pull and is has difficulty focusing on you, a front-attaching harness or head halter that controls the direction of the head will help you to train attention.

For a hands-free leash, try The Buddy System (www.buddysys.com). Head halters, harnesses, and bait bags can all be found at your local pet retailer or online

TRY THIS EXERCISE

Between dinner and bedtime, count the number of times other family members give Rover a command or cue that he ignores. Each word in repeated commands counts, so for example "Sit!sit!sit!" counts for three times.

Chapter 15

Say Please By Sitting

No jumping on guests, no chasing cats, no sampling food off the dinner table, no dragging humans down the street during daily walks: With so many rules, it's no wonder that Fido is having trouble developing the good social skills he needs to survive in a multi-species society.

Luckily, it turns out Fido can learn most of life's rules if you just teach him several basic behaviors—Say Please by Sitting, Leave it (which is an extension of Say Please by Sitting), Watch Me, attention on walks, and Come when called. All of these exercises focus simply on keeping your dog's undivided attention. When he consistently can execute the five exercises listed here at full attention, you have most of the basic skills needed to having a four-legged expert at dog-human etiquette. (The five exercises are covered in Chapters 15 to 20).

Teaching Say Please

The first and most important pleasantry all pooches should learn is to be polite by Saying Please. Dogs say "please" by sitting patiently while awaiting the go-ahead from you.

First, remember to avoid saying Fido's name. If you need to get his attention, make a smooching sound instead. Start with a ravenous dog either on a leash or in a small room devoid of distractions. Let him see that you have the treat so that he knows what he can earn, and then just hold the food hidden in your hand. At first, he'll wonder why there is a delay in treat delivery. If he's a go-getter, he'll try to get your attention doing what's worked in the past. This probably means a few pogo-like pounces on you and a "woof, yap, yip." In fact, he may bounce around more than usual at first if he goes through an **extinction burst** (see page 58). Rather than barking back an English equivalent of "No" or placing a hand on him to keep him down, make like an icicle and freeze so that he knows you're ignoring him. Be completely quiet and hold as still as a thousand-year-old tree stump (Figure 15.1).

This will puzzle your punchy pooch and give his wheels a workout. If he weren't attached to you by a leash or stuck in a low-distraction room, he might give up and find a simpler game. But since he's hungry for your special treat and strapped to you by his leash, you can just wait him out. Eventually he'll sit. If you're on the ball, you'll catch him in the act and within a split-second give him a treat before he has a chance to get up. Now he has his first clue. Quickly give him one or more additional treats for remaining seated while looking at you (Figure 15.2).

Next, back up or walk away a few steps while hiding the treat in your hand, then repeat this exercise. If his mind wanders, get his attention by making a smooching sound with your lips. Don't bother using his name unless you're 100 percent sure he'll look at you immediately. Otherwise, you'll just be teaching him to ignore his name. If making a sound doesn't

Figure 15.1   Figure 15.2

immediately get his attention the first or second time, then hold still and just wait (sometimes for quite a while) until he gets bored and figures out that he'll continue to be bored until he sits again and gives you his attention. If he's attached to you via a hands-free leash, he can't go anywhere to find something more interesting. In fact, if he does blow you off, perform this exercise with him on leash. It's as important for him to learn that behaviors other than sitting and focusing on you get no reward (negative punishment) as it is for him to learn that saying "please" earns rewards (positive reinforcement).

Once you have his attention again and he decides to make another try for the treat, he'll still start with the old song-and-dance routine. When it just earns a cold shoulder, he'll start thinking about the last clue you left; not barking, not pogo-like pouncing, not standing and staring at the hand with the treats. As soon as he sits and simultaneously looks at your face, send the treat express-delivery before he stands up and then give a few additional treats for remaining seated while focused on you.

Practice this 10 or 20 times in row, and Fido should clearly have the concept. In fact, see if you can get 10 sits in a minute. If it takes longer, don't worry, just practice in additional sessions throughout the day, or wait until he's hungrier for the treats or food you're using. Alternatively you can always just randomly catch him in the act of sitting near you and reward him. Once he has the exercise down, practice in different locations—first in the house, and then outdoors—so that he starts to suspect that you want him to say "please" in many situations.

Reinforcements, Not Bribes

As soon as Fido gets the idea that when he wants something he should sit, make it a point to hide the treat. You can do this by:

- holding your treat hand right against your belly button so you don't accidentally hold it out as a lure;
- putting your hand behind your back, and as soon as he sits and simultaneously looks at your face, get it to him within a split second; or
- placing your hands in your pocket until you need to deliver the food reward.

Be sure to deliver the reward in a way that causes Fido to look up towards your face—so that you're rewarding eye contact—instead of looking away from you.

You might wonder why bribing is bad. When practicing exercises under more distracting situations, people often lose patience and start to bribe instead of reward. They show the dog the food to remind him it's there and even wave it around. While this seems harmless at first and even gets Fido to sit faster a few times, if you make this a pattern, pretty soon, for each task, Fido's going to ask you to "show him the money." If the money's not good, he'll take a pass. Instead of a song and dance to get his attention, go back to silently standing and wait for him to finally figure it out. Then let the treat or praise just suddenly appear. Remember that you can also control the environment and his access to other reinforcers by putting him on a hands-free leash. Also, decide on the exact behavior to expect, and stick to your standards. If he sits too slowly, repeat the task, and only reward the appropriately speedy sit. Training sessions are where your pooch pits his brains against yours. Make sure you're training Fido instead of Fido training you.

Progress to Variable Ratio Rewards and Wean Off Food Rewards

In general, it's quickest to start with food when training, but once Fido sits consistently switch to variable ratio rewards and rewarding with just praise, petting, or whatever Fido most wants in the given situation. That is, when he's regularly sitting when he wants something from you, switch to rewarding with treats every one to three or more times. That way he never knows which time he'll be rewarded. When doing this, you may choose to use a marker word that you have trained, such as "Yes," whenever he performs the correct behavior—even if he's not getting a treat. Also, occasionally replace food with praise or whatever Fido wants. If he wants to go out the door, then reward him by letting him out the door. If his goal is to have a toy tossed, reward him by tossing the toy. For dogs who don't care about praise or petting, you may need to pair these things with food until they also become a good motivator. The overall goal is to systematically cut down on your food-using frequency.

Avoid the Sit Command Most of the Time

Notice that in this exercise, we never gave a command. If you teach Fido to wait for a command before being polite, you may always have to tell him to say "please." In this exercise, we've purposely omitted a cue word, because we want Fido to just behave politely out of habit, rather than having to tell him each time. He should know that when he wants something and you are just standing and waiting, he should be polite and automatically sit to say "please." For dogs who are not so great about offering new behaviors or just happy to stand but know sit really well, for a day or two you can whisper the word "sit" to help them along. But after this they should sit automatically.

Add a Cue Word for Sit

While Fido should sit in designated situations automatically, we will sometimes want him to sit on verbal cue. To teach him the cue word for sit, just call him over and say, "Sit" in your regular speaking voice, just before he starts to automatically sit. Then reward him with praise or petting (if he's motivated by these things) or with food once he sits.. By uttering the cue word right before the action a few dozen times, you'll teach Fido that "Sit" should be followed by a sit. You can test whether he really knows what the word means (versus him reading your subconscious body language) by turning your back to him and then seeing if he still responds to the verbal "Sit." Alternatively, once you've taught him one of the other exercises listed in this book, you can alternate between cues for various different exercises and see if he performs the correct behavior. Once he knows the cue word, remember to use it sparingly. In most situations Say Please by Sitting should be automatic, such as to go out of the car, get treats, get a leash on, or have a toy tossed.

The Learn to Earn Program

When should dogs Say Please by Sitting?

Once Fido can perform Say Please by Sitting in the house during a training session, it is time to teach him to automatically be polite at all times. The goal is to train Fido that no matter how excited he is, to get what he wants he must say "please." As a result, he'll learn self-control rather than acting on impulse, and to look to you for guidance— especially when he can't get what he wants or doesn't know what to do. If you work through this program diligently for even just several days you'll see a huge change in your dog's behavior. (To see video of this topic, go to "Stellah Learns to Earn" http://www.youtube.com/watch?v=ct_uYoQx12A; or find "Stellah Learns to Earn at www.DrSophiaYin.com under the "movies" section.)

Start by measuring Fido's daily allotment of food and treats, so that you can carry it around with you in a bait bag or have it conveniently located around the house during the day. If your dog has a tendency to blow you off or walk away when you're hoping to train him or hoping he'll stick near you, you'll also need to keep him on leash at all times when you're home with him. He'll be tethered via his leash so he has to follow you around the house (or he can be tethered to furniture if you're nearby). The purpose is to prevent him from being rewarded for blowing you off.

To start the program, randomly reward him with treats (kibble) for sitting near you. For instance, if you're working at your desk and he sits and looks at you, then give him some treats. Or if you walk to the kitchen and clean the counters and he sits, reward him with a series of treats. Since most dogs get about 100 to 200 pieces of kibble per day, he'll earn 100 to 200 rewards for sitting and looking at you throughout the day; consequently he'll learn quickly to focus on you. The end result is that ideally, every time he looks at you, he should think about sitting.

Now that sitting is fresh in his mind, apply automatic sitting to everything else Fido wants.

Getting Out of the Car

If Fido tends to leap out of the car straight into danger, train him to sit before exiting instead. Open the car door a crack and block his route out. If he tries to make a dash for it, quickly sidestep or step forward (like a basketball player on defense) to make your block. (This exercise is easiest if he's already learned the Leave-it exercise from Chapter 16). Each time he makes a move, thwart him by positioning yourself in his path. Eventually, whether carefully planned or just by accident, he will sit. Immediately give him a treat while he's still sitting and then give a few more for remaining

Figure 15.3

seated. When he's been looking at you for several seconds let him out. You should be able to move completely out of his way, giving him a clear path out of the car and he should stay seated until you give him the word. Again, if he makes a move to get up, just block his path quickly enough so your intentions are clear. The first few times you try this technique will often become a big waiting game (Figure 15.3). Some dogs are perfectly comfortable standing around with a blank stare, especially if they aren't yet used to Saying Please by Sitting in many situations in the house. If your pooch is a slow sitter and he's already good at sitting on verbal cue, you can say "sit" in a whisper. Once he's sitting make sure you give him a string of rewards. Then make sure you practice 5 to 10 times in a row and also practice the Leave-it exercises. If you're rewarded him enough he should be sitting automatically on his own within several days. You can also just wait him out a few times and then shower him with a string of treats once he's sitting. The wait is well worth it, because when the light bulb turns on, it shines bright. Five to twenty trials in a row over the course of a few days will result in a relaxed exit after his car ride to the park.

TURN SIT INTO A FUN GAME

Training dogs isn't just about giving treats, it's about moving in ways that make your message clear and make focusing on you fun. (Dogs like MTV, not *Masterpiece Theater*.) So if you're pokey or your movement is sloppy Fido's bound to lose interest and look like he has a low attention span. You may incorrectly attribute this to thinking he doesn't like playing games—when he really just doesn't like playing games with handlers who are boring.

Quick Repeat Sits Going Backwards

Fido already knows how to follow you and sit when you stop. Now, from a stationary position, start with Fido sitting, then suddenly run backwards several steps (Figures 15.4 and 15.5). Make sure you move enough to make it clear that Fido should get up and sprint after you. Then suddenly stop (Figure 15.6). He should stop and sit (Figure 15.7). The purpose of the distinct movements is to make it clear what you expect Fido to do. Repeat this exercise five to ten times in a row always going backwards. Note that you can back up in any direction you want as long as Fido is facing you and you move in a straight line. Ideally, Fido should have his eyes glued to you throughout this routine. This exercise will also help prepare Fido to Come when called and is a good exercise to use when he's about to bark or lunge at something. Just do the repeat sits going in the direction opposite to the distractions until you can keep Fido focused on you more easily.

Figure 15.4

Figure 15.5

Figure 15.6

Figure 15.7

Quick Repeat Sits to the Side

Next, teach Fido to keep his eyes on you when you move to the side. Again start with him sitting in front of you and then suddenly run several steps to the side as if you're playing football and dodging a tackler. Then suddenly stop and wait for him to sit (Figure 15.8). Fido should have his eyes glued to you throughout this whole routine. Remember to hide the treat in your hand so that you're not bribing Fido. If he's starting to jump, then take fewer steps or run just a little slower. Stop running before he jumps and gradually increase your speed. This game will help prepare Fido for both heel and come.

Figure 15.8

Up the Excitement with "Suddenly Settle"

Now we can up the excitement more with "Suddenly Settle." Run to the right or left while cheering, waving your arms, and otherwise encouraging Fido to romp excitedly (Figures 15.9 and 15.10). Then suddenly freeze and watch him sit (Figure 15.11). Like a child's game of freeze, he should go from rowdy and rambunctious to silently sitting as though you have him on an on/off switch. You can reward with food, praise, or calm petting while he's in a sit.

When you can perform these games, your dog will really think Saying Please by Sitting is a blast. Have races with your friends, practice during play sessions, and remember to reinforce with praise, petting, or treats (whichever he responds to best) on a variable ratio. When you go onto a variable schedule, you may choose to use a marker word such as "Yes" to tell him when he's performed the behavior right.

Figure 15.9

Figure 15.10

Figure 15.11

Waiting to Go Through Doorway

This same technique applies to waiting to go through doorways. Instead of letting Fido rush past you, first wait until he sits to open the door, then block him from coming out (for more information read Chapter 16, Leave It).

If you time it right, he won't even get close to the opening before he sees the opening narrow. Every time he makes a move, make your countermove. After he finds that a mad dive won't do it, he'll look for other solutions, one of which will be to sit. Then, you should be able to open the door wide without him trying to dash out. Every time he starts to make a dash, counter with a quick move to block him. Only let him go through after you've given him a verbal or visual cue that tells him to go. Soon, he'll know just a small movement by you means he can't get out.

Before You Toss a Toy

When Fido wants to play fetch, wait until he sits to toss the toy to him. If he has huge arousal issues around toys, then teach him to sit or lie down and remain seated to get the toy. Go to Chapter 16 for instructions on how to do this.

To Greet Guests and Family Who Enter the House

When you come home and Fido tries to jump on you, remove your attention and turn into a tree until he sits. If he's big, turning your back on him will help you keep your balance. Reward him with food when he sits, or even with a pat on the head. If he gets up, which he's likely to do if you praise him too exuberantly, immediately stand straight and ignore him again, and then reward him with one or more treats in a row when he sits. If you're consistent, he'll soon learn that he only gets attention when he's seated. Note that you can also preemptively lure him to sit with the first treat, and then reward with treats for remaining seated. Practice many times in a row so that he gets the idea quickly and forms a new habit. Next, set him up by having a few friends come over and give them treats. When he sits for them, the treats can either come from you or directly from the guests (Figure 15.12). If you expect him to always give good greetings and never reward him for jumping, this seated greeting will quickly become a handy habit. You can extend the time he sits for guests by waiting longer periods of time to give him the treat, and by giving him

Figure 15.12

several treats in a row each time he sits and then gradually increasing the interval between the sequential treats.

To Be Petted

For persistent jumpers and for dogs who are dubbed hyperactive, overly energetic, or as having attention-deficit, expecting them to stay seated to be petted can turn them from a four-legged fury to calm canine sitter overnight. Doing so gives them an instant "off" switch. Thus, even when maximally excited, they learn to control themselves in order to get attention. This exercise is the most challenging for owners to perform consistently, because owners tend

Figure 15.13

to pet their frisky Fido as he stands or wiggles around, not just when seated (Figure 15.13). Instead, you should withdraw your hand and stand up straight so that you're clearly removing attention. When Fido's sitting calmly without wiggling, you can pet him (Figure 15.14). Again, if your dog's really exuberant and energetic but likes being petted, it may take 5 to 15 minutes for him to learn that he has to sit politely to be petted. By petting him in a slow, soothing massage only when his derriere's on the ground, you're rewarding him for being calm. You can give him treats while he's seated and you're petting him in order to speed the sit-to-be-petted process. If your dog seems to have a low attention span or completely lacks focus, you should perform this exercise with him attached to you via a hands-free leash. Again, while this is probably the most effective exercise for giving a friendly Fido some focus, it's a challenge for owners to keep from giving in. One way to change the human habit of reinforcing unruly behavior with petting and attention is to have a competition to catch family members in the act. Take note when family members are petting Fido when he is standing, and see who can change their behavior the quickest. Note that an extension of rewarding the calm sit behavior is in the chapter on teaching your dog to lie down. You can speed this process up by giving him treats while you're petting him—give them frequently at first and then slow the rate down. (For video demonstration, go to http://www.youtube.com/watch?v=ct_uYoQx12A "Stellah Learns to Earn.")

Figure 15.14

Chapter 16

Leave It

If Fido slurps up slimy surprises during his daily walks, nearly takes your hand off with each food treat you feed, or fights dynamically over dropped scraps, this exercise will save you from all types of trouble. The goal is for Fido to wait for your permission to go to objects that are lying on the ground or in your hand. These exercises will help teach Fido self-control, and can be used as a foundation for training Fido to wait to come out of the car, go through the door, wait to grab a tossed toy, focus back on you when he gets to the end of the leash, and more.

Food in Your Hand

This is a good exercise for teaching Fido to take treats nicely. Put a treat in one hand and hold your hand out in a fist. Let Fido sniff and lick and try to get the treat, but keep your hand perfectly still (Figure 16.1). When he moves his head back for even a second, open your hand, move the treat closer to his mouth, and let him take the treat (Figure 16.2). If your timing is good, after only a few 5- to 10-minute sessions, he should automatically keep his teeth and nose away from your treat-holding hand until you open the hand and push it up to his face.

To teach Fido to look at you for guidance before taking the treat, hold a second treat in your other hand and place it near your forehead. When he moves his nose away from the treat hand that is closed in a fist, give him the treat that you're holding near your forehead, followed by the treat that's in your closed fist (Figure 16.3). He'll know he can have this second treat because you'll open your fist and put it under his nose.

When giving the treat from your close-fisted hand, you can first draw the treat up to your face, so his gaze remains on your face when he gets this second treat, too. After 10 to 50 trials over several days, he should be looking at you immediately for direction.

Next, remove the forehead treat and just give him the fist-held treat after he's looked at you for direction. You can also continue to take the fist-held treat and draw it to your forehead before giving it to him.

Add the Leave It Cue

When he's close to 100 percent consistent about moving his head away from the treat in your hand, add the verbal cue "Leave it." Use the cue as he sees you put your hand out, but only when you're sure he will move his nose away. Once he understands this phrase means to remove his nose, you can use it for when you're not in position to give him the synonymous body signals or cues. For instance, if he's sniffing food on the coffee table, tell him "Leave it" and praise him exuberantly for looking at you, while providing a better treat.

Also, although your body language tells him when he can have the treat, you can also teach him a cue such as "Take it," so he also has a verbal cue that you can use in other cases. Just use the phrase "Take it" each time you let him have the treat. Later use this cue in cases where it's not so clear that he can have food that's lying around. You can also use a verbal release word, such as "OK," "Break," "That's all" or "All done" to mean he can have what he wanted.

The Open Hand Variation

For a variation on this exercise, hold your hand open with the food in it. If Fido makes a move to sniff, close it into a fist. When he moves his head back, open your hand again. When he's held

Figure 16.1

Figure 16.2

Figure 16.3

How To Behave So Your Dog Behaves

his nose away for a few seconds, either hand the treat to him so he knows it's okay or tell him "Take it" and let him take the treat. Remember, you can also draw the treat to your head and then immediately give it to him. The direction that the treats come from will be the direction he will want to look.

Once he has this exercise down pat, you can use this cue to tell him to keep his nose away from taboo items. He'll think it means, "Move your nose and you'll get a treat from me instead."

Leave It From the Ground: Blocking Method

In this exercise, show Fido a treat and then drop it on the floor behind you (Figure 16.4). As he starts to rush after it, block him with your body by taking small steps to the right or left (like you're doing a basketball block). If he outmaneuvers you and gets around, quickly step on the treat so he doesn't get rewarded for his superior athletic ability. When he Says Please by Sitting and looks at you, give him a string of treats until he has a stable gaze on you. Next, move out of the way so that he has clear access. Give treats to reward him for remaining seated and focused on you, and block him if he makes any movement to go towards the food on the ground. When he has a stable gaze on you, either pick up the food on the ground and hand it to him while telling him "Ok," or give him his release word and let him get the treat.

After about a dozen or so successive trials on your part, he'll stop rushing full-speed toward the treat, and it will be easier for you to block his path. Several more 5 to 10 minute sessions and he'll automatically look to you for direction. Once he's good at the behaviors you can add the

Figure 16.4

"Leave-it" cue word. At this point put the reward on a variable schedule of reinforcement. That is, he doesn't have to get the treat on the ground every time. During practice sessions sometimes let him get the treat and sometimes don't.

Now you can also use blocking in other situations where you want Fido to learn to sit and look at you before he runs off to do something else. For instance, block him when training him to wait patiently before coming out of the car, before going out the front door, before chasing a toy you toss inside the house, or when he wants to rush to get to a family member.

Leave It From the Ground: Food Tossed Outside of Leash Range

In this exercise Fido needs to be on leash. Toss the treat outside of the range of the leash and when Fido gets to the end of the leash, just stand still like a tree (Figure 16.5). When he realizes you're not budging and he can't reach the treat, he'll come back and sit in front of you. He'll do this because he already knows the Say Please by Sitting exercises and knows that's how he gets what he wants. When he sits in front of you give him a series of treats until his gaze is consistently on you (Figure 16.6). When he's looked for about two seconds without treats, then say "Ok" and point to the treat and walk towards it fast enough so he stays on a loose leash. This exercise is great for teaching Fido that when he gets to the end of the leash, he's not going to go

Figure 16.5   Figure 16.6

anywhere (negative punishment because he won't get rewarded for pulling). Add the cue word once he knows the exercise well and also switch to a variable ratio or reinforcement—during practice sessions he doesn't always get the treat on the floor. This exercise comes in handy in any situation where Fido may want to pull on leash. You can also use toys instead of treats tossed on the ground to teach him self-control around toys.

Practice, Practice, Practice

Play this game during everyday situations: On walks, randomly drop treats and then block Fido's access if necessary. Or, if he's on the leash, stop just out of reach and stand stationary. Let him strain and tug like in the "walks nicely on leash" exercise (Chapter 18). When he finally figures that he can't get to the food, make a smooch sound, and when he comes to you, you can give him a treat. You can then go and block access to the item you planted on the ground for him to try to eat. Wait until he looks to you for permission or Says Please by Sitting, and then pick the treat up and give it to him.

At home, whenever scraps drop on the floor, make Fido wait prior to picking them up. Then, either give him the scrap (if that was your intention), or give another treat so he doesn't feel like he's missing out. That way he will learn to automatically wait when he sees food and realize that objects on the ground are off-limits. As an added bonus, if all household hounds learn this game, then competing members will learn to wait instead of diving for the food and getting into fights.

Around the Food Bowl

Practice this same technique when putting the food bowl down, and soon Fido will learn to sit patiently while you prepare and place his food.

Chapter 17

Watch Me

All of the cues you've used so far, including smooching and using your dog's name, should cause Fido to look to you. The following exercises will teach him to keep his eyes on you until you tell him it's okay to look away.

Teaching Watch Me

Make the smooching sound you usually use to get his attention, and when Fido looks up at you, give him the treat before he looks away. Then give him three or four more treats in rapid succession before he looks away. If he looks away before you give him all the treats, quickly run backwards a few steps so he has to follow and then repeat the exercise again. Once he's good at keeping his eyes on you for all the treats, then increase the interval between treats by one to two second increments at first. Once he performs the behavior well five times in a row, you can increase the interval between treats. If you have problems getting Fido to look up at you when you smooch, start with the treat either at your forehead, where you want him to look, or at his nose level, and quickly bring it up to your eyes (Figure 17.1). Again, when he looks up at your face, immediately give him the treat. You should only need this lure two or three times.

Once you're sure Fido gets the idea, you can add a specific cue phrase such as "Watch me" if you like. Say the cue right before you smooch so that it predicts that you will smooch and give a treat. If he tends to look automatically when he hears your voice, you can omit the preliminary

Figure 17.1

Figure 17.2

smooch. Soon he'll learn that "Watch me" alone means to look up at you in order to receive a treat, but you can always just stick with the smooch sound as your cue.

Reinforcements, Not Bribes

Once Fido knows the cue and looks up at your face immediately upon hearing it, use the food as a reinforcer rather than a lure. Hide it in your hand or behind your back and give it to him after he looks at you, but before he looks away (Figure 17.2). You can even hold the treat in your hand out to your side. Initially he'll probably look at the hand with the treat, but when he finally looks to your face, immediately give him the treat. If you have problems with him looking away, try drawing the treat up to your forehead the instant before you give it to him. This often helps ensure that he keeps his eyes glued to your face, rather than staring at the treat.

Increase the Time

Gradually increase the seconds that you expect him to watch you prior to getting his treat, as well as the interval between sequential treats. The goal is to get the treats to him before he looks away. If he looks away, you waited too long. Work up to about 10 seconds before the first treat and between treats, and then start giving the treats at irregular intervals. Next, add distractions, but first lower the standards to only a few seconds. Then gradually increase the amount of time with distractions.

When to Use Watch Me

The primary purpose of this exercise is to teach Fido to keep his attention on you for extended periods of time while stationary, in preparation for focusing his attention on you when you're moving; however, you can also use this exercise in other situations. For instance:

- When Fido's waiting with you in line and you don't want him sniffing around, play the watch me game instead to keep him occupied and out of trouble.
- If you're walking along and he wants to inspect something that's off-limits, ask him to watch you instead of looking at the taboo item.

Chapter 18

Walk Nicely on Leash

Every year, scads of dog owners envision the great times they'll have with their new dogs—early morning jaunts in the park, after-dinner strolls around the neighborhood, weekend trips to the beach. Then, after several months, they realize that something's not going quite right.

Rather than showing the social skills befitting a pup who has attended the finest puppy preschool, he acts more like a fresh-off-the-farm Fido. In his hurry to get there faster—wherever the end of the leash goes—Fido strains and lurches like a sled dog in a weight-pulling contest. And if he's on a choke chain, he gags and sputters as the chain tightens around his ever-strengthening neck.

In an attempt to put some dignity into this daily escapade, some owners opt for power steering—the pinch collar. This multi-pronged bit of metal looks like a medieval torture device, but it's actually safer than a choke chain, because it distributes pressure around the neck more evenly. The problem is that even when used correctly, it can cause your dog to be scared or develop a bad attitude when walking with you; and the corrections, especially when not forceful enough, may not be effective in the long term.

At this point, small dog owners are still in good shape. They can save face by switching to a harness—a virtual pull-training device. This stops the coughing and hacking, but not the pulling. Then, to fake a good dog-walking technique, they add a retractable leash, a leash that expands and retracts with a flick of your finger. Now Fido can run all over without dragging his owner or gagging but may trip or jump on pedestrians and dogs who are within 15 to 20 feet (4.5 to 6 m). Large-dog owners who try these methods aren't so lucky. Most who try a standard harnesses find that one or two rides is enough. Only the most avid enthusiasts of extreme activities stick with this method for long. And a harness plus a flexible leash can be even worse—this combo just means Fido can pull from farther away.

So what do you do? Well, by this stage, most owners give up. That means a life of backyard confinement for their Fido. But it doesn't have to be that way. You can easily teach a dog to walk nicely on lead, and all you need is a leash, a regular buckle or snap collar, and patience.

Teaching Walk Nicely on Leash

Plan your first walk in a familiar area, such as right outside your house, at a time of day when there are few distractions. Warm up by doing a few repeat sits—reward him with treats and then when he's sitting, position yourself so that he's on your left side with his front feet even with yours. On walks, he can normally just walk on a loose leash by your side or a little behind, since that's the best location for him to pay attention to your cues. Since he's on a loose leash he'll still be able to sniff trees and plants when you allow him to.

While the left side isn't set in stone, it's the side that most dog trainers use to start. You can choose the left or right side (or train both sides later), but when you walk the dog should stay only on the side you designate unless you tell him to walk on the other side. When you're first

Figure 18.1

learning, stick to one side. After you have the techniques down you can add the other side. In this book, we'll start with the left side.

With Fido's leash hanging in a loose "U" that doesn't quite touch the ground, take off at a power-walk pace so it's clear to him that you've started the walk. As soon as his front feet get ahead of yours and way before he hits the end of the leash, stop dead in your tracks (Figure 18.1). At first Fido will pull because it's worked before, but because you're not budging, it'll be like he's hooked to a tree. He's not going anywhere. Eventually, he'll turn and sit in front of you just like he does in the Leave-it exercise. Reward him with a treat within a split second for sitting at attention, and then sometimes reward him a few more times for continued attention (Figure 18.2). Then resume power-walk pace. Don't expect to go far. By the second step (or the fourth or fifth if you're walking fast enough), he'll probably be near the end again, and you'll have to stop. In fact, your whole walk will be a series of starts and stops, like a ride in a junker ready to conk out.

Don't feel bad if it takes 20 minutes to go all of a few blocks. The goal is for Fido to understand that the criteria for where he should be positioned is always the same. Each start and stop must be distinct so that Fido understands what causes forward walking and what causes stopping. That is, always stop right as his front feet get ahead of yours and then when you start walking again, walk briskly so it's clear to him when you're starting and when you're stopping. When Fido understands the new walking rule, he will immediately stop before he gets to the end and turn to show he's paying attention to you (Figure 18.3).

Figure 18.2

Figure 18.3

If, at the end of 20 minutes, you haven't made a dent, your timing is probably off, meaning you're stopping too late, you keep changing your definition of the distance Fido can go, or the speed at which you walk makes it difficult for Fido to understand when exactly you've started walking. It can also mean he's not motivated for the food rewards. If, however, you save his entire meal for short walks during the day, and toss any food he isn't willing to earn, his treats and kibble will be more valuable to him. Within several days he'll understand that pulling doesn't work anymore so he'd better get focused back on you for the increasingly desirable food rewards.

If you stick strictly with the plan, before long, you'll notice a huge change. By the second or third walk, Fido should be a different dog. Where he used to strain relentlessly, now he'll stop at the slightest tug on his flat collar, even at the beginning of his walk. The better you are at putting on the brakes, the clearer the message will be: Tight leash means stop; loose leash means go.

Ways to Speed Up Training
Hands-Free Waist Leash

Using a leash that wraps around your waist, such as the Buddy System (www.buddysys. com), will speed up Fido's understanding of the correct signal. This is because the leash will immediately go tight when he reaches the end (Figure 18.4). When the leash is in your hand,

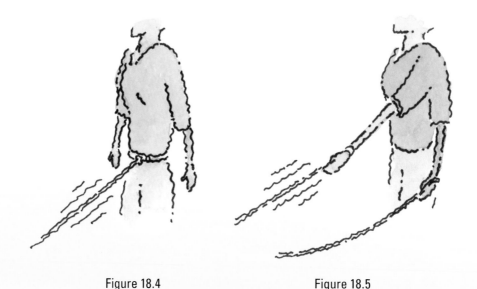

Figure 18.4   Figure 18.5

you have a tendency to extend your arm out as the dog pulls rather than holding your arm tightly against your side (Figure 18.5). This makes it unclear when you want him to stop and also teaches him he can pull a little.

Front-Connecting Harnesses and Head Halters

For those of you wary of dealing with even short bouts of tugging by your experienced leash puller, add a front connecting harness or a head collar to the picture. With the front-connecting harness (such as the Sensation harness or Gentle Leader harness) when Fido gets to the end the leash, which is connected to the front of the harness, it causes his body to turn back around towards you. The head halter (such as the Gentle Leader or Snootloop) is even more effective in this respect. Like a horse's halter but made for dogs, a head halter works on the idea that where the head goes, the body must follow (Figure 18.6). When the dog gets to the end of the leash he walks right into his head halter and it actually turns his head back around to you. Now when you repeat the training procedure, Fido won't be able to pull so hard.

To get Fido used to a head halter, give him treats for just putting his nose through the loop for the first day or so. Then, when he's comfortable with this stage, put the collar all the way on. Be ready to work on the games he already knows and likes, such as Say Please by Sitting. This way he has something fun to think about other than the odd contraption on his head. If he paws at it, just gently guide his head up so that he learns that pawing causes his head to be pulled up. Then, when he relaxes, immediately release the tension and get his attention with treats and games that earn rewards.

With this collar, as with haltered horses, gentle guidance rather than sharp tugs works best. Because sudden changes in direction can send Fido to the chiropractor, make sure you teach

Figure 18.6

WHAT SOME DOGS LEARN AND HOW TO FIX IT

Some dogs learn the following behavior chain—pull, stop, run back for a treat, and then pull again. If Fido has figured this trick out, instead of giving him the treat when he runs back to you, do a 180° about-turn and power walk in the opposite direction. At first, practice this move without your dog. Start by walking in a straight line. When you decide to about-turn, plant your left foot, turn around toward your right 180°, then jog several steps in the direction that you came. Once you're comfortable doing this, practice with Fido. When he catches up to you after your about-turn, reward him with a treat while continuing your power walk. Next, work on U–turns—walk around your dog so that you can turn and head back the direction in which you came. To do this you have to be slightly ahead of Fido first. As you're walking, with your left hand place a treat lure down at his mouth level to stop his forward movement. Once he's stopped, make your U turn around him. Give him the treat once you and he have completed the U turn. Throw U turns into the mix frequently so that Fido learns to stay slightly behind. Also, once he knows the exercises, start rewarding on a variable schedule rather than every time.

him the "walk nicely" game so he knows to pay attention to your moves. You don't want to use the head collar just as a way to contain strong pulling without teaching Fido to pay attention to you. Because if you suddenly change directions with any speed, or if Fido sees something distracting that he wants to chase, he may get a big jerk that can injure his neck. (For complete head halter protocol with photos go to www.lowstresshandling.com to the online book and download the handout called "Training Dogs to Love Their Gentle Leader.")

Treats to Reward Continued Walking by Your Side

You can speed the process even more by rewarding your dog with treats when he's by your side and looking at you. If Fido tends to look at you but then looks away before you have a chance to give the treat, you can use a marker word, "Yes" (if you've already trained it), right when he looks at you in order to buy some time. Make sure you deliver the treat with the speed of someone smacking the "yes" buzzer in a game show.

Be Consistent

Remember that every time Fido is on leash, you must be sure that he walks on a slack leash (Figure 18.7). Every time he gets close to pulling, be sure that you stand as stationary as a post. If your dog is inconsistent about walking on a loose leash, it's because family members are inconsistent about requiring him to walk on a loose leash.

WRONG.

RIGHT.

Figure 18.7

Chapter 19

Paying Attention at Your Side (Heeling)

Now that Fido knows how to say "please" and how to pay attention outside, he's ready to learn to walk at attention by your left side. The key here is that he pays attention and is focused on you. On walks, he can normally just walk on a loose leash by your side or behind you, since that's the best location for him to be attentive to you. You should at any time be able to get him to give you eye contact while walking politely by your side. That way when a distraction—such as a cat, dog, person, or anything else Fido wants to bark at or investigate appears—you'll be able to get his attention back on you and keep him politely at your side.

Now walks will be a time to bond with and play with him rather than a time for him to blow you off or wish you didn't move so slowly. As for the loose-leash walking exercises, for the purpose of this book we'll start with all of the exercises on the left. We'll also start with Fido on a hands-free leash, since keeping your hands free will allow you to concentrate on your dog and on proper reward delivery instead of the leash.

Method One: An Extension of Say Please by Sitting

Your dog already knows that when you sprint a few steps to the side or run around rambunctiously, these are cues for him to mirror your direction. He also knows that when you stop, he should immediately Say Please by Sitting. First, warm up by sprinting to the side a few steps with Fido's gaze focused on you the whole time, and then reward him for sitting once you stop. When he can do this consistently, start with him in a sit, turn to your right so that you and he are facing the same direction, and start walking at power walk speed. The speed is important because it will help him understand that you want him to follow. He should automatically know to mirror you and should catch up almost immediately. With your left hand, give him a treat as soon as he catches up. He should be standing and you should still be walking as you give the treat (Figure 19.1). And to make it clear when he should take the treat, walk with your left arm bent 90° and by your side. Then when you decide to give the treat, just straighten your left arm so that the treat is delivered right to your dog's mouth within a split second.

If Fido's unsure he should try to keep up with you, next time smooch to get his attention as you start to power walk, or hold the treat in your left hand at your left side as soon as you start walking. Then give it to him when he catches up (Figure 19.2). This is luring, which will work at first, but if you continue to use it over and over, your dog will get greedy down the road and only perform when he sees a treat he likes at that instant. After the first few times that you lure him, he should get the idea. Next, hide the treat in your left hand where it will still be ready, and then let the treat suddenly appear once he catches up.

When you can get these first several steps of attention, which with the proper groundwork should only take a handful of tries, you can continue to walk briskly after the first treat and reward him for continuing to walk at attention at your left side.

Your goal is for his eyes to be glued to your face at all times. If he looks away, smooch, speed up for a few steps, and give him the treat as soon as he responds appropriately. If he tends to look away immediately after he gets a treat, start with four to five treats in your hand and give them in rapid succession, before he has a chance to look away. When you're out of treats, stop

Figure 19.1

Figure 19.2

the exercise and reload. Systematically increase the number of steps before the first treat and between treats, while always expecting him to look directly at your face when heeling. It's important to increase the number of steps from, say 3 to 5 and then to 7, 10, 15 and every half block, and then to a variable rate quickly so that you can ultimately make heeling a habit that doesn't require treats.

Marker Words

If your dog tends to look at you for an instant, but you can't dispense the treat to him before he looks away, take a step back and work on say "please" by sitting and running to the side.. Another option is to add the marker word "Yes" to buy some time. Remember to say the marker word to mark the correct behavior and then follow with the treat, rather than saying "Yes" as you give him the treat. When done correctly, this game will teach him to walk in the special spot on your left and pay close attention.

If you're timing is right, Fido will focus more and find his position, because it earns him rewards. Once he's keeping his attention on you, you can go longer and longer between treats. This way, you'll reward him for keeping his attention on you for longer periods of time. The goal is to reward him before he looks away rather than waiting too long.

Method Two: Targeting

Another way to teach your dog to walk nicely by your side is to use targeting. The first step in this method is to teach him to touch his nose to a target that you make with the first and second fingers of your left hand. Hold your left hand out like a karate chop so he can touch his nose to the tactile side of your fingers—the side you usually use to touch things. Now you know which side he should touch. Next, place a little bit of canned cheese or peanut butter on your fingertips to lure him to sniff your fingers (Figure 19.3). Start with your left arm bent and your hand held

Figure 19.3

Figure 19.4   Figure 19.5

up by your side (Figure 19.4). Then straighten your arm and place your target hand just a few inches from his nose (Figure 19.5). When he touches, remove the target to its original position out of his view and simultaneously give him the treat.

Repeat this in short 5 to 15 trial sessions. When he responds reliably at a few inches, move the target farther away, so that he has to take a step, and then repeat the trials (Figure 19.6). Most hungry dogs in low distraction environments learn this exercise within 10 trials, which is virtually immediately. If your Fido seems slow, have someone watch you, or watch yourself in a mirror in order to evaluate your technique. Be sure that you're holding the target low enough for Fido to see.

Reinforcement, Not Bribes

If Fido is responding readily and as fast as you put your hand out, you can remove the cheese or peanut butter lure and see if he touches the target. Make sure you start by presenting the target just several inches away to make it easier, and that you hide the treat. You should still have the treat ready, though, in the treat-delivery hand. You'll know when your treat in the treat-delivery hand is accidentally out of place and consequently distracting him, because he'll look at that hand instead of your target hand. If he does respond correctly a number of times, then increase the distance you expect him to move. First, expect him to move one step to touch the target, and when he's good at this, increase to two or three steps. He should be running to touch the target.

To make his movements crisper, be sure you make the target suddenly appear and disappear—like doing a karate chop. In other words, rapidly straighten and extend your arm and the target out so it suddenly appears (Figure 19.7). Once he touches it, reward him while simultaneously

Figure 19.6

making his target disappear. If you leave it out for him to take his time, he will. If you move it closer to make it easier for him, he will train you to do this regularly. Instead, if you've chosen the wrong distance, make the target disappear and then reappear at a closer distance.

Now you're ready to use targeting to teach Fido to walk at attention on your left side. With Fido in a sit or a stand, start walking, and stick your target out on your left side in line with your hip, exactly where you would like his nose to be. He should run to reach the target, at which point he'll be in a perfect position at your left side. When he touches the target, remove it and simultaneously give him a treat while you continue walking.

With his nose targeting to your hand, you have a way of telling Fido exactly where you want him to walk. Whenever he's a foot or more behind you, speed up and simultaneously target him to tell him to get into place. When he's at your side paying attention, you don't need the target; just randomly give treats for being at attention at your side. If he's too far ahead, you can do an about-turn and target him to catch up. You can also do any of the exercises you used in the last chapter to keep him by your side—like stopping and waiting for him to sit or U-turns.

Using Targeting to Get Back to Heel Position

Another way to get Fido back to heel position when he's ahead is to abruptly stop, take a step back with

Figure 19.7

your left leg, then target farther back on your left side. If you target far enough back, when you start walking forward he'll be aligned with his shoulder at your hip. Intermittently reinforce his paying attention to you and being in position at your left side.

If Fido tends to cross over behind you to your right side, whip your left-hand target out conspicuously so he sees it and heads back to the left side. Then intermittently reinforce heeling at attention in this correct position. Remember to smooch when needed to get his attention, rather than calling his name.

Adding the Heel or Let's Go Cue

As soon as Fido reliably walks at attention at your side, you can add a cue word, such as "Heel" or "Let's go." The cue word means that Fido must hang with his shoulders roughly near your hip and at your left side while focusing all of his attention on you. Only use it when that's what you expect.

To teach the cue, say the word "Heel" or "Let's go" in a happy voice and immediately start walking briskly in a manner that you know will cause him to run to heel position. When he quickly catches up, give him a treat and praise, if he responds to praise. Use the cue word every time you start off briskly (and know he'll get into position quickly) and soon he'll understand that "Heel" means to be in the heel position.

Adding Fun Footwork

As stated earlier, one purpose of heeling is to make walks fun. While treats are fun, an equally important aspect is controlling how you move. So now, instead of just walking forwards when working on heel, you'll throw in sudden direction and pace changes. Make these changes unpredictable. If you fall into a predictable pattern or pace Fido will be lulled to sleep or find something more interesting to do. If you focus on how you're moving and how Fido's responding, then your walks will turn into a bonding time for you and your pooch. For best results you'll need to work without your dog first.

Pace Changes

First, try walking your regular power walking pace, then suddenly jog for just three to four steps and then return to your regular pace. Now try it with Fido. When he races to catch up, give him the treat. Once he's good at catching up, give treats intermittently for catching up. It's important to jog just a short distance because it's the initial change that makes it fun. If you keep jogging, then Fido may get bored. Also, practice suddenly walking really slow for a few steps. Fido should perk up and mimic your sudden change.

180 ° About-Turns and U-Turns

Throw in plenty of about-turns and U-turns. By performing a lot of U-turns you'll be able to quickly cut down on the amount of treats you need when just walking on a loose leash (Figure 19.8). As with the pace changes, once Fido knows the U-turn and about-turn well, then only reward intermittently. For instance, reward the about-turn or U-turn every 1 to 5 times. Once you go to intermittent reinforcement you may want to use a marker word or rewards with praise so that Fido always has some confirmation that what he has done is right.

Figure 19.8

Right Turns

Draw an imaginary 10 x 10 foot (3 x 3 m) or larger square at the park or in your front yard. Feel free to use the lines on a basketball or four-square court. First walk in a clockwise direction. When you get to the corner, plant your left foot and then cut right like a wide receiver. Run three steps, then slow to your regular power walk. Practice this until you don't have to think about your feet, then try it with Fido. Right before you make your run to the right, say, "Let's go" or "Heel" in your best "party's over there" voice to remind him something is going to happen where he needs to work to stay at your side (Figure 19.9). When he catches up, give him a treat. Your goal is to get him to gallop happily alongside in this funny game. If you've done your homework up to here, then he should immediately respond to your direction change without being left behind.

Mix It Up

Start by moving in straight lines—power walking forwards, doing about-turns or U-turns, right turns or suddenly run to the right or left. If Fido's good at these, then add circles to the right

Figure 19.9

or left at a brisk pace. You can spiral down from a large circle to a small one or serpentine in and out of trees. Speed up for a few paces, then suddenly walk in slow motion, and remember to reward intermittently. Fido should always have his eyes glued to your face. If he looks away, smooch to get his attention back, or suddenly change your direction and pace.

Troubleshooting

If you're having problems keeping Fido's attention, take a few steps back. Start by keeping his attention for the first two steps. Then, when he's consistent, expect attention for 5 steps, then 7 steps, then 10 steps. Now go on to a variable ratio of reinforcement; that is, sometimes reward him every 3 to 5 steps and other times reward him every 10 to 15 steps so he never knows exactly when the treat's going to come. Then increase the requirements even more. In this manner, you can quickly build up attention. Once you can regularly get attention at about 10 steps, you're practically home free.

Be aware that in more difficult situations (e.g., the part of your walk where a gardener suddenly appears, dogs are barking, or people who want to pet him walk by), you'll need to be ready to play the fun heeling games and give treats at a higher rate. The more you practice successfully in these high-distraction situations, the faster you can cut down on the food rewards in these contexts.

When to Use Heel

Now that Fido knows how to heel attentively on your left side, you have the tools to handle all kinds of problems. These heeling techniques can be used on dogs with many bad behaviors. In counter-conditioning, you train the dog to perform a behavior that's incompatible with the problem behavior. At the same time, because you're using food and praise, you're teaching the dog to associate good things with situations that may have once been fearful.

On Regular Walks

Fido should just stroll at ease on a loose leash. But in a clutch situation, you should be able to bring him back to heel position with the soft utterance of the magic word. For example, when you need to pass a pedestrian who doesn't like even leashed dogs, a well-timed heel for several yards should ensure that he or she can pass your dog safely. This game will also spice up ho-hum walks and make them more interactive. Sprinkle the strolls with a fast-paced game of heel. Vary and blend the methods whenever you want.

When He's Aggressive With Other Dogs

If Fido sees other dogs and growls and lunges, go back to this heel exercise using either the first or the second method, whichever works best. Start at a distance where the technique works and gradually move closer and closer to the distraction. If you do this regularly, Fido will learn that it is more fun to play the game with you than to pay attention to the other dog. (For more, go to www.lowstresshandling.com/dvd/dogaggressivedog.php.)

When He Wants to Chase or Lunge

If he's chasing or lunging at bikes, skateboarders, cats, and rollerbladers while on walks, again go back to the attention basics. Instead of playing the chase-the-people game, he can learn to play the chase-the-food game while walking at attention.

When He's Afraid of Objects, People, or Dogs

Try the same technique again. Fido learns that when he sees these objects, he gets to play that fun game again. He learns to associate these fearful objects and people with good things.

Note that in all of these clutch situations, if you can't keep Fido's attention while heeling, then switch to doing repeat sits backwards away from the distractions. Also consider using a head collar, as this will cut down on the amount of running around and quick movements you'll need to keep Fido focused on you.

Chapter 20

Come When Called/Recall

Getting a good recall is simple, but making it a solid habit requires lots of practice. Of all the exercises that people should teach their dogs, this is one of the most important but least appreciated, as well as the one involving the greatest waste of an owner's breath. For example, twice one week during a jog with my dog, a Standard Poodle came bouncing across the park. "Fanny, come! Fanny, come! Fanny, come! Fanny, come!" yelled the owner, standing stationary half a football field away. Based on the Poodle's response, one might have guessed that Fanny was some other dog, but the owner's gaze gave himself away. "Fanny! Fanny! Fanny!" he continued, as if commissioned to alert the entire area of Fanny's presence, or maybe just to alert me that he wished Fanny would come back, even though he was too lazy to walk over to get her. After following us for several hundred yards, Fanny finally broke off and headed to her handler in a roundabout way.

While this episode led to no harm, consider the following case instead. Say you're walking a dog with mild dog-dog issues, or pushing a baby carriage, or you have a healthy fear of large four-legged beasts that barrel into your personal space. So when you see Bowser bounding over, you head the other direction or call out, "Please call your dog!" Unfortunately, several "Bowser!"s later you realize you should have yelled, "Please come GET your dog…NOW!"

Well, if there's no knocked-over baby carriage or no dog fight ensues, what's the big deal? That's what owners of one large off-leash dog thought, until one day they came upon my mom walking her Scottie, Meggie. Meggie has a hereditary disorder that unpredictably affects her ambulation. One minute she's running around full throttle and the next her muscles go haywire and suddenly her front legs are churning in third gear while her hind legs are stuck in first. At this point the slightest shove can topple her off her two-inch stand. Even for a Scottie, she's poorly equipped to defend herself, though because of her oversized head, she does have an abnormally loud bark. Unfortunately, only blind dogs are fooled, and the German Shepherd Dog who ran up to her was not blind; however, he did predictably play deaf when his owner called. Then, in a show of poor socialization, after a second of nose-to-nose indecision, the dog grabbed Meggie and flopped her like a fisherman tossing a striped bass into his boat. My mother fell, and Meggie marched off as quickly as her discombobulated legs would allow. Luckily the Shepherd's owner was finally able to leash him.

While there were no broken hips and Meggie recovered after several days, the scene could have been much worse. Just as a key fall during a Superbowl riot can quickly turn a victory celebrator into a trampled victim, a fall accompanied by screams in the presence of aroused, fighting dogs can turn a human into the new target.

These are only a few examples of things that can go wrong when Rover's lacking a good recall. Here's how you fix it.

Getting Started Teaching the Recall

In the say "please" by sitting exercise, Fido learned to perform the behavior multiple times when you took a step or two to the side or backward. In the recall, you'll first practice the sit and "please" by taking three to four steps backward and expecting Fido to follow attentively.

To extend this into a full recall, start with Fido either standing or sitting. Say, "Fido, come" and then backpedal quickly so that Fido races to catch up and performs Say Please by Sitting (Figure 20.1-20.2). Although he should be used to sitting when you halt (because he has practiced the "Suddenly Settle" exercise earlier), some dogs occasionally get distracted or forget what they are supposed to do when you run this far. These dogs can be lured into a sit using a treat the first several times.

Once Fido is steady and he keeps his eye on you at all times, place him in a quiet setting and walk with him, making sure the leash is slack. Then suddenly run backwards and say, "Fido, come!" in your best cheerleading voice. This sharp change in direction, along with your encouraging call, should stimulate him to spring into action. If he looks like he's forgotten about sitting and is going to run right by, show him the treat at nose level way before he gets to you, and guide him into a sit in front of you. After luring in this manner several (two to three) times, you should be able to fade this lure out and just reward him once he sits nicely.

Randomly practice this game over and over, cheering him on while he's running to you. Your goal is to make him think it's fun by getting him going at a dead run. To do this, you can call him and turn and break into an animated run. Then way before he catches up to you and has a chance to run by, turn around so that he can sit politely in front. If this game is unpredictable

Figure 20.1   Figure 20.2

enough and lots of fun, he'll hopefully learn to choose to come even when sampling smelly items on the ground, chasing cats across the street, or barking at other Bowsers who want to play.

Upping the Ante

Usually recalls at close range with few distractions are fairly easy. To get good recalls in critical real-life situations, you have to gradually add real-life distractions. Try walking with Fido on loose leash near something he likes, such as a toy lying on the ground (Figure 20.3). Before he makes a move toward it, call his name and then run the opposite way—as if you're racing to chase a squirrel in the other direction. If he doesn't immediately come, he will feel the gentle but firm tug on his leash. Be loud and happy while you're running away as if there's a party in the other direction. Immediately give him a treat when he promptly sits in front of you. After you give him his treat, let him go back and play with the toy, too. But make sure he's on a loose leash on his way to the toy so that he doesn't get to practice pulling.

Repeat this game with different distractions. Make the game easy by using mild distractions at first so that he can be successful and come without feeling a tug. If he fails to come immediately, it's because the distraction was too big for his stage of the game, or you called him after he was engrossed in the object. Take a step down to an easier level, or improve your timing. Once Fido is an ace, he'll come even when he's in the middle of something else that's fun.

Graduate to a Longer Leash

Next you can use a leash that's over 10 feet (3 m) long. Retractable leashes work especially well for this exercise. Let Fido walk around on the lengthy lead. Then, making sure it's not tangled, depress the button on the handle that retracts the leash and then call him and run in the

Figure 20.3

RECALL TIP

After they've come running and collected their treat, some dogs lose interest until the next recall and go off on their own thing. To keep their attention, give several treats in a row, and gradually increase the interval between treats in successive trials. Alternately, move directly into another exercise such as heel or target, or try the "watch me" exercise.

opposite direction at full speed (Figure 20.4). You may need to pull him gently but firmly so that he knows you're in a rush to get to the party in the other direction. But if you move fast enough, your energetic movement will also incite him to chase you. When he catches up, guide him into a sit in front of you using a treat as a lure (if needed) the first several times. Then give him treats and lots of praise (if he's motivated by it) so he's sure he made the right choice. You can also play tug with a tug toy (like the ones Nylabone makes) if he knows to let go when you say leave-it.

When he comes immediately 100 percent of the time, give him even more slack on the leash, or add distractions. But only make one of these changes at a time. In the case of distractions, start with easy ones at first, such as stationary objects. Then graduate to more engaging ones, such as moving toys or other dogs on leash. In the case of doggie distractions, make sure the other dog can't run alongside Fido as he's trying to make his way to you. As usual, when he reaches you and sits, give him a treat, praise, and the opportunity to play with the other dog. That way he learns that coming when called never means missing an opportunity to play.

When to Practice Off Leash

Your ultimate goal is for Fido come when he's not on lead. After all, if he's on leash, the recall is not such a problem. If you've already been practicing other exercises with the hands-free leash, and actually kept the leash both slack as well as free of your hands, you've been preparing Fido for off-leash work. If he's not focused on you during all exercises already but lazily waiting to get a tug on his leash, he's not ready to be off leash. He must jump to attention whenever you ask for it.

Practice off-leash recalls in your house and in your enclosed yard. Only call Fido when you know he will come. Every time he hears

Figure 20.4

"Come" and does his own thing, he learns to that it's okay to do his own thing.

Practice in public places on a regular-length leash and during everyday walks, and practice with a retractable leash at the park. Let him sniff and explore the park, and when he gets far enough away, randomly call him and run in the other direction. When he catches up, give him one or more treats in a row. Repeat this intermittently throughout the walk. If he wants to play with another friendly dog, let him play while on his retractable leash, or hook him up to a long leash that you let drag on the ground. Then intermittently call him back and give him a slight tug as you run the opposite way, if needed. When he sits in front of you, give him a string of treats and then let him play with the other dog again.

When he reliably comes from strong distractions every time you call, try him off leash in a dog-safe area. Again, only call him when you know he will come. Set Fido and yourself up for success. Note that in high-distraction situations, if he can't focus on you doing repeat sits or heeling then it's not likely that you'll get his attention for a come when called. So you may need to go back and practice this in distracting situations.

When to Use the Recall Command

Use the come command in the following situations to keep Fido out of trouble:

- When play between Fido and his four-legged playmate is getting too rowdy, call him back before a scuffle ensues. Then reward him for coming and let him play again, but this time call him back before his arousal level rises.
- If you spot something smelly that all the other dogs are rolling in, call Fido back before he starts rolling. Well-trained dogs come even if called while they're rolling. Of course, they still stink, so it's better to catch them before the first roll.
- When he starts running over to strangers or kids, call him back to your side. These people may not feel comfortable with strange dogs investigating them or their children. Even if they do like dogs they might not like getting jumped on.
- If he sees something that he might chase, such as a bike or skateboarder, call him before he becomes fixated. If he doesn't come, you waited too long to call him or he is too close to the stimulating object.
- In the house if he barks at someone passing by or at a neighbor dog in the yard, call him and then reward him for coming and follow up with additional treats for remaining near you for a while.

Note that if he's unable to focus on you doing repeat automatic sits in the above-mentioned situations, he's not likely to have a good come when called. So go back and work on the Say Please by Sitting exercises from Chapter 15.

Chapter 21

Teaching Your Dog to Lie Down

Just as sit is a great way for dogs to say "please," lie down is a great way to teach dogs to settle for extended periods of time. Consequently, down can be the second most important exercise for those dogs who we label hyperactive or overly energetic or who love to jump on people. In this section, you'll learn how to get Fido to lie down, and in the following section, you'll learn how to extend this into a down-stay.

Method One: Watch the Wheels Turning

One of the most interesting ways to see Fido's brain in action is to teach down the same way you taught say "please" by sitting. Take a treat so that Fido knows it's time to try something. Now just wait for him to try different things. At first he'll sit. To show him that's not what you want, turn your head, ignore him and say, "Too bad" in a nonchalant way. This cue phrase will come to mean, "Try something else." An energetic dog who doesn't yet have a strong habit of saying "please" by sitting will eventually try different things, including nudging you, sitting in different positions and, finally, lying down. As soon as Fido lies down, give him three to four treats in a row for staying down for several seconds. Do this 50 times in 10 trial sessions over several days, and he'll soon get the idea. In fact, if he likes the rewards you're giving, he'll soon be throwing downs faster than the average advanced obedience competition dog. Once he's offering downs regularly and quickly, add the cue word "Down" just before he lies down.

Method Two: Shaping Down with a Food Lure

For dogs that just don't seem to try many different behaviors or those that have made a habit of saying "please" by sitting, shape the behavior instead. Start with Fido already in a sit and hold a treat in front of his nose but dropped down several inches closer to the floor. This will draw his nose and head down and cause him to lower his front end a little. Immediately give him the treat plus a series of treats for holding this position rather then getting up. If when you hold the lure he gets up, that means the treat was held too close to the floor; next time hold the treats higher up. When you practice this enough times so that he's bending close to the floor promptly, go to step two.

In this step, hold the treat a little lower so that he bends down a little more. If he loses interest or keeps getting up, you're holding the treat down too far. Continue this process until he's pretty good, and then increase the difficulty in the next step by holding the treat further down. Once you've gradually worked to the level where the treat is almost on the ground, take the next step by holding the treat on the ground, but a few inches in front of him. This will allow him to bring the front of his body the rest of the way down. Overall, you are moving the treat down and then away from the dog in an "L" pattern (Figure 21.1). Each time he lies down all the way, give him several treats in a row in rapid succession so that he learns to enjoy the down position.

Figure 21.1

Method Three: Make a Tunnel

For dogs that really don't like to lie down, you can try the tunnel variation. Start with both you and Fido sitting on the floor. Raise your knees so that you've made a little tunnel. Hold the treat halfway into the tunnel (Figure 21.2). To get the treat, Fido will have to bow down and reach into the tunnel. At first, he'll just bow. Reward him for this with a string of treats. Then, gradually shape the behavior in steps by moving the treat further and further into your tunnel. For instance, hold it 5 inches into the tunnel until he's successful immediately most of the time, then hold it 6 inches into the tunnel until he's accomplished at this task, and so on, until he magically bows lower and eventually lies down. Each time he lies down all the way, give him several treats in a row in rapid succession. When he lies down immediately 8 or 9 out of 10 times in a row, you can remove the tunnel and change to method two.

Figure 21.2

Switch From Lure to Reinforcement

Once you're confident that Fido will lie down with a lure every time because he does it at least 8 or 9 out of 10 times in a row, you can stop using food and either wait for him to offer down in method one, or you can use the hand motion to signal the down command. Use the same hand motion in the "L-pattern" you used for luring him, but this time do it without a treat in the signaling hand. Once he's down, give him three to four treats in a row from your other hand while he's still lying down. Eventually, he will learn to stay relaxed in his new position.

Adding the Cue

At any point when Fido's predictably lying down with the hand signal, add the cue word "Down" right before you give the hand signal. Make sure you say the cue distinctly but in a happy voice. Also, make sure you say the cue word before you give the hand signal that he already knows. If you present the two at the same time, a phenomenon called blocking may occur, in which he fails to learn the verbal cue because the visual cue (which he already knows) is more salient. That is, he will have no reason to learn the verbal cue because he already knows the hand signal. On the other hand, if you present the verbal cue first, then it will predict that the visual cue is coming. Once you present the verbal cue prior to the visual cue enough times and follow with a reward, he'll respond to "Down" by lying down. You can test whether he's lying down due to the verbal cue or whether he's going on a visual cue by standing perfectly still with no body gestures and uttering the cue "Down." If he lies down on a vocal cue while you're otherwise perfectly still, then he knows that "Down" means lie down.

If you taught down by just waiting for Rover to lie down and then rewarding the good behavior, then you can teach the verbal or visual cue by giving it right before you know he's going to lie down. After many pairings, he will understand that these cues mean that he should lie down.

Games

Here are a few games that can teach Fido how to Down.

Game 1: What Does "Down" Really Mean?

If you've been practicing the cue word "Down" a bunch of times in a row, Fido may indeed know that "Down" means to lie down without needing a visual cue, or he may just think "Down" means to perform whatever behavior he's been working on for the last 5 to 10 trials. In order to test or train Fido to distinguish between different words, try the following game. Walk around the room and then stop and tell Fido, "Down." If he sits, ignore him and wait 5 to 10 seconds, then try again. If he messes up again, repeat the last procedure. Repeat four to five times until he lies down. If he doesn't lie down, then go back to the step of adding the visual cue. If he does lie down, give him a treat and then walk around the room again and ask him to lie down again. When he's good at this, then switch between the cue to lie down and the cue to sit. If he performs the correct exercise, give him a treat. If he performs the wrong exercise, then wait 5 to 10 seconds and repeat. If he reliably performs the correct behavior when you randomly alternate between the two cues, then he knows the difference between the verbal cues of "Sit" and "Down."

Figure 21.3

Game 2: Advanced Version of "Suddenly Settle"

Any dog can learn to lie down, but lying down fast can be a fun game. Start with Fido standing up and just wait for him to lie down (as with method one). When he lies down, give him three to five treats in a row. Then walk a few steps, stop, and again wait for him to lie down before giving him several successive treats. If he is extremely motivated for the treats you're using, he should start lying down immediately when you stop. Once he's going down superfast, get his energy level up between exercises. Once he's good at this, you can also practice using the same exercise with the cue word "Down." Walk with him focused on you, stop, and suddenly tell him "Down." If he goes down quickly, give him several treats in a row. If he's too slow, then wait 5 to 10 seconds and try again, only rewarding him when he goes down quickly. Once he's going down superfast, get his energy level up between exercises. Loudly praise him and cheer him on so that jumps up and down (but not on you!), or runs by your side. Suddenly stop and ask him to lie down. When he has this down, you can switch between having him sit or lie down on cue. If you work on this exercise after you've worked on the down-stay in the next chapter, he should really love lying down and throw himself down quickly. You may need to practice this exercise with Rover on a hands-free leash first.

Game 3: Rewarding the Calm Down

For dogs who are hyperactive, overly energetic, or dubbed attention-deficit, you've already worked on the say "please" by sitting for praise and petting. Now extend this exercise to the down. For several days, concentrate on providing all attention and petting when Fido is in a down (Figure 21.3). If he wiggles or paws at you or tries to roll over when you're petting him, immediately remove your hands and stand up straight so that he knows you're ignoring him. Once he's calm, resume your petting in a relaxed, massaging manner. If you do this consistently, your dog's behavior can change overnight. Again, if your dog has a low attention span for focusing on you because he finds so many other things exciting, you should start with him attached to you on a hands-free leash. For dogs who are anxious without you, tether them to furniture with a leash and stand or sit several feet (m) away. Only approach and reward them once they've laid down. The goal is that they learn that lying down calmly is what makes you come back to them.

Game 4: Lie Down to Have Toys Tossed

You can also reward Rover with many other motivators. For instance, you can expect him to lie down before having his toy tossed during fetch. In fact, if you want a fantastically fast down, you can require that he lie down in all of the situations in which you'd like him to say "please" (instead of just Saying Please by Sitting).

Chapter 22

Sit- and Down-Stay

Picking up poop during dog walks is part of the regular routine, but when Fido steps in it instead of standing politely while you clean, things can start to smell foul. If you've ever experienced any such situation, you'll be happy to have this sit- or down-stay exercise under your belt. But of course sit-stay and down-stay have an infinite number of other uses. For instance, if Fido begs when you're eating dinner, a down-stay in his doggy bed might make your mealtimes more peaceful. Or if you have to inspect your dog's skin, ears, or other body parts, a sit- or down-stay will ensure he holds still. Once your dog has these exercises down pat (even with distractions), you'll find many creative ways to use them.

Teaching the Sit-Stay

Because Fido is used to all variations of Say Please by Sitting, we'll start with a verbal and visual "Stay" cue immediately. With Fido sitting in front of you, put your hand out facing him in a lopsided, universal stop signal while saying, "Stay" (Figure 22.1). Then bring your hand back to a relaxed position at your side while taking a step backward, followed immediately with a step forward so that you're back in the starting position (Figure 22.2). Give him a treat before he stands up. For some dogs, you may have to start by rocking your weight back instead of actually taking a whole step backward. Then rock forward into your starting position and give him a treat. The trick is to move backward and then get back before Fido stands so that you can reward him for doing the right thing. This may be a little confusing to Fido at first, since he's used to mirroring your moves in the Say Please by Sitting. If you're having any problems at all with the first step, then teach the down-stay at the end of this chapter first. Or give him a treat as you're stepping back and then another when you return.

Figure 22.1   Figure 22.2

Increasing the Distance

Once Fido stays put for one step back and then forward, you can graduate to two steps. An easy way to do this is to have 5 to 10 treats in your hand, and rather than ending the exercise with each treat, step away, come back, give a treat, and then repeat the exercise at the same level you've given all 5 to 10 treats. Once you've completed one or two 5 to 10 treat trials in a row, you can increase the distance by one step. You can also keep the distance the same and just increase the time. The goal is to get back to Fido before he gets up. If he gets up, then you went too far away or were away too long.

Another possibility is starting with a step to either the right or left side and, using the same technique as before, work your way around to the back of your dog. Then increase your distance away from him.

Adding Distractions

In everyday life, you'll want Fido to sit-stay at a distance and while the rest of the world keeps moving. This can be achieved by adding distractions into the exercise and also by building up the distance. To build the distance past the length of your regular leash, start with a long leash that's 20 to 30 feet (6 to 9 m) long for safety. Then just continue the earlier sequence of building one step at a time. While this sounds like it would take a long time to train, but it's really fairly simple. Practice walking away with your back to the dog, walking in a serpentine pattern, spinning, walking fast, or running a few steps. Each time you add a different exit as you walk away, drop the distance or time that you leave. The goal is to do just enough to make it more difficult, but to get back before he gets up.

Then, work in other distractions, such as toys or friends walking by. At home, practice sit-stay while another family member knocks on the door, or practice out on walks, or at the dog park between play sessions. Remember that each time you add a new distraction, you should decrease the distance and time so that Fido can be a success. One way to do this is to start by standing near him with 5 to 10 treats in your hand and giving treats every three seconds while a second person makes a distraction. The distraction should happen just as your dog is getting his treat. If the dog can focus on you instead of the distraction for several trials of 5 to 10 treats in a row, the distractor can then make the distraction more randomly. When your dog is good at this step, you can incrementally increase the time interval between treats by several seconds for each trial, until you're able to go 30 seconds between treats. Once you can go for 10 to 30 seconds, you can start increasing your distance from Fido during the distractions. Repeat this procedure for each distraction and each intensity of distraction—starting with the distraction far away at first and then moving it closer with each trial.

Out of Sight

If Fido's sit-stay is solid, even with devious distractions, you can practice off leash and walking out of sight. Practice in the safety of your home first and just disappear for a second or two before you come back with a treat. Then move to dog-safe areas outdoors and follow the same protocol. Hopefully, you'll never need this behavior, because it's not safe to leave Fido outside unleashed and unsupervised, but you'll have it just in case.

Teaching the Down-Stay

The down-stay is exactly the same as the sit-stay, except that some dogs have to practice an intermediary step first. For dogs who stay down after you give the signal but pop into sit or stand once you stand straight up, practice first giving a series of treats while they are down and you're kneeling at their eye level. Start with about 10 treats in your hand and give them every two to three seconds, until it's clear that your dog is comfortable staying in a down. When you're out of treats, end the exercise, reload your hand with treats, and repeat the trial. When your dog consistently (and in a relaxed manner) stays down for 10 treats, then practice giving him treats while you're changing positions to a stand, and then back to a kneel (Figure 22.3). Make sure you deliver the treats low to the ground so that you don't lure him into a sit or stand. When he's comfortable at this step—that is, when he performs it perfectly for at least 5 consecutive trials or 8 or 9 out of 10 trials in a row—then the next step is to stand, and remain standing while giving him his treats. Once he reliably stays down while you're standing up, you can start building your distance away. Practice at one distance for 5 to 10 treats in a row before going on to the next step.

Figure 22.3

That is, you can start by taking one step backwards or to the side and getting back to give him a treat; then, rather than ending the exercise, just repeat this 5 or 10 times. If he consistently stays down, increase the difficulty to two steps. This is a quick way to simultaneously build up both time and distance. You'll be able to build up both quickly as long as you don't skip any steps. You can also practice adding in distractions using the same technique as with the sit-stay.

Practicing at Home

Once Fido knows the long down-stay fairly well, you can take a shortcut to help build the down-stay duration. During dinner or some other time when you're sitting at a desk, have Fido lie down next to the table and step on his leash so he can't get up. Give him a few treats in a row for staying down and then rely on the leash to keep him in position if needed. Randomly give him treats throughout the meal when he's lying down nicely.

Alternatively, you can take him 5 to 10 feet away, ask him to lie down, and then tie a very short leash down low to something so he physically can't get up. Then intermittently go back when he's lying down politely and reward him with attention or a treat. With these methods, Fido can quickly learn long down-stays in the house, and you can use your time efficiently.

Practice this exercise in all cases where you need it, both outside and around the house. For example, have him lie down when guests come over and for short spells during walks, or when he gets too rowdy during play.

Games

For most people, the sit- and down-stays are boring to practice, but if you throw in some games, you can make it a virtual party.

- **Friend Challenge:** Challenge your friends to see who can get the farthest from their dog in 20 seconds while their dog remains in a down-stay or a sit-stay. The winner is the one who gets the farthest away but whose dog remains in place until the owner comes back.
- **Down-Stay Aerobics:** See if you can do jumping jacks, spin, and run circles around Fido while he's in a down-stay or sit-stay. Your stay is solid if he ignores your antics. Try this with a friend, and see if you can trick your friend's dog into getting up while your dog stays calm. Remember, the goal is to always get back to your dog with a reward before he gets up. You can speed up the training if you have one person giving treats at a regular interval and another person making the distractions. At first the distractions should come while your dog is getting the treats, and then more randomly.
- **Other Dogs:** Test to see if the dogs also sit and stay if other dogs walk by or if toys appear out of reach. Remember to start with easy distractions and gradually up the ante so that you and Fido can be a success.

DOWN-STAY AND THE MANNERSMINDER DOG TRAINING SYSTEM

A systematic and easy way to teach Down-stay is using the MannersMinder Dog Training System (www.MannersMinder.net). This system contains a remote-controlled food dispenser that can give treats to your dog while he's lying down away from you. The system tells you how frequently to give the treats at each given step, and can also give treats in an automated fashion at different measured intervals. The system comes with a DVD that takes you through the clinically tested protocol for Down-stay and Down-stay with distractions.

Chapter 23

Go to Your Place

When Spot feels the need to get underfoot in the kitchen, freeload at the dinner table, stick his nose in your guests' faces, or hound the visitors at the door, there's no need to lose your temper. Just teach him to go to his special place where he can do a down-stay. You should perform this exercise after Spot knows down and performs it instantaneously on verbal cue. Better yet, you should practice the down-stay in his special place before you even teach him to go to his place. That way he'll already associate his place with lying down and getting treats.

Method 1: Teaching "Place"

Start with a doggie bed, blanket, or other distinct surface that's large enough for Spot to lie down. From about 5 feet (1.5 m) away from the bed, briskly walk with Spot toward the bed. When you get about a foot or two away, toss a treat onto the bed in such a way that he has to climb all the way in and encourage him to get it (Figure 23.1). Most likely, because you've started with movement and tossed the treat, he'll immediately grab it and gobble it up. If he doesn't go for it because he's confused it with the leave it exercise, point to it and give him the release cue that he learned in the Leave it exercise (Figure 23.2). Once he eats the treat, give him the verbal cue to lie down. He will most likely turn around to lie down facing you. As soon as he lies down, give him several treats in a row for staying down. Practice this in sessions of 5 to 10 trials in a row. If you're already practiced down-stay on his bed or rug and he's received lots of treats, he should learn this placing behavior quickly. When he gets to the stage in which he runs over immediately when you head in the direction of his bed, you can add the cue word "Place." Start with Spot 5 to 10 feet (1.5 to 3 m) away from the bed, and say "Place" right before you start heading for the bed. He should start running to the bed. Then, as before, toss the treat onto the bed, and once he eats it, give a sequence of treats when he lies down on verbal cue.

Figure 23.1

Figure 23.2

Once Spot consistently runs to his place on cue, you can omit the first treat that you toss on the bed and just follow him to his place and give him the treat for lying down.

Method 2: The Easy Way

A more systematic and easier way to teach "place" is using the MannersMinder Dog Training System (www.MannersMinder.net). The steps are shown in the MannersMinder DVD. Basically, the machine provides an easy target so Spot knows exactly where to go. Plus it saves you a lot of the variably-placed treat tosses and walking back and forth.

How Do You Know When He Knows the Cue?

You know Spot has a clue about the cue when you're able to say "Place" and he runs right over to it even though you're standing stationary. Once he lies down, you should walk up to him and give him his several treats in a row. At this stage, you can add a down-stay with distractions to the "place" exercise.

Increase the Time and Distractions: A Variation on Down-Stay

Now, as with the down-stay in the last chapter, increase the time that Spot stays on his bed. Once you send him there, give him about 10 treats in a row for staying in place. With treats coming at about every three seconds, you can add in distractions such as knocking on the door, or people running around the house or making distracting noises. Once he's good at a given distraction for several 10-treat trials in a row, work on trials where you increase the interval between treats while the distractions are still coming.

When to Use Place

- When Spot's getting in the way or guests come over, just send him to his place to sit or lie down quietly, but still be in the middle of the action.
- When the doorbell rings and Spot barks, let him bark several times and then send him to his special place. You can specifically train this by sending him to his place, giving a treat for staying, and then heading to the door but returning before he gets up. Then reward him for staying down in his spot. Gradually increase the difficulty by actually walking up to the door, touching the door, knocking on the door, or opening the door to look out. You can even purchase a wireless doorbell and practice ringing it when he's in his place, or you can ring it first, then send him, to his place and reinforce him for a down-stay. The MannersMinder Professional Dog Training System protocol was specifically designed with the doorbell situation in mind (www.MannersMinder.net, Figure 23.3).
- When housetraining your dog, you can use the place command to send him to his crate.

Figure 23.3

Section 4

Five-Minute Guide to Solving Common Canine Problems

Fidos with piddling problems in the house; Bowsers who bark for hours on end; Rovers who bite seemingly of the blue. While these common pooch problems may have been a mystery to you in the past, now that you know more about how dogs communicate and learn, you probably have an inkling of the cause. In this section, everything we learned earlier will be put to use, in order to understand what's causing these "canine crimes." With your current knowledge, and the five minutes it takes you to read each chapter, both the cause and the solution will soon be clear. (Although, in cases where aggression is the issue you should also seek the advice of a veterinary behaviorist or certified applied animal behaviorist; and if health is a possible issue, your regular veterinarian should be your first stop.) Overall, good leadership—which is gained without coercion or force through the "Learn to Earn Program" found in Chapter 15—is key in all cases, but for some problems, certain exercises and techniques are more important than others. Once again, you'll see that bad behaviors are repeated because they are reinforced, and the keys to success include good timing, consistency, clarity, and the correct rate or reinforcement so that Fido knows that you have the ability to guide him. You may also need a coach or trainer to watch your form and to help you refine these skills. Equally important is the dog's emotional state. To fix the overall issues, we do want to address the underlying motivational state that's driving the behaviors. And—just as a heads up—the most common motivator for aggression is *NOT* a need to be "highest ranked," but rather the most frequent motivator for aggression is fear.

Chapter 24

Crate Training and Housetraining Your Dog

Crate Training

To those who are new to the concept of crate training, confinement in such a small space surely seems like some sort of medieval torture. However, dogs trained properly can see it in a whole different light. To them, it's a safe haven, a place to call their own. It can be like a modernized den or lair.

Crate training can save your sanity in more ways than one. For owners of pups in the potty training stage, a crate can be their savior. During this piddly life stage, there are only three safe sites for the young pup: outside in a dog-safe area where the pup is free to do his duty; tethered via a leash to your side so you can take him outside at the first signs that he has to let loose; or inside a comfy crate. When you can't watch your puppy with an eagle eye, or if your puppy piddles even when attached to you on leash, let him rest in his kennel that's roomy enough for him to move but small enough so that he holds his urge to go.

Crates can have myriad other great uses, too. These portable dens can serve as a private place to rest when company is around, or a safe nighttime spot out of trouble. For any pet who travels or stays with a friend when you travel, crate training allows you to bring the pooch's home wherever he goes. Now Fido, who normally bounces around in the car, or who doesn't know what to do in the hotel room when you're on vacation, or who needs a safe spot when he's staying with a friend, can feel more familiar or comfortable with the new situation.

How to Crate Train

Training pets to call their crate home is simple, even for cranky cats and adult dogs. It's all about teaching them that great things happen when they are in their kennel. The great thing we will use is food.

If your dog really dislikes being confined, start by feeding him his daily meals just outside the crate. When he's comfortably eating his meals in this new location, move the food just inside the crate so that he has to stick his head in to eat. Within a few days, you should be able to move the feeding location farther in the crate so that he has to step in with his front feet. In this manner, move the feeding location farther and farther in. Once he easily goes in and out on his own, you can start shutting the door while he's eating or putting him in with a special toy, which can be a Nylabone chew or a tasty bone. As soon as (or just before) he's finished, open the door to let him out. You can also randomly place secret food surprises for Fido to find in his crate. Try peanut butter smeared on the back wall of the crate or pieces of hot dog under his blanket. This process sounds like it will take a long time, but in reality it usually takes less than a week, even with adult dogs who don't like the crate.

Once Fido starts entering the crate to eat, teach him to go in using food as a reward instead of a lure. First show him a treat and after he goes in give it to him. Block him from getting out by shoving another treat right up to his nose. Give a sequence of treats to him when he's stationary in the crate. Better yet, have him lie down or sit, then move aside and call him out. Then repeat the exercise, but this time just point into the crate. When he goes in, again block him from coming out by shoving a treat in his face. Then give a sequence of treats again for remaining stationary in a stand, sit, or down. Repeat this step until he consistently goes in when you're pointing. Generally this just takes one or two short sessions. Next add the cue word "Kennel" by saying the word right before you point. Also practice training this cue word randomly throughout the day by walking over with him toward his crate saying "Kennel," then rewarding him when he goes in.

A Variation on Go to Kennel

A variation for teaching dogs to go into their kennel on cue without a food lure is to start by saying "kennel" and then tossing a treat in. Make sure to say the cue word before you toss the treat in so that it predicts that a treat will be tossed. The tossing motion is, in effect, a visual signal. If you present both visual and verbal signals at the same time, your dog will preferentially learn the more meaningful cue (i.e., the visual cue) and may not learn the verbal cue. (This phenomenon of only learning the more obvious cue when two are presented together is called overshadowing.) Once he goes in, toss more treats to the back and then block him from coming out by shoving a treat in his face to block the way out. Then continue with the food rewards for remaining stationary in a stand, sit, or down. Next, you need to turn the food lure into a reward so that Fido learns to run to his crate whether or not you have food. Walk with him toward his kennel while hiding a treat behind your back or in your hand. That way he sees and receives his reward only after he's gone in. You can also gradually increase the distance from which you send him to his crate.

Once you progress through all of these simple steps, you'll have a hound that thinks his crate is a heavenly haven. (For a visual demonstration of additional methods, go to www. DrSophiaYin.com and watch "Pepe Crate Train" on the "movies" page.)

Housetraining

Anyone with kids knows that potty training can be a long process, and bedwetting is just part of the deal. But when it's a puppy that eliminates enough times outside the preferred zone, family members are bound to be less forgiving. And worse, when it's an aged Mastiff making the messes or an adult Airedale with occasional accidents, it doesn't take long to reach the end of your rope. Luckily, once you know the cause of the soiling, the solution is straightforward.

The number-one cause of these potty mistakes is just incomplete housetraining. The problem is that some people think that potty training is as easy as just keeping the pooch on a regular eating, drinking, and potty-outing schedule where he is taken out every several hours. Or they think that the pup will be completely housetrained in just a week or two. For some precocious pups this might be so. But many pups taken through such a lax abbreviated potty protocol remain only partially housetrained. They learn that outside is a good place to go but don't understand that inside is off bounds. In fact they may even come inside after an extensive play or exercise period and then relieve themselves on your expensive carpet. If you want to avoid the drama and headaches of multiple messes during the day, you'll have to execute the full potty-training protocol, rather than the lax, abbreviated plan for potty training geniuses.

The Full Potty Training Protocol for Young Pups

The process starts with a comfy dog crate big enough for the pooch to lie down in but not so roomy that he can make one end the outhouse. You may need to temporarily place a box in the crate to adjust the crate size. The crate will be the pooch's designated nighttime abode and a safe daytime retreat for times when you can't watch him like a hawk.

The next step is a rigid schedule that goes something like this:

- When the pup wakes up, let him out of his pooch palace or crate.
- Immediately carry or run him out on leash to the preferred potty spot outside. Note that if you're letting him walk on leash, this walk should not be a stroll where he has a chance to dilly dally and then pee. Rather, it's an emergency power walk or sprint to get outside safely.
- Once you're outside, stand stationary and silent until little Fido's both peed and pooped. Because he's on leash he won't be able to run around and play.
- As he's about to potty you can say the cue word "potty" just once so he comes to associate the word with the action; then you can reward him as he's finishing. But otherwise you're silent so you don't distract him from doing his duty.
- If he's done both then he can come in and have a meal and play session or go for a walk on leash. If he has not peed and pooped, then he goes back into his crate for 15 minutes after which time you try again.
- Repeat this process until he's peed *and* pooped, or he'll just potty inside as soon as you've taken a break and strayed from the plan.

During the Day

When Fido has earned a free-time session you can let him loose in a small area—if you can keep your eyes glued to him. As soon as you take your eyes off him he's sure to have an accident, just as sure as your pasta water will boil over as soon as your attention is diverted elsewhere. Because virtually everything—waking up from a nap, playing, extended chewing on a Nylabone, slurping a big drink—makes little Rover want to go, you'll need take him out after any of these potty-inducing situations. Signs such as sniffing the floor, whining, panting, circling, and wandering away from you are also your cue to escort him outside. You'll also need to take him out 15 to 20 minutes after he's eaten or drank water.

During the rest of the day, repeat this cycle:

- An hour or two in a potty-safe area such as his crate, an exercise pen, or attached to you via leash so you can keep an eye on him.
- Then he's taken out to do his duty.
- Then if he does his duty, allowed supervised play.

You may need to repeat this process 6 to 10 times a day.

Note that some young puppies will potty in the blink of an eye with minimal signs—even when tethered to you. And for others pottying seems like a favorite pastime—urinating once an hour, or five minutes after they drink, or any time they get the slightest urge. If your pooch is like this, you will need to rely on an extremely rigid plan. Once he potties outside, you can play with him outside for a variable amount of time or inside for a short time (10 to 15 minutes) where you supervise him intensely. Then crate him for several hours at a time so he learns to start holding his urine (he should spend no more hours in the crate than his age in months). At the end of the crating period, repeat the procedure of taking him out to potty and then rewarding with play, exercise, and training games—even a walk if he needs more exercise. Since he is getting crated for several hours at a time during the day it's essential that you make sure he gets enough exercise. If you calculate the hours, it's still a lot of time on your part. In a 16 hour day, that's 6 to 8 potty and play sessions, and if each session is even just 15 minutes long, that's 1.5 to 2 hours of your undivided attention.

HOW LONG CAN HE SPEND IN THE CRATE?

In general, puppies can be crated the same number of hours as their age in months.

At Night

While housetraining is labor intensive during the day, at night you get to relax.. About 30 minutes before little Fido's last outdoor excursion, remove his water until the next morning. If Fido can't make it through the night for several nights, that means you may need to remove his water sooner. It could also mean that he has a medical issue making it difficult to hold his bladder and should visit the veterinarian.

After Two Weeks

After two weeks of this protocol, your pooch should have the schedule down pat, but that doesn't mean he's fully trained. In fact, at this point, he probably knows that outside is where he should go, but doesn't yet know that inside is a no-no.

Now you should gradually give him more supervised freedom during his play sessions. Start with just one room, then increase the time he can be loose in that room while you're present. If he can go for several hours, you can systematically add additional rooms—but at first only when supervised. It's important to systematically add rooms so that he specifically learns where else not to go. You have to be consistent enough so that he just develops a habit. This may take longer with little dogs living in big houses. Every accident that you let happen through poor supervision delays the habit from forming.

Accidents

If Fido has a bout of confusion inside and you catch him as he's starting to go, startle him with a sharp "Aaah!" to temporarily stop the flow and then whisk him to his potty place. Be careful not to scare or punish him, or he will just learn to go out of your sight. If he has an accident when your back is turned, just clean it up with an enzymatic cleaner and watch him more closely next time.

If your pup has an accident in his crate, clean his crate thoroughly so he doesn't learn to be dirty. You likely left him there too long, or his crate is too big. He may also have a health problem that prevents him from controlling himself. These problems include intestinal worms or other gastrointestinal disorders causing diarrhea, and urinary tract abnormalities or conditions causing lots of drinking and consequently lots of urinating. Ask your vet during one of your regularly scheduled visits or make a special trip to your vet if you suspect something might be wrong.

Housetraining your pup may seem like a lot of trouble, but compared to diapers for three years and changing bed sheets for more, this is a virtual cakewalk. Most puppies can be somewhat housetrained at a young age; however, they are not fully housetrained until they have no accidents for 12 weeks, which generally doesn't occur until they are about 6 months old.

Housetraining Adult Dogs

If your adult dog has accidents in the house, go back to puppy potty school. Remember that any time a dog goes to a new house, he may no longer know the appropriate potty locations, and

PIDDLING WHEN GREETING PEOPLE

Never fear; your pup's peeing problems will soon disappear. While little Fido's bladder control or lack thereof leaves much to be desired, he's in a phase that most puppies pass through. He may be a little behind in housetraining, but the problem is likely to eventually evaporate as he matures. In the meantime, you can take several steps to speed the process along.

If you've identified Fido's problem as occurring upon first greeting family and friends, and you've correctly observed that he piddles out of excitement, the solution is simple: Don't get him so excited.

Because piddling occurs when family and friends come to visit, instead of petting and playing, they should ignore the little guy for several minutes, or until he has calmed down. Or, they can reward a sit with treats before he has a chance to piddle. Once he's standing or sitting serenely, they can try some placid petting. They should start with slow, even strokes paired either with silence or soft, soothing speech.

If the pup lets loose at this stage, the petting session started too soon, was too exuberant, or lasted too long. The people petting should gauge his behavior. If your dog starts to wiggle and squirm in excitement, they should quickly remove their attention and treat him as if he doesn't exist. Then, as soon as he's still, they can reward him with petting.

Expect immediate accidents the first few times because the pup is used to his old routine—see friends, greet excitedly, and urinate. But, surprisingly, if all greeters stick to the new routine, the piddling problem might be solved in only a handful of sessions.

You can speed this training up by working on sit or lie down to be petted. This way Fido learns that even when he's maximally excited, he has to control himself and calm down, which decreases the likelihood that he will get so excited that he will piddle.

you may have to do a crash housetraining course again. Also, sometimes older dogs go through lapses in earlier training; other times, they may have medical problems. Some dogs develop incontinence in adulthood or diarrhea due to internal problems. If your adult dog suddenly develops loss of housetraining, take him to your veterinarian to rule out medical causes, such as urinary tract infections, diabetes, and other common conditions.

Chapter 25

Mouthing Off:
Chewing and Nipping

Chewing

Baby gates, cabinet locks, seats with straps—these are normal necessities for anyone with a baby. Barely mobile but full of mischief, these little tykes try their mouth on any object within hand's reach. Luckily, as part of the same human race, new parents are usually at least partially ready for the oral onslaught.

Puppies go through a similar exploratory phase, but their teething targets may be a bit different and harder for humans to predict. They try their mouth out on toys, but they'll also try shoes, sofas, and the ultimate interactive squirt toys: the outdoor irrigation system. From their naïve point of view, everything's a chew toy until they're told otherwise. Here's how to keep the little chewer out of trouble.

Control the Environment

As with human infants, the first rule is to control the environment. Keep tempting chew things out of reach either by locking them up or disallowing doggie access to areas where these things reside. Keep shoes in the closet, towels in their drawers, and magazines on their higher shelves.

Keep Appropriate Toys Available

- Keep appropriate playthings available at all times, such as rubber squeakies, tennis balls, and stuffed toys. It's best to keep four to five toys out at a time since they like to switch between different toys. Rotate with different toys every few days so that Fido views the toys as a valued resource and doesn't get bored by having them all available at all times.

Supervision

Until Fido is destruction-free, supervise him at all times, just like you would supervise a young child.

When He's Chewing on Something Inappropriate

If he starts to nibble on or has an inappropriate item in his mouth:

- Utter a sudden "Ah," loud enough and sharp enough to get a startled response or an immediate stop in his behavior. If you don't get this type of response don't bother trying it. Just rely on the second portion of this technique (see next bullet).
- Quickly entice him with an appropriate toy by waving the toy like prey. Encourage him to grab it, and when he does let go of the offending item, praise him (if he responds to praise). Alternatively, give him a treat for letting the taboo object go, then give him an appropriate toy.
- In the cases where Fido runs away as soon as he sees you heading his way, avoid being sucked into the chase, which is fun for him. Instead, ignore him or pretend to play with something better until he leaves the object on his own, or have him perform an alternate incompatible behavior—Say Please by Sitting, come when called, targeting, or Leave it (covered in Section 3).
- To just release items you ask him to hand over, probably the most useful solution is come when called followed by a food trade until it becomes a habit.
- Another alternative is to put foul-tasting products such as cayenne pepper, bitter apple, or bitter orange, which you can purchase at the pet store, on things he shouldn't chew. Smear these on the potential problem chew things. Dab good-tasting things such as beef bouillon, mint, and peanut butter on appropriate chew things, such as Nylabones.

Exercise and Attention

Chewing serves as a natural way for dogs to engage their minds and explore their surroundings. Make sure pup gets enough exercise and attention. The more regulated his exercise, the less he'll have to entertain himself. Also, consider feeding some of his meals in a treat ball that he has to roll around, or freezing his meal in hollow chew. This immediately makes his meal a way to exercise his mind.

Some dogs chew as a way to relieve the anxiety or stress of being left alone. If you think Fido falls in this category, train him to enjoy staying at home on his own.

Older Chewers

Some dogs continue chewing for over a year and even when outdoors will always find items, such as the interactive drip or sprinkler system with its moving parts, more fun than the stationary toys they see every day. These dogs should be confined in dog-safe areas when they can't be supervised, exercised well to help them burn off steam, fed out of puzzle toys that give them mental and physical exercise, and trained through the "Learn to Earn" program from Chapter 15 so that they can learn to settle and focus on you.

Nipping

If you have a pup who nips you when he plays, you're probably hoping it's just a phase.

Unfortunately, it's one that could last his entire life. Even if it's mild, you should address it as soon as possible. If you accidentally reward the nipping by shouting and waving your arms around like a squeaky toy, you can train the puppy to play in a rude, overly aroused manner. In some puppies the nips can progress to bites.

Here are several methods to deal with nipping. They all start with training the Say Please by Sitting (found in Chapter 15) so that the puppy will have a more appropriate behavior to perform when he wants to ask you to play.

Method One: Ouch!

This method works best on young puppies, but can also work on adult dogs that are sensitive to your tone of voice or that already have a clue. It mimics the learning that should have occurred back in the litter when the pups roughhoused with their siblings. During this first seven to ten weeks, pups learn that wrestling and gentle mouthing are okay. But if one pup gets too rough, a sudden yelp from his victim marks immediate cessation of play. Even for a pup, it's not too hard to figure it out: Play nice or go away.

Humans can parrot this "yip" when they feel tooth on skin by emitting a loud, sharp, but not angry, "Ouch!" If you utter the "Ouch" with enough verbal force, the way you would if you unexpectedly stubbed your toe, the pup should startle and suddenly release. Immediately praise the pup, give a treat, and then swiftly shove an appropriate chew toy, like a Nylabone, in his direction. Or reward with a string of treats for sitting, and then perform a few more repeat sit games to remind him that sitting is fun. If he starts nipping again, repeat the exercise; but if his response is not dramatic or clear cut, then avoid this technique and go onto one of the other methods.

Once Spot learns the routine, you can switch from the word "Ouch" to the word "Out." Now "Out" is your new cue word for Spot to release things from his mouth. Remember to always follow with a toy or treat. If you have to repeat this exercise more than two or three times in a row, it's not working, so try the second method.

Method Two: Make Like a Tree

For dogs who couldn't care less about a loud-sounding "Ouch," or for owners who just can't say the word sharply, try method two—the tree technique. Every time Spot nibbles, immediately stand up silently and make like a tree, so that it's clear you're not rewarding his behavior by accidentally playing (negative punishment). Hold perfectly still and even look away so that he can clearly see that you're ignoring him. The minute he sits, give him a string of treats for sitting and remaining seated (positive reinforcement). Then move on to other repeat sit games.

Once he's finished the treats, if he goes right back to nipping, go right back to imitating a tree. The puppy will quickly learn that his interactive human chew toys turn into a boring tree when nipped. This step will go even quicker if Spot already knows say "please" by sitting.

Method Three: Play the Leave It Game

Another option is to teach him the "Leave it" game from Chapter 16. When you say "Leave it" you will also have to perform the "be a tree" body behavior (see above) that tells him you're not going to interact with him (Figure 25.1). Once he has the knack, you can use this cue to tell him to keep his teeth off your skin and other taboo items.

Figure 25.1

Chapter 26

Separation Anxiety:
Canine Style

In Jack London's classic novel *White Fang*, the main mutt (W.F. for short) developed one strong bond with his man. So tight was this bond that when master departed temporarily, W.F. refused to eat and chose to pine away in agony. As a kid, I was enamored by this romanticized display of loyalty between dog and owner. But now that I know better, when I recall the story I just wanna shout, "Hey! That dog has separation anxiety. He needs help."

London's main canine character is not the only dog who ever had separation anxiety. He's not even a rarity. In fact, separation anxiety is one of the most common reasons for a trip to the animal behaviorist. It comprises 20 to 40% of all canine cases seen by behaviorists in the U.S. and Europe. Unlike W.F. though, most of these dogs don't display their despair in such poignant fashion. Instead, they rip the house to shreds, bark incessantly, and leave accidents in conspicuous places—and for their worry all they get is the label "spiteful." Unfortunately for most dogs, owners wait until the problem becomes well-established before seeking help. Then, after thousands of dollars in damage or complaints from neighbors, the situation is now a life-threatening emergency to the pet.

Social Animals

Why would a dog get so upset about being left alone?

It all has to do with the group mentality. As social animals, dogs love to hang out with their peers, and when raised with people they view people as their peers. Usually this isn't a problem—we humans like the attention. But some dogs are a little too dependent on their two-legged friends.

Often you can spot these dogs right off. They follow their owners from room to room never letting them out of sight or even out of reach. It's as if they're afraid that their human could vanish at any time. These dogs may ask for constant reassurance by perpetually leaning on their owners, climbing into their laps, and whining or barking for attention. In essence these pooches have a sort of doggy low self-esteem.

But this isn't the only type of dog who succumbs to feelings of angst upon an owner's temporary departure. Any dog who is used to having a person with him at all times or has never been trained to be relaxed when separated from people, playmates, or access to whatever he wants, is prone to despair when abruptly left alone. (These dogs who are anxious because they've never learned any impulse control and are used to getting things immediately when they want are not technically cases of separation anxiety, but the behavior modification scheme is the same.) Separation anxiety can crop up quickly with sudden isolation—perhaps when the human companions who are always home get a new job or school starts and the kids are no longer home.

Here's an example of how it might happen. Fido, a dog who tails his favorite family member from room to room as if attached by Velcro notices something different—people getting ready to leave the house all at once. After a melodramatic good-bye, the owner leaves Fido alone for the first time. Fido's puzzled. "Hey. Where'd you go? You forgot me. I'm in here! Hey! Hey!" Of course to the casual listener it sounds more like this: "Woof! Woof! Ruff....... Owooooooh!"

After ten minutes, Fido figures he wasn't just forgotten—he's been abandoned. Now he's really worried. He tries to get his mind off the situation by chewing on something convenient—the dining room table—but it doesn't work, and what's more, all this worry is giving him an upset stomach. He goes to the bathroom on the carpet. Finally, he can't stand it anymore. "I gotta get out and find him!" So he starts frantically digging at the front door.

When the owner comes home she arrives with a big fanfare—showering Fido with praise and petting out of guilt for having left him alone. Fido reciprocates, dancing and jumping to celebrate the big event. Or alternately, the owner sees the mess Fido has made and yells or reprimands him, which only makes the previously panicked dog more anxious.

In either case now Fido knows that when he sees his family members getting ready to leave it means they're about to disappear. The departure cues—grabbing keys, putting shoes on, and rushing around the house in a hurry—now come to signal the scary event. As a result Fido will now act anxious or fearful when his family members prepare to leave.

Dealing With Separation Anxiety

So how do you deal with a dog who is too dependent on you?

Well, punishment is out of the question. It only increases the anxiety in an already frightened Fido. But surprisingly, a sympathetic streak can make things worse too. Coddling actually deepens Fido's dependency. You can tell, because the petting and talking often make him whine more or act more anxious. What Fido really needs is a chance to stand on his own four feet. Here are some ways to boost Fido's independence and teach him to remain calm in your absence.

Train Fido to Associate Your Departure With Good Things

A simple solution for easy cases is to leave Fido with a favorite toy, food puzzle, or stuffable chew, such as the ones Nylabone makes. Put down the chew 5 to 10 minutes before you leave, then remove it when you arrive home. Goodies should be given well before departure and must occupy Fido for a while when he's alone. This method is not as powerful as actually training a calm down-stay or sit-stay behavior (discussed below), because it relies just on distracting the dog. However, when it works it saves you a lot of training time. Also, when Fido does start eating the treats, it indicates that his anxiety is decreasing.

Teach Him What Works

Teach Fido that whining and anxious behaviors don't work; rather calm behavior and emotional control are what bring him rewards. The quickest way is to take Fido through the "Learn to Earn" program from Chapter 15, which teaches him self-control and to trust your guidance. Require that Fido automatically Say Please by Sitting and remaining seated for everything he wants, especially for praise, petting, attention, and things that generally elicit overexcitement. This will immediately build in some self-control. (To view these exercises, visit www. DrSophiaYin.com "Lucy Says Please, Rewarding Calm Behavior" and "Teaching Dogs to Learn to Earn").

Once he gets these exercises, which should only take a few days to a week, practice tethering him on leash so that he can only get within a foot or two (.5 m) of you. Pet him for five seconds at a time when he sits or lies down and remains in that position. This will teach him that sitting or lying down calmly is what causes you to come over to him and pet him. You can systematically increase the distance so that he's farther and farther away, and then even out of sight. Then leave the room for an instant and come back, but wait until he sits when he sees you to actually walk back up to him. Again, he's learning that sitting or lying down calmly is what makes you come back; he's learning that he can have what he wants if he controls himself.

Train for Independence

At the same time as you're working on the tethering exercise you can work on the sit or down-stay away from you (see Chapter 23). That is, you can purposely ask him to sit or lie down and reward him with treats or petting for doing so. First just move away a step and get back to reward him before he gets up. Do this 5 to 10 times in rapid succession. Then increase the distance to two steps, three steps, and so on.

One way to speed up this process is to use the MannersMinder Dog Training System (www. MannersMinder.net) and just follow the protocol for the down-stay and down-stay with distractions. For the distractions portion of the protocol you practice walking around—away from him and back while he's getting treats from the MannersMinder. The goal is to walk pretty quickly and in a relaxed manner and return often enough so that if he looks up from the machine that's doling out treats, he never sees you walking away for long. Before he starts to get anxious, you head back. With both methods, systematically increase the distance and time between rewards until he can lie away from you in the same room for at least a half an hour.

Next train him that out of sight is not out of mind. If Fido's further along, then start with short departures from the house (several seconds) and try to return before he gets anxious. It's important that you get back before he's anxious—we want to completely avoid the anxious state. If he has a history of getting anxious soon after you leave, then place him in a down-stay (which he should already be good at), and treat departing like a distraction. Start by jiggling the door handle, opening and shutting the door, or walking out the door but coming right back to Fido to reward his good behavior before he looks anxious. Repeat the distraction at one level until he's consistently calm for 5 to 10 consecutive trials. Then increase the intensity by actually walking outside or staying outside longer than before—but make sure he looks relaxed the entire time. We want his experience when you're gone to be only positive. The MannersMinder (www. MannersMinder.net) can help because it can dispense treats on an automated basis so that Fido can be rewarded for a calm down-stay when you're out of the house.

Overall, the goal of these exercises is to teach Fido that good-byes are okay; they're followed shortly by hellos. Note that during these practice sessions you can walk in and out of the house many times. Systematically increase the amount of time you're gone so that he can remain calm for at least a half an hour.

Stop the Greeting and Departure Drama

Cut the drama out of greetings and departures and turn both into ho-hum events. Ignore Fido for 20 minutes prior to leaving and after returning home. But if in spite of your efforts Fido tends to pace anxiously as you're getting ready to leave, or runs around in a solo celebration when you return home, then reward him repeatedly for lying or sitting calmly for the length of time it takes him to calm down and remain calm. Do this before you leave and when you arrive home.

Desensitize and counter-condition Fido to departure cues. If there are some departure cues that really cause Fido to switch from calm to anxious, then it's a good idea to desensitize and counter-condition him to them. For instance, if grabbing keys makes him pant and drool regardless of the time of day and what you're doing, then start by picking up keys quietly so as not to incite a full-blown response, and then toss him a treat. The goal is that when he notices you pick up keys it comes to mean that he's going to get a really tasty treat. Pick the keys up over and over—maybe 20 to 30 times per day with at least 5 to 10 times per session—followed by tossing the tasty treat. Systematically increase the loudness of the key jingling. If your technique is good, you can generally train this new association within a few days.

Manage Fido When You're Gone

Find a way to manage Fido temporarily when you are gone. Ideally during behavior modification Fido only has good experiences when you're gone. Consequently, if you need to leave him alone in the house you may need to send him to doggy day care or a friend's house, have a pet sitter babysit, or put him in a boarding kennel if the damage when you're gone is severe. If he's not yet to that point and you're only gone for a short time, you can still consider a crate—once you've trained him to love his crate. If Fido tolerates his crate, you can work on making it his favorite place well before you leave him alone. (See Chapter 24 for more on crate training.) This will involve ignoring him when he's outside his crate and lavishing attention, treats, and praise when he's in the crate. (For a visual aid, see "Pepe Crate Train" at www.DrSophiaYin.com on the "movies" page.)

The treatment plan for separation anxiety seems straightforward, but if you've ever lived with a needy dog you know it's really not. Some dogs turn around within days while for others the problem drags on for months. Many people need coaching on the technique and a plan tailored to their specific dog. In some cases Fido may even need medications; unfortunately, even separation anxiety drugs like Clomicalm or Reconcile, are not a quick fix. They need to be paired with behavior modification and are not effective in all dogs. And, just to throw a wrench into the process, dogs showing individual signs of separation anxiety may have a different behavioral or medical problem instead.

The good news is that if you perform the techniques described above at the first sign of anxiety—for instance when your dog whines and barks a little to get out of his crate, or when separated from you by a gate or door, or at the first sign that he's destructive when you leave—you can often prevent him from developing separation anxiety down the road. If you are not experiencing clear success or at least marked improvement with the individual steps fairly quickly (such as within a week), you should get help from a certified applied animal behaviorist (www.animalbehaviour.org), your veterinarian, or a veterinarian who also practices behavior modification.

AVSAB

Veterinarians who are not versed in behavior can receive guidance through the American Veterinary Society of Animal Behavior (www.AVSABonline.org), on my website (www. DrSophiaYin.com), or by joining the Veterinary Information Network (www.vin.com).

Chapter 27

Dominance Aggression:
A Struggle for Status

With 800,000 reported (and many more unreported) dog bites in the United States each year, do you ever wonder why and who all these Bowsers are biting? Over 20 years ago, we tended to attribute all aggression to dominance, a word that had vague meaning. We called every dog who was misbehaved, spoiled, unruly, or aggressive "dominant." Since then the science of animal social hierarchies and of wolf behavior has advanced, and the behaviorists educated in science now attribute most aggression to fear. For example, most dogs who bite unfamiliar adults or kids are fearful due to inadequate socialization during puppyhood. They bite because these victims accidentally threaten them or because they've learned the offense is the best way to keep these "scary" people away.

On the other hand, dominance aggression is aggression between individuals fighting to establish priority access to multiple types of resources. Dominance is a relationship between individuals and a dominance-submissive relationship does not exist until one animal consistently defers to the other.

Given this scientific definition, which dogs are actually dominant aggressive? The typical dominant-aggressive animal is confident and aggressive over many types of resources. As the top dog, he's outgoing and rarely shows fear postures or what one might call "apologetic" behavior. One moment he's as charming as a Casanova on a first date. The next minute he's throwing more barks and bites than a prizefighter at a pre-fight press conference. Sound like a dog you know? If so, read on.

How Can a Dog Become So Unpredictable and Bossy?

This high and mighty behavior starts in puppyhood when the pooch is treated like a prince. He gets praise and petting for his slightest deeds, and free food delivered on request like room service at a swanky hotel. He wins tons of toys without even trying and has the best human beds and couches on which to rest his bum. Most dogs who live the high-life just become spoiled, unruly brats—they are not considered dominant aggressive.

But for some dogs with a more aggressive personality, this life without leadership or predictable and consistent rules creates a furry monster who aggressively claims ownership to any resource—food, toys, sleeping places, access to attention—that he wants. In essence, some Fidos claim the household to be under their dictatorship.

This diagnosis dominance aggression is actually not that common. More frequently, even with dogs who are aggressive to family members, the dog is just possessive over one type of resource. Or the dog is aggressive because he's been punished by an owner who fails to provide a behavior that the dog should perform instead. Since the dog has no alternative to behavior to perform he reacts defensively.

Ending Rover's Reign Using Brains Rather Than Brawn

You might think that like wolves in a pack, baboons in a troop, or lions in a pride, the way to take charge of a dominant-aggressive dog is by calm, assertive force or even violence. The problem is that an animal's reign is often short-lived, lasting only as long as they have the physical strength to prevail. Similarly, only the strongest, most skilled human members of the household can win physical altercations, leaving the majority of members to fend for themselves. Furthermore, such a butting of heads can temporarily suppress the aggression while making the underlying emotional state much worse. Since emotions guide behavior, the dog may outwardly hide his resentment when he's not strong enough to fight, all-the-while seething inside. Then when he can't contain it any more, he bites. Luckily, because *we humans have bigger brains*, we can swiftly carry out a non-violent, long-lasting coup while changing Bowser's entire attitude.

Keep Yourself Safe

The first step is to keep yourself safe—avoid all situations that trigger a battle. This is a war of wiles where you supposedly outsmart your less cerebral companion. If furniture is one of the resources Fido guards, then all human furniture is off bounds. Deny access to the room containing the cherished chair, barricade the bed with uncomfortable books, or booby trap it with the electrostatically charged Scatmat, or just keep Rover on leash so you can pull him right off. Just be sure to do it in a ho-hum manner. For instance, nonchalantly take the leash and walk away unemotionally. Then reward him with a treat for following you off of the forbidden furniture.

Take Control of All Important Resources

Take control of all important resources, including food, furniture, toys, and anything else Rover likes, such as petting, praise, and playtime. Instead of him controlling these items, you'll ration these resources selectively. Also control Rover's freedom of movement by putting him on leash. For the next several days or week, he should be attached to you or tethered to a tie down in the house whenever people are at home with him.

Teach Rover to Say Please by Sitting

The next step is to teach the ruling Rover to Say Please by Sitting patiently in order to get what he wants (as described in Chapter 15). Once he learns to sit for treats and enjoys the repeat sit games go to the next step.

Apply the Automatic Sit to Everything Rover Wants

From here on, Rover must automatically Say Please by Sitting for everything he wants, instead of automatically taking it for free. Wait for him to sit and look at you politely before tossing his toy, letting him out the door, or giving him a treat. Put his dog bowl in storage and make him earn each piece of kibble and pat on the head by performing sit and other behaviors

GET HELP

If you are concerned that your dog may bite someone you should consult with a veterinarian with special interest in behavior (www.AVSABonline.org), a certified applied animal behaviorist (www.animalbehaviour.org) or certified pet dog trainer (www.ccpdt.org) who is experienced in such cases and uses techniques similar to those described here.

that he knows. The goal is that he learns that this is how his world now works. It has order and predictability. When he wants something, he doesn't have to worry about guarding it. He'll get what he wants when he sits politely and looks to you for permission.

Train Rover to Enjoy All Handling Procedures He Dislikes

Many dominant-aggressive Fidos also growl and snap when you handle or restrain them. They require desensitization and counter-conditioning to handling in different ways. For instance, if he dislikes having his feet handled or toenails trimmed, work first on touching his feet or leg in a way where he barely responds, and pair this touching with treats. In order to make it clear that touching the feet equals tasty treats, only touch the feet while Fido's getting treats, and stop touching the feet as soon as he finishes the treat. When he consistently allows this level of handling then increase the intensity—for example gently squeezing the toes, or holding the toenail trimmers near his feet. The goal is that at each step he ignores the handling and is only focused on the food. By only going to the next step of handling when he's non-reactive at the current level, Rover can improve quickly, even over just several days to a week. (For a visual aid, watch www.lowstresshandling/dvd/samples/toenailtrim/php.)

The Attitude Change Can Be Fast

At first these changes are a challenge for owners. They want to pet the pooch when he pushes his way into their laps instead of ignoring him until he's polite. Or they accidentally let him barrel by to get out the door rather than waiting for him to drop his derriere and look to them for direction. But by bearing down and making all the changes at once, you make the message black and white. Once Rover gets the rules you've conveyed to him through your actions, the weight of trying to be in charge will be lifted off his shoulders. Furthermore, once asking politely is Rover's new habit, you'll only reward him when you decide he should have the reward. That way you remain the one in control.

Chapter 28

Food Possessiveness
and
Toy & Treat Possessiveness

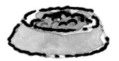

Food Possessiveness

What's up with the dog who eyes people who approach his food bowl or stiffens and even growls, snaps, or bites if others interrupt his meal? Doesn't he understand that you're the provider of the things he wants and not a threat to him?

Like many dogs who are otherwise easygoing, this type of Fido has a food fetish, and he feels it's his duty to guard each bowl as if it holds his last meal. While this behavior may seem odd for owners who provide plentiful amounts of food for their pooches, anyone who's watched free-roaming and stray dogs in developing regions (such as Bali or Costa Rica) knows that this type of behavior is common. These street or village dogs have to search for their food and never know if they'll have enough. As a result they may defend food with the vigor of a dog whose life depends on it. This food defense behavior may then just become a habit whether the dog's hungry or not. Pet dogs can develop the same behavior starting in puppyhood, especially if they experienced strong competition for food.

Often in cases of food bowl aggression, our instinct is to show Fido who's the boss. For instance, some trainers recommend that you force him into submission by holding the dog down on his side. After all, they say, that's what a higher-ranked dog would do. What they neglect to

BALI DOGS

For more information about free-roaming dogs in developing regions, read my articles on Bali dogs at http://askDrYin.com/blog/2009/10/01/bali-provides-a-glimpse-into-how-dogs-evolved-alongside-man/.

point out is that in many cases where a higher-ranked dog tries to take food away from a lower-ranked one, a fight can and often does occur. The fight may only involve loud growling, spit, and drool—or it may include an actual bite.

Similarly, the problem with humans trying to force dogs into submission in an attempt to show the dog who's boss is that the boss may turn out to be Fido. If so, the showdown could be ugly and dangerous as well. Even if it ends quickly and you're injury-free, the situation may not be resolved. Rather, you may be in for multiple rematches, because now your dog knows each mealtime means a fight.

What's even trickier is that sometimes after one all-out battle everything looks okay on the outside, but get into Fido's head and you might see trouble waiting for your guard to drop. Instead of learning goodwill around the food bowl, Fido has just learned to hide his inner anxiety. He smiles on the outside but he simmers and seethes on the inside when you're in his feeding space. Then, when he can't take it anymore, rather than warn you with stiff posture or growls and nips (like he did before), he breaks out in a full-blown bite.

A third scenario for those who battle this bad behavior with brawn, is that while Fido may decide you are top dog when it comes to the food bowl, all other humans have to fend for themselves. Fido may even behave nicely around the bowl when you're there to back up guests and other family members, but if you're out of sight he may tell them how it is.

So what can you do? Instead of teaching Fido that mealtimes will be a fight and that his fear of having food taken away will come true, train him to associate the presence of people around his food with even better things happening to him.

Method One—For Easy Dogs

At every meal, while Fido's eating his plain dog food, stand a safe distance away and toss a steady stream of bite-sized treats (10 to 30) that he loves. Then, when he's finished and has nothing left to guard, move closer and toss more treats to him or into his bowl. Note that you'll have to cut back on his regular food so that he gets his normal daily caloric allotment of food.

After a few meals using this method, move a bit closer each day, always staying outside Fido's defensive range. If Fido tenses up or even growls, then you've moved too close too quickly, so watch his body language closely. The key is that he stays relaxed at all times around the bowl and learns to expect even better treats from you. If this method takes you more than a week, then you should go to Method Two (below).

Method Two—For More Difficult Dogs

A variation on this method is to teach Fido to sit for special treats when he's eating his meal. Before you can attempt this exercise you'll need to work on two other exercises first. Start by teaching Fido to perform Say Please by Sitting away from his food bowl and during non-meal times (see Chapter 15 for more details). This way he'll learn some self control. Next, train the Leave-it exercise where you apply the automatic sit to getting other things he wants (see Chapter 16). Train both versions of Leave-it with food dropped on the floor found in that chapter.

Start with the safer version—where he's on leash and you toss treats out of his range, then when he pulls to get to the treat you stand your ground firmly. Once he figures out that no matter how hard and long pulls he's not going to get to the treat, he'll turn to you and sit. When he does, get a treat to him within 0.5 seconds! Fast! Continue to give him a string of treats every 2 to 5 seconds for sitting and looking at you. They should come fast enough so that he just wants to focus on you. Continue until his gaze is stably fixed on you so it's clear he's no longer thinking about running to get the treat on the floor, and tell him "ok" or use some other release word. Then point and simultaneously walk towards the treat on the floor making sure that you get there fast enough so that he's on a loose leash (For the more detailed version go to Chapter 16). Alternatively you can continue giving him treats for remaining seated and looking at you while you walk over to the treat on the floor, pick it up, and give it to him. Use that alternative if you decide you never want him to pick up food from the ground because he may get into a race with someone else who tries to grab the food off the ground.

This Leave-it exercise will teach Fido that he will get what he wants if he just exhibits some self control, therefore he has no need to be possessive. It also teaches him that he gets a lot of things he likes when he's calmly sitting and looking at you. Once he's good at immediately sitting and looking at you when treats are tossed out of range, you can also teach him the cue word "Leave-it" by saying it in a happy voice, as if it's a game, right as or after you toss the treat out of his range. In training, only use the cue word if you're sure he'll sit within a second or two, otherwise it will take a long time for him to learn to associate the word with the actual behavior. Work on this game often so that it becomes a habit within just a day or two.

You can also work on the second version of Leave-it from Chapter 16, where you block him from getting to the treat that's dropped on the floor. Most food-possessive dogs will not become aggressive if you stand in front of them without reaching for the object on the ground, since the object is not yet in their possession. But if you are unsure how your dog will respond, then skip this exercise for now.

Learn to Earn—For Everything He Wants

If you feel your dog is an extremely difficult or dangerous case, you should also put him through the full-bore "Learn to Earn" program, where he learns he has to control his impulses in order to get what he wants. That is, he has to automatically Say Please by Sitting to earn every single kibble when you're home with him, to get his leash on, to go out the door, to get petted, during the Leave-it game, to have his toy tossed, and for everything he wants. In essence you're using everything he wants to your advantage in order to teach him that he only gets what he wants if he controls himself and looks to you for permission.

It's not about the human trying to be the boss, it's about the dog learning that politely asking permission gets him what he wants—when it's ok with you. Of course you'll also want to seek professional help if you feel your dog could actually nip or bite.

Specific Food Bowl Training

When Fido's good at the automatic sit and leave-it exercises, expect him to sit to receive his meals, too. If he's a particularly difficult or aggressive dog, tether him on leash away from where you will place his bowl so that he can't lunge and injure you.

Hold his food bowl, which contains his boring kibble, and wait for him to sit. Put the food bowl down outside of his leash range and tell him "Leave-it," just once. If he gets up, that's okay because he's on leash and can't get to the food. Just wait for him to sit. When he's sitting, give him a few treats and then unhook his leash and give the release word and let him get his meal.

Make sure you're standing outside his defensive/protective zone (the zone he guards around his food bowl) when you release him, so he doesn't feel threatened. Just let him eat his meal in peace. When he finishes the meal, slowly approach with a mouth-watering morsel and stand right outside his food-bowl protection zone. When he Says Please" by Sitting, give him a tasty treat. Note that to make this treat special, it has to be one that he only gets during these practice sessions. Peanut butter on a dog biscuit or a piece of real meat are good choices for the early sessions.

Now make this your new daily feeding routine. When Fido regularly sits every time you approach after he's finished his meal, you can up the ante by approaching during mealtimes—but just to the edge of his feeding space at first so that you don't cause him to feel defensive. Then give him a treat or two when he sits and then walk away. We want your approach to mean

PROACTIVE PLAN

As a proactive plan, you can perform the feeding game with puppies and newly adopted dogs so they don't become protective of their food.

something good to him, and your walking away to signal he can resume eating his meal. Again, if he consistently sits immediately upon seeing you approach, you can move closer the next time.

Always wait until he sits to go all the way up to give him his treat. The benefit to this Say Please by Sitting technique is that you can better judge what Fido's thinking. If he sits and looks expectantly to you for treats as you approach, then he sees your approach as something good. Conversely, because you're only allowed to approach him when he sits and looks expectantly to you for something better than his meal, you're not likely to mistakenly approach him when he's feeling he has to protect his bowl.

Speeding Up Your Progress

To speed your progress, during the first several sessions you can start with one-fourth of your dog's meal in the bowl so that you can get four practice trials each meal. Once Fido gets the idea that he should sit when you approach you can go back to putting the entire meal in his bowl, and then practice approaching him with something better during his meal (1 to 4 times during his meal).

Later you'll want to practice having other family members go through the same routine. He should generalize to them almost immediately unless he has some underlying fear of them. The goal of the training is that Fido learns that people approaching him while he's eating means something good. He'll get something great and still get to eat his regular food. As a result, his underling motivation for being protective will disappear and he'll be good in general to people approaching him while he's eating out of his bowl.

These plans may sound too good to be true, but stick with it, practice patiently, practice with different people, and Fido's food bowl fetish will gradually fade away.

Toys and Treat Possessiveness

Dogs commonly protect their food bowls and, not surprisingly, they sometimes like to protect other possessions as well. If your dog stiffens and snaps when people approach his toys or treats—even if they may not take them away—then he's too attached to these things. One option is to just avoid the situation by calling a moratorium on all special chew treats or playthings that trigger the possession aggression. The problem is that this will only work if you can guarantee with 100% certainty that for the rest of his life he will never get close to these items—especially around a child.

GET PROFESSIONAL HELP

If your dog is aggressive to the point where you fear he may lunge, nip, or bite, enlist the help of a veterinary behaviorist, veterinarian with special interest in behavior (www.avsabonline.org), certified applied animal behaviorist (www.animalbehavior.org), or certified pet dog trainer (www.ccpdt.org) who has worked with many food-possessive dogs and uses similar techniques.

Sometimes there can be other contributing medical and behavioral factors that need to be addressed and often owners need coaching at how to perform the techniques skillfully.

Keep in mind there are additional variations that professionals might teach.

Alternatively, if you can't 100% guarantee that you can avoid putting these items into your dog's possession, you can address the problem directly. Don't worry, as the smarter species, we don't have to bone up for a fight. Instead of using muscle or trying to force our will on our dogs, we can teach Fido that he has no reason to feel possessive. Good things happen when he gives us objects from his mouth, and he often gets those objects back In our example below, we'll discuss the guarding of a prized toy, but the treatment is the same if the object is a bone or other treat.

As with food bowl possession (discussed in Chapter 30), you'll work on say "please" by sitting and leave it first. Then we'll expect Fido to sit for all treats, toys, and attention. Once he has this

down, which should take no more than several days when done correctly, we can start on the object exchange game.

The Object Exchange Game

Start with an extremely hungry dog, irresistible treats, and a low-value toy. Give Fido his toy, and then immediately hold the yummy treat directly in front of his face. If you've chosen the right treat and he's hungry enough, he should eventually drop the toy to eat the treat. To prevent him from diving right for his toy, give him several more treats in a row. If he won't even let you get close to him and his prized possession, instead of handing him treats, toss them to him one by one.

Practice this treat-tossing in several sessions. At this stage, never take his toy away unless he's abandoned it himself and is relaxed. When he consistently drops his toy as soon as he sees your tasty treats, and remains relaxed while looking expectantly for additional treats, then go on to the next step. Now, work on touching, and later taking his toy while he's eating his treat. When he drops his toy, feed him a treat and simultaneously touch the toy. When you can repeatedly do this and he remains relaxed, you can progress to taking the toy. When he's finished with the treat, wait for him to sit, then give him the toy back. In this manner, he gets two rewards—a yummy food treat followed by his object back. He won't have to be possessive about the toy because he thinks he'll never lose it. Practice this game hundreds of times with different objects in different settings. Gradually select objects that Fido values more and more. Your dog will learn that giving you his possessions is fun.

Leave-It Game With Toys

Another game to work on is the Leave-it game discussed in Chapter 16, which used the technique of leaving food on the ground, but here you can use a toy instead. You can work on both versions: blocking him fom getting to his toy, as well as dropping the toy out of range of his leash. Both exercises will teach him self control around his toy. You can also work on having him automatically sit to recieve the toy.

Chapter 29

Keep Safe Around Kids

"Six-Week-Old Girl Dies After Mauling By Family Dog" the headlines blared. The LA County Sheriff's Department reported the familiar scenario. A family member had left the baby unattended on a bed for a few minutes and returned to find her head encased in the dog's mouth.

Sounds shocking, but this isn't the first time an infant has fallen prey to the family pet. According to the Centers for Disease Control and Prevention (1997), of the 279 dog bite-related fatalities in the US that occurred between 1979 and 1994, most involved children younger than ten years of age, with infants making up a disproportionately high percentage. The most common bites occurred when infants were left alone with the family pet.

What type of dog would perform such a deed? While many would immediately conclude that it must have been the much-maligned Pit Bull mix or a rogue Rottweiler, not so here. In the case above, it was a Pomeranian—a pocket-sized dog known more for being babied than biting babies. And although due to their size, large dogs are usually to blame for fatalities from dog bites, other little dogs—Dachshunds, Westies, and Cocker Spaniels—have all committed the same crime. Even Labrador and Golden Retrievers are on this ill-fated list. So the word is out—all dogs can bite, and a few will even kill.

ADDITIONAL READING

For more information about children and dogs, read *Raising Puppies and Kids Together: A Guide for Parents* by Pia Silvani and Lynn Eckhardt and *Living with Kids and Dogs: Parenting Secrets for a Safe and Happy Home* by Colleen Pelar.

Why Pets Attack

But why would a pet attack a family member, especially an innocent child? The whole situation seems senseless, but once you take a moment to think like a dog, the pieces come together.

Prey Drive

One day life for Jake the Jack Russell Terrier is just ho-hum, and then suddenly a surprise arrives. A five-pound (2 kg) squeaky thing moves in, triggering his predatory instincts—the same ones that cause him to "kill" fluffy toys and squeaky balls, and to chase relentlessly after squirrels. The mystery object enters hidden in a bundle of cloth. It smells like a mammal and squeals like live food, yet Jake never really learns what it is. It also jerks and gurgles like wounded prey. This secret toy is off-limits but always tempting with its presence. The longer it hides from Jake, the higher his frustration and drive.

Older toddlers and young kids incite this instinct too. They run around yelling and flinging their arms like the ultimate interactive squeaky toy. Then when the dog gets loose he chases just to play, but when the kids get scared and scream and flail more, Rover's arousal gets out of control—sometimes leading to a bite.

Fear

While prey drive can cause dogs to bite tiny infants, in actuality the most common cause of bites to youngsters is fear. This can be very surprising, especially in cases where Fido loves all adults. But what commonly happens is that Fido was socialized to adults when he was young but didn't see many kids. So while adults are filed in his brain as being "safe," infants and kids are categorized as "alien." Often parents are completely unaware that their Fido is afraid of their infant. Because an infant is relatively immobile, Fido can just stay away; but when he becomes a crawling or walking toddler, then the aggression begins. The toddler keeps approaching Fido, ignoring Fido's warning lip raises or growls. In fact, when owners note these postures, they may even punish Fido instead of thanking Fido for giving a warning sign. This punishment serves to increase Fido's anxiety and possibly to hide his warning signs. So instead of a warning lip-raise, growl, and then snap when he gets cornered, he holds it in until he can't anymore and lets out a full-fledged bite.

Even when Fido isn't afraid of kids, kids can drive dogs to the boiling point. Parents are often proud that their dog is so tolerant that he puts up with toddlers sitting on him or poking their fingers in his ears. But they don't realize that just like humans, dogs can only take so much. Imagine how you would feel locked in a room with a bunch of screaming kids who have no concept of your personal space—plus, you have no control over when you can take a break. You might be okay for a few hours or a day or even a week. But at some point they're going to irritate you enough to yell at them or even become more violent. As protectors of both our dogs and our kids, it's our job to train kids to play and interact with pets. The pets should look like they enjoy the experience rather than just tolerating it.

Change in Status

One last cause of bites that's not very common but does occasionally occur is when Fido doesn't like his new position playing second fiddle. No more walks, no more talks—everyone's focused on the new addition. Like older human siblings, each dog responds to this situation differently. Some dogs don't mind their new status on the fringe; others long for signs of their owner's affection. They watch plaintively but politely as new parents fawn over the newcomer. Still others seethe at this object that is hogging their owner's time and attention. If the offender were another dog, this Fido would make it clear that he gets first dibs. He'd nudge or even force his way into position—and if the message still wasn't clear, a flash of teeth would be sure to set things straight. The problem is that toddlers don't read or heed the warning signs and back off. And if adults notice them they just punish the dog, making him even more upset. Like siblings whose parents constantly reprimand them for bad behavior towards each other (instead of setting the situation up for success and then rewarding appropriate interactions), the dog learns to associate the toddler with his getting in trouble. Needless to say, this is not good for their relationship. He may direct his aggression to the child when owners are not present to supervise.

How to Prevent Problems

Knowing the causes of infant and child attacks can help us avoid a serious disaster. Dog bites to infants and kids can be prevented and the steps started before baby comes home.

- The first step is to make sure your dog knows his manners and self control. Does he come when called, sit when asked, and wait patiently for your next cue—even when he'd rather grab the toy you just tossed or snatch that piece of food that just fell on the floor? If not, put him through the "Learn to Earn" program where he learns to Say Please by Sitting for everything he wants. The Say Please by Sitting exercises not only reinforce self control, but provide structured fun time for Fido, which you'll be able to continue once the baby arrives. Also, make sure he has a good come when called so that you can call him out of danger. He should also walk nicely on leash by now, since walks will be more complicated when you're pushing a baby stroller.

- Next, make sure Fido has safe place where he can rest and be away from the baby. A crate, exercise pen, baby-gated area, or his own room are good options. It's best if the place can be an area he can choose to go to on his own and the baby will be taught to avoid.

- Train Fido to enjoy all of the bad things that might accidentally happen—just in case they do. For instance, train him that when people approach his food bowl good things happen to him (see Chapter 30 for more on food-bowl aggression); and that it's fun giving people his toys because he gets treats and the toy back (see Chapter 31). Train him to love being touched and handled all over, including his paws, ears, and tail. Although you'll ultimately spend every day teaching your toddler to stay away from Fido while he's eating or sleeping, and to only touch him gently, invariably the child will make a mistake and that's what we want to train Fido to tolerate now.

- Get Fido used to baby sounds by playing recordings of babies. Ask him to play some games, such as targeting or Say Please by Sitting, if the sound seems to bug him. Make sure he gets lots of treats. Also, if he reacts strongly to the sounds at regular level, start with the recording at low volume and gradually increase it.

- To prevent cross-species sibling rivalry, do the unthinkable—start paying less attention to

Fido a week before the expected day. Continue his exercise, fun training games, and Say Please by Sitting exercises throughout the day, but otherwise treat him like a ghost at home. That is, don't lavish extra attention or have long periods of petting. We don't want him to associate a big decline in attention with your bringing baby home.

- When the baby does arrive, bring a blanket or something else with the baby's scent, and let Fido get used to the smell. If he ignores it, that's fine, because it shows the smell doesn't bug him. Then when you bring the baby home, let Fido get used to her. While holding the baby safely out of his reach, have him sit quietly and reward him with treats for being calm. That means no whining and no straining or jumping up to reach you. The ideal behavior is for Fido to act relaxed, like a baby is not a big deal. In other words, you're training him to perform his sit games and practice self control while the baby's around.

- As a matter of habit, ignore Fido when the baby is away and reward him for good behavior, such as sitting, when baby is nearby. Soon he'll learn there's nothing to fear when the little infant is near. He'll just know that good things happen to him when baby is around. As a bonus, he'll also know that he should remain calm and controlled around the baby, and that the baby does not mean removal of attention for him. Instead the presence of the baby means that he's going to get rewards.

- Lastly, no matter how petite or perfect your dog is, never leave him alone with an infant or small child. Things can go terribly wrong—even when you're in the same room. It's up to you to recognize the signs and know when Fido needs a rest and your toddler needs more rules.

While it sounds labor intensive, by failing to take these precautions one bad day and a lapse in your attention and tragedy could occur.

Chapter 30

Aggression Toward Non-Family Members

A 1998 FBI report lays it out—139 murders and 24,000 violent crimes committed by kids 15 years of age and under. "He's never done anything like this before," say the puzzled parents of one young offender. "He's a good kid. We don't know what happened."

Imagine if city officials proclaimed, "Juveniles must be banned from public places. They're a danger to society." Clearly this is a preposterous plan, but if the criminal element has four legs and big teeth, some citizens only see red. One side says they are unpredictable and a menace, the other side says, "Not mine." Both sides are searching for answers to no fruitful end, because the problem is not with Fido. It's with Fido's best friend.

With over 74.8 million pet dogs in the US and an average of only 16 fatalities from dog bite attacks per year, your dog is not likely to be the dirty one in a fatal crime. But the fact that dog bites are among the top ten causes for emergency room visits tells us it's time to wake up and open our eyes. The signs are always clear to those who see; those who don't may be setting Fido up to bite inadvertently.

The fact is, dogs don't come out of the womb knowing how to bite aggressively. As with other skills, they learn to bite hard because they've had lots of practice and the precursor behaviors have been rewarded. Even dogs bred and selected specifically through temperament tests for police work or protection dog sports require lots of practice before they're confident enough to handle controlled bite work. Most family dogs that bite even the first time have also had plenty of practice leading to the full-on event.

How Biting Behavior Develops

Here's one example of how bite behavior could develop. It may start with the dog barking at joggers, cyclists, and squealing kids running by, then progress to lunging while on leash or chasing when off. The first 5 or 10 times might be just a game, but with a heightened chase or the wrong move by the pseudo-prey, teeth can explode faster than fists at a hockey fight. With each barking episode, Fido is gaining confidence, building his aggressive repertoire, and practicing overarousal and lack of self-control.

The dog's territorial nature, coupled with owner encouragement, can also place Fido in a fix. For instance, owners often think it's good for Fido to be protective around the house, especially at the door, so even if he's barking out of fear they praise him in these situations when he's young. Then, as he matures, he takes it upon himself to say who belongs on his territory or near his human family, when it should be up to his owners to decide. Why not trust Fido with these choices? The decisions seem straightforward: bark at the mail carrier, the UPS delivery person, or strangers at the door. What's the harm? But if Fido gets out, then what do you do? Should he speak his mind, or deliver his message in person? Or if your friends drop by, maybe Fido should keep them out, too. Due to poor leadership or guidance, these decisions are no longer up to you.

The situation goes from bad to worse if Fido's also received inadequate socialization to people and dogs (which should have started well before vaccines are complete and continued through the first year of life). A lax socialization plan can doom Fido to a life of fear. And, not surprisingly, fear is the most common cause of bites. This paranoid pooch sees an unfamiliar person or dog and registers a threat. At first he backs away or freezes and hopes the threat will go away. But after several experiences where a yellow Lab mobs him as his owner yells, "He's just playing," or a person leans over to hug him (which he views as a death grip), he tries a

different strategy—he barks or growls. Now barking and growling are his new behaviors when he feels threatened. Whereas before people and dogs could pass him on the sidewalk, now as soon as he sees them down the street he preemptively warns them to go away. When he breaks out in a battery of barks, the owner either tells him everything's okay, which he ignores, or yells, "No! No!" In both cases, Fido misunderstands and continues to focus on the people or dogs—in his mind he's hearing, "You're on the right track" and "Go! Go!"

How to Prevent Aggression Problems
What do you do to prevent your pooch from becoming another terrible statistic?

Find a Good Match
First, start off with the right dog. A conscientious breeder carefully matches pups to owners with the appropriate personalities. That means no exuberant pony-sized puppy with a person who's too frail or too busy to train, and no shy, flighty Fifi in a household with hyperactive tots. Equally important, there should be no adoption of multiple puppies to a household at the same time, since two puppies are exponentially more difficult to manage and train than one. And if you're using them as babysitters for each other, they generally learn to bond with each other and ignore you. When you want them to focus on you, they blow you off and get rewarded by puppy play instead.

Leadership Exercises
Once the correct match is made, it's up to the owner to make it clear that she sets the rules and has the ability to guide Fido. Work on the three leadership exercises: Say Please by automatically sitting for everything he wants (Chapters 15 and 16); attention on walks (Chapters 17 and 18); and come when called (Chapter 19). Make these the behavioral norm. Remember that the key point in all these exercises is to make Fido think that you're more fun than any of the naughty things he wants to do. Remember you set the rules and need to stick to them (i.e., don't randomly change the rules), so you must be certain of what you want. This way, your dog sees you as dependable and as someone who can guide him.

The exercises are so simple that even a young puppy can learn to perform them perfectly, provided his owner gives good direction and all household members are on board. If you treat all interactions with him as training sessions, so that you not only reward good behaviors consistently but also remove or avoid accidentally rewarding bad behaviors, then Fido's bound to learn to follow the rules quickly.

Socialization

Next, start the young Fido in a puppy socialization class that includes plenty of greetings with polite puppies and with all kinds of people bearing treats. When it comes to meeting people your goal should be to give him 100 positive experiences with 100 unfamiliar people in 100 days. This includes men and women of all ages, ethnicities, and sizes carrying and wearing different things such as hats, sunglasses, and umbrellas. That way Fido learns to associate all kinds of people with good things, instead of developing a fear of those that look different than what he's used to. Of course, he should sit politely for all greeting so that he learns early on not to jump. Later he can learn to only go up to people if you give him permission.

When it comes to meeting other dogs, your puppy should meet a few new friendly, calm, polite dogs of different ages each week. Note that I emphasize the personality of the other dogs. Most people don't realize that puppies can learn all kinds of bad behaviors when socializing with other dogs, even in a supervised puppy class. For instance, if play is just free-for-all, scared puppies can become worse as they get pounced on. What they learn about is defending themselves. Rambunctious friendly dogs can be equally harmful, as puppies will learn that it's fun to mob and leap onto other dogs. Then when they use this impolite greeting in a real-life situation, the Rover they run up to may be fearful or just not like it. The ensuring growl can then lead to a fight, and now your previously friendly Fido learns that other dogs aren't so nice.

Lastly, if the puppy class doesn't put enough emphasis on focus, then the puppies can learn that playing with other puppies is way more fun than focusing on you. This can lead to you no longer existing for your dog whenever there's a pooch on the scene. So choose your puppy class carefully and don't be afraid to change if the current one is not suiting your puppy's needs.

Continue Practicing

Puppy socialization is just the start. Follow up with adult dog classes, where you can continue to practice your leadership in the presence of dogs and people. Also, be sure you continue letting Fido say hello to people with a proper greeting out on the street, and make sure he continues to greet polite pooches in public.

How to Fix a Developing Problem

What do you do if Fido is already untrustworthy around people? Some people wonder if protection work will help. Protection dogs are selected for their nerves of steel and are under perfect "on-off" control. You wouldn't want to encourage a dog who's showing uncontrolled aggression or fear to bite any more than you would want to put an unstable person on the police force and show him how to use a loaded gun.

The owners of dogs showing even subtle signs of aggression to unfamiliar humans can take immediate action, though. They can work on the same leadership exercises just recommended for puppies above. Once the owner has Fido focusing on her like she's the most interesting thing in the world, she can start working with Fido around the things that make Fido lose control. The owner should start with these distractions in the distance where he or she can get Fido's attention, using games such as targeting, rapid repeat sits going  backwards or running to the sides, recalls at full run, and attention on different heeling patterns. When done correctly, it should seem like Fido doesn't notice the distractions. When he's good at one distance, work closer and closer to the distracting stimulus—as long as Fido remains focused on the owner and the fun games. The goal is that when Fido sees these things that used to get his attention, instead he turns to his owner to engage in games that are more fun.

Realistically, on a given walk you won't have people who stand around for 10 minutes while you work with your dog around them. Rather, you'll work around one person at the distance where you can keep Fido happy and focused. Then when that person heads in a direction away from you, you'll go back to having Fido walk on loose leash until another person approaches.

You can also use a head collar, like the Gentle Leader, to speed things up add some safety to the routine. When Fido lunges or pulls, the head collar controls the direction of his head. It also tightens around his mouth, making it more difficult for him to bark and bite.

This same aggression protocol works for aggression to other dogs, barking at cars and buses, chasing cats or birds, and virtually any other case where you have trouble keeping Fido's attention. However, because this training is a technical skill and requires a good understanding of dog body language, you may want to hire a certified applied animal behaviorist (www. animalbehaviour.org), a veterinarian with special interest in behavior (www.AVSABonline. org) or a certified pet dog trainer (www.ccpdt.org) to help you evaluate Fido and come up with a more specific plan.

Chapter 31

Feuding Fidos

It sounds like a plot from a cheap made-for-TV movie. Two siblings raised together for years. Competition suddenly creates a deadly rift between them. Trapped together under one roof they're forced to fight it out.

Unfortunately, this plot is not ripped from the headlines, it's more likely playing at a home nearby. But it doesn't involve people—rather it's a story about their pooches. Dogs who fight primarily in their owners' presence.

While most people hope their dogs will get along like best friends, frequently these Fidos fight like arch enemies. The typical scenario is that a pup or younger dog comes into the home and takes a place as second fiddle. He respects Older Rover and gives him preferred access to all resources—such as toys, attention, and treats—by backing off and letting older Rover go first. But as young Fido reaches adolescence or starts to feel more at home, he wants to cut to the head of the line. So like serious shoppers at a 12-hour sale the day after Thanksgiving, the two dogs rush to grab a toy or to get petted first instead of politely waiting their turn. When neither backs off an altercation involving teeth and skin can ensue.

Or, in a spin-off of this main plot, younger Fido doesn't purposely want everything first, he's just overly rambunctious and doesn't know when to stop. He pesters Older Rover, treating him like a moving four-legged chew toy—sometimes at random or just when he's most excited. Older Rover may occasionally enjoy this whiff of new energy and join in the play, but all the time is just too much. He may often respond by running for cover, but like an innocent bystander trying to avoid a dogged salesman he just can't get away. He may voice his opinion, somewhat politely, by putting ears back and lowering his body, turning, and growling and whining in a half-hearted attempt to fend of the junior Fido. Owners often mistake these signs of anxiety and think the older dog likes to play until one day, maybe several years down the road, Older Rover finally decides to fight back more than just verbally.

Should the Dogs Just Duke it Out?

Even when they notice that the dogs are starting to get into fights, owners often wonder if they should let the dogs duke it out to determine who's the dominant one. Or that Older Rover should take matters into his own hands and put Junior in his place. This happens in the wild, but may involve injuries, and when frequent or severe enough one dog often elects to leave. Additionally, each altercation that does not result in a clear, permanent rank establishment just sours the relationship between the dogs.

As humans we theoretically occupy the top spot on the totem pole so it's our job to decree that family members are not allowed to fight, just as the CEO of a company would take charge and not allow employees to fight. And because we have a more developed brain, we can do this without exerting force or using pain.

How to Change the Relationship

One recommendation is to choose which dog gets to be higher ranked and allow this dog to have priority access to your attention, petting, food, toys, and everything else. The problem with this approach is that in many cases this causes the higher-ranked dog to become even more aggressive. That may seem odd, but imagine this: if you give a movie star brat even more privileges than she already has and demote everyone else to lower rank, the movie star brat could easily become more of a bully than before.

So, rather than trying to give more privileges to one dog and punish the other, your approach will be two-pronged. You'll first establish that you're the leader and the dogs should follow some house rules. Next, you'll repair the relationship between the two by teaching them that good things happen when they are around each other. This way they learn to associate each other with good things. In serious cases, the two dogs should be kept completely separate so that all daily interactions can be planned and part of specific training sessions. Then they'll have no chance to fight, and their only experiences with each other are those that teach them good things.

For now avoid all altercations by rewarding alternate appropriate behavior first. And keeping them apart in cases where you aren't 100% sure that you can control them (e.g., you don't have treats ready, there's too much going on in the house) you'll quickly change their habits around each other so that they can once again get along.

Here's the general approach.

Step 1: Follow the Learn to Earn Protocol

Up to now, many altercations have probably been over your attention, with both pushing their way in. The dogs will now learn that they can only earn your attention by sitting politely, instead of rushing around and pushing each other out of the way.

You'll first teach them to automatically Say Please by Sitting for treats. (The following is just an overview—see Chapter 15 for detailed information.) When they sit, reward them with several treats. Then repeat the exercise over and over until both dogs understand that the only way to get what they want is to politely Say Please. Although this sounds like it might take a while, it's usually only a matter of 5 to 15 minutes for them to get the idea. You can start by training both dogs together, but if you're concerned about fighting in this situation start with each dog separately.

Once they get the Say Please command down pat, expect them to use it all the time whenever they want something from you. When they want to be petted, eat, go outside, or play with their toys, make it clear with your actions that they must be civilized. You'll have to practice Say Please by Sitting in each of these situations until it becomes a habit. Once you do, you'll notice a huge difference.

They will sit politely instead of racing around wildly to go through the gate first or to get the most petting. Specifically plan to give them treats for sit/please in situations where they tend to fight. For instance, if they fight when you run up the stairs, practice sit/please at the base of the stairs and then run up halfway and practice there. Start with just one dog and then work with two together when they have the game down individually.

Step 2: Teach Them to Leave It When Food Is Dropped on the Ground

If the dogs fight over dropped food, teach them to Leave it, which we discussed in Chapter 16. The goal is that they never race for dropped food because they have to sit politely and look at you anyway. Make sure that once they have this exercise down in the practice situation, you randomly drop treats in more realistic situations, such as when you're preparing dinner. If you practice 15 food drops per day in real-life situations (with the dogs apart first), and do so for several days in a row, the behavior will quickly become a habit.

Step 3: Come When Called

The third exercise for indoors is to bone up on come when called (see Chapter 19 for full protocol). First practice this with the dogs separately and call them only when you know they'll come running or when they're on a leash. To turn convert Come to a fun game of chase, run the opposite way and give the dogs treats when they catch up.

Once you have this down, if you see the dogs tense up or observe that one's getting too rowdy, call them apart before an altercation erupts. Then engage them in alternate appropriate fun activities.

Step 4: Teach at Least One Dog to Run to a Rug and Lie There to Get Treats

You can train the Go to Place exercise found in Chapter 23. If you teach both dogs, then they should have separate rugs or areas to run to. Training can be performed with treats given by hand or using a MannersMinder (www.MannersMinder.net), (Figure 31.1).

Once at least one dog knows how to run to his rug, lie down, and stay—even with high excitement—whenever you think chaos is about to break out, send him to his "place," which he already loves. This rug can be in the same room or a different room in the house. (If you use the MannersMinder it dispenses treats at that location so you don't have to worry about running back and forth with treats when you send the dog there.)

Step 5: Ignoring the Dogs When They're Apart

To speed the training up even more, you can up it a notch by ignoring the dogs when they're apart and only playing these and other fun games with them when they're together. This will help them learn that the best things in life occur when they're polite and in the presence of each other.

Figure 31.1

Chapter 32

Taking the Bark Out
of Bowser

A *San Francisco Chronicle* reader once asked me, "How can a dog bark for great lengths of time? If I yell and scream for a long time, I lose my voice."

Luckily, before I set out on an extensive review on the scientific literature on the canine vocal apparatus, I read the next part of his question, "I live between two houses with a dog on each property. Dog A barks at anyone who makes the slightest noise and continues to bark long after people go into our houses. When I try to shush him, he barks louder and faster. Dog B barks when other neighborhood dogs are barking. She's friendly and stops barking when I ask, but resumes after a short time. What can I do besides telling the owners to keep their dogs quiet during certain times?"

That made the solution much simpler. Actually, it would be easier to solve if the boisterous barkers belonged to the question-writer. Then, my recommendations would have been: Keep them inside with the family, exercise them regularly so they're not looking for trouble, and teach them some manners by rewarding good behaviors and removing rewards for bad. When they belong to someone else, it's a whole different ballgame. Here's what you might try.

Plan A: The Direct Approach

Go to your neighbor and say, "Hi there. Did you know that Fido barks a lot when he's outside by himself? I hear that when they do that it's often because they need more exercise and mental stimulation or they have separation anxiety. Have you thought about taking Fido to doggy day care, hiring a dog walker, enrolling him in obedience or agility classes, or even just keeping him inside?"

Hey, it could work. You never know. Some neighbors don't know their barking dogs are a disturbance. But if you hear Fido's owner laughing uncontrollably as he closes his door, proceed to Plan B.

Plan B: The Gift That Keeps on Giving

Go to the pet store and buy Fido a Nylabone or chew that you can stuff with treats, and next time you see the neighbor, bring it over to him and say, "Hi there. I brought this for Fido so he'd have something to do all day. My vet said it's a good idea to rotate between different toys each day. One day he can have a bone, the next day he can have a toy filled with low-calorie frozen treats, and so on. And she said that it's a good idea to feed him his dry dog food meals by putting them in one of those toys that they have to roll around to make the kibble fall out. You get them at a pet store."

Then hurry away before he asks why you, a person who owns no pets, are seeing a veterinarian.

Plan C: Stealth Training

Say Fido's good for a day or so but then starts barking again. Now you have to play dirty. You're going to have to take matters into your own hands. And it'll cost you—money for dog treats and time for training. Yes—you're going to do some training behind your neighbor's back.

But, first, one more conversation with the neighbor: "Hi there. You know, my friend just told me about her dog who had bad diarrhea from a food allergy. I didn't know dogs could have food allergies. Have you ever heard of that? Does Fido have any food allergies? How about heart problems or diabetes? On any medications?"

Once you get the scoop on any medical conditions, you can depart. But not too suddenly; he might get suspicious. If Fido has any special dietary considerations, your cover's blown. You'll have to confess your plans with your neighbor so that you can find out what treats are safe to use. Otherwise, proceed as follows.

For Dog B who already gets quiet on your "Quiet" cue: When he barks, tell him "Quiet," and when he stops, as he always does, immediately give him a treat. Better yet, give him 10 to 20 small treats in succession and space the interval between treats out as far as you can, without giving Dog B a chance to bark. Then walk into the house, and before he barks again, go out and reward him for being quiet. Keep repeating this, and gradually build up the interval between treats. The trick is to always get the treat to Dog B before he barks again. If he ever barks between treats, you know you waited too long.

If he doesn't already know "Quiet" quite as well as you thought, instead of saying the cue, start by just waiting patiently for him to shush down. The instant he's quiet, toss him a treat. Next, wait a few seconds and toss him a second treat. If he barks before that, toss him the treat a little earlier. The goal is to toss treats before he barks again, so that you're rewarding him for being quiet. Repeat this step and gradually increase the length of time he has to be quiet before receiving a treat. This seems like it might take a long time, but according to one pilot study that my undergraduate students performed in an SPCA kennel, most dogs take less than 10 minutes and 30 food reinforcements to learn to be quiet for several minutes. Once you have several minutes, you're home free, because you can just lengthen the time by rewarding for longer periods of quiet. And if the dog needs to learn the "Quiet" cue, all you do is wait for him while he's barking and say "Quiet" in a normal tone of voice the instant before you're sure he'll be quiet. Do this regularly, and he'll soon know that "Quiet" is his cue to shut his yap and get a yummy reward. Once he knows the cue, his behavior is now under your control at a distance.

For Dog A, the dog who barks louder when you holler, don't holler. To the dog, you might as well be barking back. He may feel threatened by or afraid of you and any noise on your part will up his arousal more. Instead, whenever you go outside, just toss treats to him continuously even when he's yapping. The goal is that you change his underlying fearful state so that he's not afraid. Be sure to toss treats fast enough so that once he starts eating them he'll just remain quiet. Also be sure to avoid sudden movements that might scare him into barking again. We want him to be in a calm, happy mood while you're out with him. Pretty soon, at least if he likes the treats, he'll be your friend. He'll associate you with good things, and he won't have any reason to bark at you. Then, whenever you notice he's quiet, randomly go outside and toss him some treats.

Now for a money-saving tip: When you first use treats, make them big and tasty so Fido notices them even in his excitement. You may have to peek over the fence to show the loot first. Once Fido gets the idea, go to the smallest treat that he notices and can eat in one bite.

Additional Steps

Obviously, these instructions are really for the owners of the barking dog, not for their aggravated neighbors. Of course if it's your own dog, the easiest course of action is to leave him inside where he can be part of the family. But in the event that he barks even when he's inside, or barks on walks or when you occasionally want him outside when you're home, here are the steps you would take in addition to the steps mentioned earlier.

- First, make sure he gets plenty of physical and mental exercise so his energy is channeled toward appropriate activities, rather than being pent-up inside.
- Next, make sure he thinks that say "please" by sitting, attention at heel, and come when called are his favorite games. Now when he barks at people walking near the house, you can just call him over and reward him for coming, and then keep his attention on you until the territorial threat has gone by.
- If he's barking at other dogs or a cat he wants to chase, practice the attention games from Section 3, so that playing with you is more fun than barking at the other exciting object.
- Last, make sure you address any underlying issues. If he's barking because he's afraid of people and other dogs or because he has separation anxiety, those are problems that need to be worked out through desensitization and counter-conditioning.

Always remember that barking in dogs is normal, just like talking is in people. To make "quiet" the more common situation, you have to make "quiet" the more rewarding condition.

Chapter 33

When Behavior Is Not the Problem

When Bowsers behave badly, it's not always purely a behavioral issue. Many medical problems in pets masquerade as bad behavior, and potty problems are high on the list. For example, when someone tells me, "My dog used to be potty trained, but he just started urinating in the house," my medical radar goes on full alert. Some owners might assume that their Dozer is being spiteful, but a quick check in the doggy manual of mayhem and revenge says that while dogs may mark their territory, they don't defecate or urinate on property to make their enemies mad.

No, spite doesn't even make the list here. Sudden loss of potty habits are more likely to point to one of a slew of medical problems, from diseases such as diabetes, kidney failure, and liver insufficiency, to drugs such as diuretics, to the common urinary tract infection, bladder stones, or bladder tumors that give dogs the constant urge to go.

Then there's the dog with a neurological disease that can't control his bladder or doesn't know he's dripping. Dogs can even develop cognitive dysfunction, which is somewhat treatable with a prescription diet or medications early on. These dogs visit their outdoor outhouse but forget what they went there to do. Then they come back in and forget that the outhouse was outside.

Other behavior changes are constantly throwing owners off track. For instance, even barking can be a sign of medical disease. One strange case that I saw was an elderly random-bred Rover who barked a lot when he was alone. Says his owner, "We just moved to a new house where we keep him in the yard a lot. Now he barks some during the day and barks a lot at night." At first this looked like a clear case of separation anxiety, but then I found out that Rover ate when the owner was gone, barked even when she was in plain sight, and was happy to sit sedentary rather than keep a constant eye on the owner—in other words, not a dog who was pining away for his favorite person. The answer to one question clued me in to his problem.

"How does he get along with your other dog?" I asked. "He follows Shadow around like a shadow," she said.

This statement made me wonder if Rover was using Shadow as his personal seeing-eye dog. Because dogs can't read eye charts—not even the ones with the pictures of bones and dog toys—I opted for a makeshift obstacle course in the exam room both in the dark and in full light. This, plus an examination of his retinas, told the story. He was blind at night and close to it during the day, and in the new house and yard he couldn't quite find his way around.

The number of diseases and their odd related behaviors abound. Dogs who act depressed because they're holding their head down may have neck pain, and those that suddenly dig through cabinets to gobble everything in sight could have one of several endocrine imbalances that cause intense hunger.

In short, a good deal of behavioral problems may be related to medical problems. But if you see a sudden behavior change or a behavior you can't explain, don't assume your dog is just acting up. Instead, take him to your veterinarian.

Chapter 34

When to Blame Genetics

Clearly, behavior is influenced by genetics. That's why animals show species-specific behaviors. It's why dogs fight with their teeth, horses kick and bite, and sheep ram each other with their specially equipped helmet-like skulls. It's also why Border Collies and Australian Kelpies tend to be better shepherding dogs than Border Terriers and Boxers. But just when can we attribute behaviors such as aggression and bad temperament to genetics?

Environmental Effects

Most people might guess that if the behavior shows up in puppyhood, it must be hereditary. Many research studies show that this isn't so, and that even early in life, there are many environmental effects at play. For instance, in their study on German Shepherd Dog puppies, J. Slabbert and Anne Rasa found that puppies that stayed with their mother through 12 weeks of age and had the opportunity to watch their mothers retrieve narcotics performed much better on narcotics aptitude tests at 6 months of age than puppies that stayed with their mothers for 6 to 12 weeks of age but that didn't have the opportunity to observe narcotics retrieval. Eighty percent of the puppies that had observed their mothers working passed the aptitude test, whereas only 20 percent of puppies that had not observed the narcotics retrieval passed. If you didn't know about the difference in early experience, you would have assumed that the puppies that passed just had a natural inborn ability.

Behaviors can be influenced by the environment even before puppyhood, too, because environmental influences start in the womb. A classic example is that of females in utero nestled between two males. Such females are bathed in high levels of testosterone, which masculinizes their brains, turning them into tomboys. Starting in puppyhood, like their male counterparts, they tend to lift their legs to urinate, spend more time on walks sniffing and stopping to leave their scent, and seeking out vertical target sites such as poles and fire hydrants. In other words, marking their neighborhood becomes a major pastime. In species such as rats, females born between two males are more aggressive with other females, but at the same time less attractive to males.

These environmental and developmental influences can have such dramatic effects that even animals with the same DNA may develop a bit differently. Probably the best example is "CC," short for Copy Cat. Cloned at Texas A&M, CC has the same DNA blueprints as her genetic mother, Rainbow. So, like identical twins, they're duplicates. That means everything's the same—but wait. A closer view in color reveals they don't actually look identical. In fact, technically they're not even the same color. Rainbow, with her speckling of orange mixed in with patches of black accentuated by a white belly and legs, is calico, while CC, who has no orange coloring at all, is a tiger-tabby.

How did this happen? The orange coat-color gene in cats is peculiar in that it is randomly inactivated in some clusters of skin cells and activated in others. When activated, the skin cells produce orange fur, and when inactivated, they produce black fur. This process usually results in a mosaic of orange and black. In CC, the orange-color gene was inactivated in all of the skin cells—thus, no orange in her coat.

The white-spotting pattern, which gives Rainbow and CC the large white areas, is also random. During fetal development, melanocytes, the pigment-producing cells in the skin, migrate across the skin starting from the back and race toward the belly. If the melanocytes get a late start on their migration, they pull up short, leaving the cat with flashy white ornamentation primarily on the underside and legs. This mechanism for expression of the white spotting gene means that even clones of a simple black and white Sylvester-type cat would sport tuxedos with noticeable variations.

While the coat color between CC and Rainbow is a marked contrast, behavior and personality are where the real differences may grow. Even after only a year of age, CC is friendlier and much more outgoing than Rainbow, because she's been handled more.

Now it's clear that two individuals with the same genetic makeup can develop differently. It also turns out that even when animals have gene variations that result in disease, they aren't necessarily destined to develop the disease later in life. For instance, phenlyketonuria in humans is a serious single-gene inherited disease. Children inheriting a copy of this gene from both of their parents are severely mentally challenged and usually die before reaching their teens. The gene works by preventing the formation of an enzyme, which, in normal people, converts one amino acid (phenylalanine) into another (tyrosine). In children with phenylketonuria, phenylalanine accumulates in the brain, causing the behavioral changes. Affected individuals can completely avoid these serious medical effects, though, just by simply changing to a diet without phenylalanine. The result is that phenylalanine does not accumulate in the brain and children are normal or nearly so. Thus, a genetic difference between normal children and children with phenylketonuria can be largely eliminated by manipulation of their environment.

Genes Interact With Environmental Effects

Taken together, what does this all mean? It means that genes are important, but they don't exactly control behavior. Rather, they interact with environmental effects to influence behavior. Consequently, if all animals in a litter exhibit the same behavioral tendencies or a very young animal exhibits an odd behavior, it doesn't necessarily mean they inherited the problem. Environmental influences could have played a major role, and all animals in a litter may have experienced the same important environmental experience leading to a specific behavioral tendency

So how do you know whether a behavior, such as aggression, in an animal is hereditary? Well, if it pops up in related siblings, breeders should be highly suspicious and should feel obligated to pursue the matter further. That is, they should closely track the behavior of other dogs in the same line and pull aggressive dogs out of the breeding pool in case it is genetic. Breeders should also look for environmental factors contributing to aggression. For instance, did they raise the affected siblings in the same detrimental way? Did they provide the appropriate early socialization to many unfamiliar people and exposure to an array of different sights and sounds? Did they handle the pups frequently on a daily basis and give them experience away from the litter? And did the owners who raised the pup follow through with proper socialization to both humans and unfamiliar dogs, as well as take them out on regular walks so that they could get used to their neighborhood?

Unfortunately, except for disorders that have already been identified in specific breeds, we can't tell whether an animal's behavioral problem has a largely genetic component. To know for sure whether the trait is hereditary, geneticists must perform pedigree or breeding studies looking at the specific trait. Once they identify a genetic component to a specific trait in a specific dog breed, if an individual of that breed with that trait is found, it can be attributed to heredity. Up to this point in time, there are no proven cases of genetically-caused aggression in specific dog breeds. Not because it doesn't exist, but because dogs are low on the list for research funding. Funding for genetic studies on both dogs and cats is primarily performed when breed clubs pool together to chip in. Once a behavior, such as aggression, is found to be hereditary, then the treatment and reversibility through behavior modification have to be specifically studied in that breed. Findings in one breed may not apply to the similar genetic disease in another.

Many dog owners are unhappy when they can't determine whether a behavior is genetic—but unless you're a breeder, it may not really matter. Even if a bad behavior is inherited, it doesn't mean owners of these dogs are off the hook—hereditary doesn't mean the trait must fully develop. Also, genetics does not mean the behavior is irreversible. So for bad behaviors, regardless of their genetic component, it's best to find the appropriate environmental conditions and behavior modification steps that will help you keep the bad behavior in check.

Glossary

Agonistic pucker: body posture in which the lips are raised revealing just the incisors and the canines.

Aversive: anything the animal dislikes or works to avoid.

Back chain: to train a series of behaviors by training the last behavior first and sequentially adding on additional behaviors that immediately precede the last one learned.

Belongingness: the concept that certain responses naturally belong with certain reinforcers such that animals are most likely to be able to learn certain responses when those responses are associated with the particular reinforcers. For instance, rats are more likely to learn to avoid certain foods when the foods are followed by nausea, but less likely to learn to avoid the foods if the foods were instead followed by a shock.

Blocking effect: prior conditioning of one cue (or conditioned stimulus) interferes with or blocks the learning of second cue for the same behavior (or conditioned response) if the two cues are presented together.

Bribing: when the owner shows the potential reward to the animal before requiring the animal to perform the behavior.

Bridging stimulus: a conditioned stimulus or cue that bridges the gap between the behavior and the unconditioned stimulus. It can either bridge the gap between the correct behavior and the food reinforcement (or other reinforcer), or it can bridge the gap in time between the inappropriate behavior and the conditioned punishment.

Classical conditioning: learning by association. When a neutral stimulus (one that initially has no meaning to the animal) is repeatedly paired with an unconditioned stimulus, the neutral stimulus gradually comes to elicit the same responses as the unconditioned stimulus.

Classical counter-conditioning: classically conditioning an association that's opposite to the association that has already been classically conditioned. Typically, when you hear the term counter-conditioning, it refers to classical counter-conditioning.

Clicker training: training that involves positive reinforcement and a bridging stimulus, where the bridging stimulus is the sound from a clicker.

Conditioned response: a response that is classically conditioned by repeated pairings of one stimulus with an unconditioned stimulus.

Conditioned stimulus: when one stimulus is repeatedly paired with an unconditioned stimulus until it elicits the same response as the unconditioned stimulus.

Continuous reinforcement: the reinforcement occurs every time the behavior occurs.

Counter-conditioning: classically conditioning an association that's opposite to an association that has already been classically conditioned.

Desensitization: presentation of a stimulus (usually an aversive stimulus) at a low level that the animal does not respond to, and gradually increasing the strength of the stimulus until the animal learns to ignore the full-force stimulus.

Domestication: the process occurring over many generations by which a population or species of animals becomes adapted to living with humans in the captive environment. During these many generations, the genetic composition of the population changes in order to make the adaptation possible.

Empirical description: a description of behavior in terms of the subject's body postures or movements.

Extinction: the process in which the particular behavior that has been reinforced in the past occurs, but is no longer reinforced, so the behavior diminishes in frequency.

Extinction burst: the initial increase in a particular behavior that may occur when a behavior that has been reinforced in the past is no longer reinforced.

Fixed ratio of reinforcement: when reinforcers are presented at an intermittent ratio that is fixed.

Flooding: full-force use of a stimulus (usually an aversive), presented in such a way that the animal cannot escape from the stimulus and eventually no longer responds to the stimulus.

Functional description: a description of behavior in terms of the functions or consequences of each behavior (e.g., submissive posture, escape behavior).

Habituation: the process by which an animal that initially responds to some stimulus (such as the sound of a train or the sight of a car roaring by) stops responding to the stimulus over time, due to repeated exposure to the stimulus in the absence of any aversive or pleasurable experience. In other words, habituation means that the animal "gets used to it."

Instinctive drift: when animals form a classically conditioned association between a stimulus (coin, ball, platform) and the food reinforcer, and consequently perform behaviors associated with finding or procuring food (such as pigs rooting, dogs biting a target, or chickens scratching the ground).

Intermittent reinforcement: when the behavior is reinforced only some of the time.

Luring: when a reward is shown to the animal prior to the animal's performing the behavior, in order to encourage or guide the animal to perform the behavior.

Mark: to distinguish or make clear. Marking a correct behavior means you are making it clear to the animal which behavior he has performed correctly, or when exactly he has performed the correct behavior.

Marker word: a verbal bridging stimulus. For instance, one can train a dog that "yes" is followed immediately with delivery of a food reward. After many trials, the "yes" can be used to mark a correct behavior because it signals to the animal that a food reward will be delivered shortly thereafter.

Motor pattern: a description of behavior in terms of the subject's body postures or movements.

Negative: in operant conditioning terminology, negative means to remove something or subtract something.

Negative punishment: removing something the animal wants in order to decrease the likelihood that the behavior will occur again.

Negative reinforcement: removing something aversive in order to increase the likelihood the behavior will occur again.

Neutral stimulus: a stimulus that has no meaning to the animal prior to pairing it with an unconditioned stimulus.

Operant conditioning: trial and error learning. Animals are more likely to repeat behaviors with pleasurable consequences and are less likely to repeat those with unpleasant consequences.

Operant counter-conditioning: training a behavior that is incompatible with the behavior the animal normally exhibits in a given context.

Overshadowing: when two stimuli (potential cues) are presented at the same time, the presence of the more easily trained stimulus may hinder learning the other stimulus. For instance, when training dogs verbal and visual cues for behaviors such as sitting or lying down, if you always present the visual cue and the verbal word cue together, the dog is most likely to learn the visual cue than verbal cue.

Positive: in operant conditioning terminology, positive refers to adding something.

Positive punishment: adding something aversive in order to decrease the likelihood that the behavior will occur again.

Positive reinforcement: adding something the animal wants in order to increase the likelihood that the behavior will occur again.

Premack Principle: states that high-probability responses can serve to reinforce low-probability responses, and a strong reinforcer is anything the animal would rather do.

Punishment: anything that decreases the likelihood that a behavior will occur again.

Reinforcement: anything that increases the likelihood that a behavior will occur again.

Sensitize: to lower the animal's response threshold to a given stimuli or increase his response to a given stimuli.

Sensitive period for socialization: time of development during which a young animal is primed to form bonds, attachments, and learn to accept objects, environments, and other animals as safe. The period varies by species. For dogs it is between 3 to 12 weeks of age.

Shaping: the process whereby you train a behavior by starting with a simple behavior that can easily be reinforced, and then gradually reinforce behaviors that are closer and closer to the goal behavior.

Spontaneous recovery: the reemergence of a conditioned response that has been previously extinguished. In classical conditioning the term used is spontaneous recovery; in operant conditioning the term used is resurgence.

Successive approximations: the sequential steps—each a little closer to the goal behavior—in a shaping plan.

Systematic desensitization: presenting a stimulus (usually an aversive stimulus) at a low level that the animal does not respond to, and gradually increasing the strength of the stimulus until the animal learns to ignore the full-force stimulus.

Tameness: a process that occurs within an individual's lifetime. In science circles, tameness describes an animal's willingness to approach humans, and is measured by the animal's flight distance. Tame animals have zero flight distance, which means you can walk right up to the animal and he won't flee. For example, a 10-foot (3 m) flight distance is one where you can approach up to 11 feet (3.5 m), but when you hit 10 feet (3 m), the animal runs away.

Unconditioned response: the involuntary or automatic response to a stimulus. It requires no prior training.

Unconditioned stimulus: a stimulus that innately causes a response. No prior training is needed.

Variable ratio of reinforcement: reinforcements that are presented intermittently when the animal performs the correct behavior, and the rate of reinforcement varies (that is, the number of times the animal is expected to perform the correct behavior before getting a reward varies).

Appendix A

Additional Reading and References

Burch, M. R. and J. S. Bailey. *How Dogs Learn*. New York: Howell Book House, 1999.

Coppinger, R. and L. Coppinger. *Dogs: A Startling New Understanding of Canine Origin, Behavior & Evolution*. New York: Scribner, 2001.

Dawkins, M. S. *Unraveling Animal Behaviour*. Harlow, Essex England: Addison Wesley Longman Limited, 1995.

Domjan, M. *The Essentials of Conditioning and Learning*. Belmont, CA: Wadsworth, 2000.

Domjan, M. *The Principles of Learning and Behavior*. Belmont, CA: Wadsworth, 2003.

Eisenstein, E. M. and A. D. Carlson. "A comparative approach to the behavior called 'learned helplessness'." *Behavioural Brain Research* 86.2 (1997): 149-160.

Karrasch, S. and V. Karrasch. *You Can Train Your Horse to Do Anything*. North Pomfret, Vermont: Trafalgar Square Publishing, 2000.

Maier, S. F., M. E. P. Seligman, et al. "Pavlovian fear conditioning and learned helplessness: effects on escape and avoidance behavior of (a) the CS-US contingency; and (b) the independence of the US and voluntary responding." *Punishment and Aversive Behavior*. B. A. Campbell and R. M. Church, Eds. New York: Appleton-Century-Crofts, 1969. 299-342.

Marder, A. R. and V. Voith, Eds. "Advances in Companion Animal Behavior." *Veterinary Clinics of North America: Small Animal Practice*. W.B. Saunders Company, 1991.

Overmier, J. B. and M. E. P. Seligman. "Effects of inescapable shock on subsequent escape and avoidance responding." *Journal of Comparative Physiol.* 63 (1967): 28-33.

Price, E. O. Animal Domestication and Behavior. New York: CABI Publishing, 2002.

Pryor, K. *Don't Shoot the Dog*. New York: Bantam Books, 1999.

Reid, P. J. *Excel-erated Learning*. Oakland, CA: James and Kenneth Publishers, 1996.

Seligman, M. E. P., S. F. Maier, et al. "Alleviation of learned helplessness in the dog." *Journal of Abnormal Psychology* 73.3 (1968): 256-262.

Serpell, J., Ed. *The Domestic Dog: Its evolution, behaviour and interactions with people*. New York: Cambridge University Press, 1995.

Slabbert, J. M., Rasa E. Anne O. "Observational learning of an acquired maternal behaviour pattern by working dog pups: an alternative training method?" *Applied Animal Behaviour Science*, 53, (1997): 309-316.

Appendix B

Resources

Animal Behaviorists

Animal Behavior Society (ABS)
Central Office, Indiana University
2611 East 10th Street #170
Bloomington, IN 47408-2603
Telephone: (812) 856-5541
Fax: (812) 856-5542
E-mail: aboffice@indiana.edu
www.animalbehavior.org

Veterinary Behaviorists

American College of Veterinary Behaviorists
   (ACVB)
Dr. Bonnie V. Beaver, ACVB Executive
   Director
Department of Small Animal Medicine and
   Surgery
Texas A&M University
College Station, TX 77843-4474
E-mail: info@dacvb.org
www.veterinarybehaviorists.org

Dog trainers

Association of Pet Dog Trainers (APDT)
P.O. Box 1781
Hobbs, NM 88241
Telephone: (800) PET-DOGS
Fax: (856) 439-0525
E-mail: information@apdt.com
www.apdt.com

Video Clips & Additional Practice Problems

Free downloadable Quicktime videos
   of training exercises:
www.DrSophiaYin.com

Hands-Free Leashes

The Buddy System
Chicks In Charge, LLC
2325 Mosswood Ct. S
Salem, OR 97306
Toll Free: (888) 363-2818
Fax: (503) 362-7203
E-mail: contact@buddysys.com
www.buddysys.com
Releash Dogmatic Products, Inc.
954 North 2nd Street, Suite B
Rogers, AR 72756
Toll free: 866-GO-DOGMA
Fax: 501-694-7711
www.dogmaticproducts.com

Appendix C

How the Science of Learning Made it to Animal Trainers
Advanced Chicken Training Camp—Hot Springs Arkansas, August 2000

I went through the picture in my head. Chicken number one climbs up the ladder, onto a-one foot-wide platform, makes a 180 degree turn, and tightropes across a narrow bridge to a second platform, where he pecks a tethered ping-pong ball, sending the ball in an arc around its post. The chicken then turns 180 degrees and negotiates a second ladder back down to ground level, where it encounters a yellow bowling pin and a blue bowling pin in a random arrangement. It knocks the yellow one down first, then the blue one.

Chicken number two grasps a loop tied to a bread pan, and with one continuous pull, drags the pan two feet. Then, in a separate segment, it pecks a vertical one-centimeter black dot on cue (and only on cue) three times in 15 seconds. The cue is a red laser dot.

Scenes from a Saturday morning cartoon? A twisted scheme of some sort? Neither of the above. It's the assigned mission at the August 2000 Advanced Operant Conditioning Workshop (a.k.a. chicken training camp), taught by Bob Bailey and psychologist Marian Breland-Bailey. Nine animal trainers from the US and Canada (including myself), are here to meet the challenge. We have five days.

The task sounds impossible, but each one of us is on a personal quest to learn the intricacies of operant conditioning.

Says Marian Bailey, "Animals are learning all the time, not just during training sessions. And they're learning with the same principles. Operant conditioning is the way that behavior changes in the real world."

As experienced trainers, we know this. We hope that with a better grasp of the principles of operant conditioning, we can catapult ourselves to a new level of training.

The nine of us form a diverse group. Some train animals professionally for theater or advertising, some have competed avidly in canine obedience trials or have been dog training instructors for years, and others just enjoy training their own assortment of pets. Despite our varied backgrounds, we all envision the myriad benefits these five days will bring forth. When we're finished, we'll return home to train our clients' animals more efficiently, accomplish more with our own pets, and instruct our students more proficiently.

For Marie Gulliford, who's trained everything from cockatoos to pigs, horses, and cows, one of the greatest benefits will be in her grooming shop. "I train the dogs who come in for grooming for my own benefit. My grooming shop is a business for profit. It's much more profitable if you can groom the dog quickly, and it's easier to do that on a dog that behaves well than on one that's doing all sorts of extraneous behaviors, such as jumping off the table or biting you."

It's no accident that we've chosen this particular training camp to help us fulfill our training goals. Sue Ailsby, a retired obedience and conformation judge who's been training dogs for 38 years, expresses the group sentiment, "This course offers an absolutely unique blend of scientific facts and practical applications thereof." Ailsby, who's trained dogs for every legitimate dog sport (and competed in most of them), and has also trained a number of service dogs (including her own), and frequently lectures at training, handling, and conformation seminars.

With her years of experience, she's chosen to train here because "the Baileys do it better, they do it faster, and do it with a deeper background."

Between the two of them, Marian and Bob have trained over 140 species of animals—which is impressive in its own right. However, their contributions (especially Marian's) to the field of animal training extend well beyond numbers. Marian and her first husband, Keller Breland, were at the forefront of operant conditioning when it was a relatively new area of study. They were among B.F. Skinner's first graduate students in the early 1940s. Their studies were interrupted by World War II, when Skinner took a hiatus from his university research and went to work for the US Navy on a project training pigeons to guide missiles. He enlisted Marian and Keller to help, and it was during this project that the two gained invaluable practical experience with the most advanced principles of operant conditioning—aspects they'd read about in their studies, but had never seen in action.

Surprisingly, it was the simpler principles that convinced them to make animal training a career. Principles such as behavior shaping, whereby you start with a simple behavior that the animal readily offers and gradually reinforce behaviors that look more and more like your goal behavior.

"Skinner had a push-button in his hand and had the electronic feeder outside of the training box," says Marian, recalling an incident during the pigeon bomb-guidance project. "At one point he took one of the pigeons outside of its training box and worked on shaping its response, because for some reason the pigeon was not pecking its target. So Skinner demonstrated the shaping process. It was then that Keller and I realized how powerful this system was. And we were very excited about it. We decided that after the war, we would get into something where we could apply this."

Because neither had gone on to get a clinical degree, they knew they wouldn't be able to treat people using this technique. But because they both liked animals, and were familiar with different kinds of animals, they decided to go into the animal business.

They started Animal Behavior Enterprises (ABE), a company whose goal was to demonstrate a better, scientific way of training animals in a humane manner using positive reinforcement. They started with dogs, reasoning that with the amount of untrained dogs in the US, owners would line up to learn their new humane way of training. Says Marian, "We thought it would be a cinch." Well, the training part was, but unfortunately the idea was too advanced for its time. Trainers shunned the new method, claiming that people had already been training dogs for centuries.

Undaunted by this obstacle, Marian and Keller headed in a different direction. For 47 years, ABE mass-produced trained animals for their own shows and for animal shows across the country. At their height, they were training about 1,000 animals at any given time for companies such as General Mills. They also worked on animal behavior research and training projects for groups such as the US Navy and Purina, as well as Marineland of Florida and Parrot Jungle—where among other things, they developed the first of the now-traditional dolphin and parrot shows. Through it all, they kept rigorous data on all of the training sessions and published several landmark papers in respectable scientific journals.

Psychologists, animal trainers, and behaviorists came to Hot Springs from all over the world to visit Marian and Keller. They trained many animal trainers, who later moved on to other places, including Busch Gardens and Sea World. Marian participated in the spread of the newest methods of humane animal training.

During their time together, before Keller passed away in 1965, they not only founded the field of applied animal psychology, but they also added many other impressive firsts, including: the first commercial enterprise (ABE) using operant conditioning (1943); the first school for teaching applied operant conditioning, including the first instruction manual (1947-48); the first dolphin and bird shows using operant conditioning (1955); the first automated commercial animal training facility (1951); the first automated (coin-operated) animal show (1953); the longest running TV commercial (Buck Bunny, 1954—ran 20 years). Their animals performed at virtually every large county and state fair in the nation.

But of all these accomplishments, one stands out the most to Marian. "One contribution was to give the science of behavior to animal trainers," says Marian. "To encourage the use of operant conditioning behavior analysis in many fields of animal work—in medical behaviors for animals, husbandry behaviors, show behaviors. Just a large number of fields have taken up the operant methods and have used them quite successfully. We've been quite gratified by this."

In fact, the methods have become so ubiquitous that trainers have forgotten where the methods originated. Says Bob Bailey, "There's one area that I think has been overlooked for a long time, and that is that it was the Brelands, even beyond Skinner and the other psychologists, who realized the significance and widespread application of the bridging stimulus. That it would be a revolution in animal training. They recognized it as absolutely key to the widespread training, and this was back in 1943."

And they were right. The bridging stimulus, usually a whistle or a click from a toy clicker, is now used in virtually all marine mammal shows, and in training zoo animals for husbandry behaviors. And, over 40 years after the Brelands first introduced it for use in dogs, it's finally taken off in the dog training world in the form of clicker training.

We use clicker training with the chickens, too, and though all of us have clicker trained extensively before, the chicken proves a particularly educational choice.

First, chickens are so quick that our timing has to be right on. The timing required to train the average dog won't hack it with chickens. A fraction of a second off, and you get a chicken that pecks near the black dot but not on it, that shakes the loop attached to the bread pan rather than pulling it, and that looks at the bowling pin instead of pecking it.

Secondly, chickens are particularly skillful at telling us that we need to up the rate of reinforcement. Failure to do so and our flappy fowl is running around on the floor in search of food, instead of up on the training table learning his tasks.

And third, because chickens peck so quickly, we get more repetitions in the short amount of time. That means we have more chances to recover from our training blunders.

Yes, even though we're in the advanced class, we still make our share of mistakes. The difference is that now we know within several five-minute sessions when we've made a mistake, because, like researchers, we take copious notes. Every session we note the chicken's performance, as well as our reinforcement errors.

It's an uphill battle for us, but we're determined to get the most out of it. And we do. On day five, after a total of 60-90 minutes of training per chicken per day, we've done it. It's a room full of poultry performing on cue like pros. Up the ladder, turn 180 degrees, across the bridge, peck the ping-pong ball, turn 180 degrees, down the ladder and then whap! whap! First the yellow bowling pin, then the blue. Click! Treat! Viola! A flock of trained chickens, and nine happy trainers.

Interview with Marian and Bob Bailey

Q) Marian, how did you first become interested in working with animals?

Marian: As a child, I was terrifically interested in animals. I was also, although I didn't know it at the time, interested in the humane treatment of animals. I read Black Beauty when I was five or six years old, and I was on a strict diet of animals stories throughout my childhood. I tried to pursuade my father to move to a farm so we could have some animals. My mother allowed only cats in the house. But my father couldn't see moving to a farm, so we didn't. But I was interested in [animals].

Q) How did you become interested in pursuing a Ph.D. in psychology? Back in the 1940s very few women were attending colleges, let alone earning advanced degrees in the sciences.

Marian: I went to college as a Latin major with a Greek minor, and I had to take a science, which I did protestingly. I took psychology. I thought it was the least painful science. I got in this special class with B.F. Skinner. He was taking a few known good students, and since I happened to have straight As, I got into his psychology class. He converted everyone. I know at least six students from that class who went onto great prominence [in the field of psychology]. He was very persuasive, and he had something exciting to work on, because it was new. There, of course, he taught the whole class on the basis of his new operant system. And so I was closely acquainted with that during my early years in college. I went on to become an undergraduate [research] assistant in the psychology department and then Skinner's graduate student after I graduated. I had added to my major, so I had a major in psychology and a minor in child psychology. I was also dating my first husband, Keller Breland. He became one of Skinner's graduate students, too.

Q) Tell me about the pigeon missile guidance project that interrupted your graduate studies during World War II.

Marian: Dr. Skinner came up with the idea because he wanted to do something for the war effort. We all left the department and went with him to this project and became research assistants on the project. We were training pigeons to essentially peck at a ground glass screen in front of them and on the screen the targets were projected. Now, the targets varied from railroad tracks to air fields. Things of that sort that were local bombing objectives. At the start of this, the navy—they were the sponsoring agency of the government—did not have a guidable bomb. So they worked away at that, [and] we worked away at the pigeons.

Q) Was the project successful?

Marian: Yes. There was a demonstration in Washington, finally, when the Navy said they were ready. And Dr. Skinner took six pigeons to Washington with the apparatus in which they had been trained—which for all intents and purposes would be the same as a nose cone for a guided bomb. And the demonstration went successfully. The pigeons knew what they had to do. They were good performers. The three pigeons in a cone was only a fail-safe situation. None of the birds failed.

Q) So if one got sick or was full, the others would still do the job?

Marian: Yes, that would be the final result. Now, if all three of them suddenly had headaches then it wouldn't work.

Q) Did the Navy ever use this pigeon system to guide missiles in the war?

Marian: The Navy turned [the project] down for two or three reasons. One, the judges who were looking at it—they were all admirals—knew the atomic bomb was nearing completion. They also knew that when that was finished, there would no longer be a need for pinpoint bombing, at least in this war. Also, they looked inside to look at the guidance system. They opened the pigeon chamber and saw three pigeons pecking away. This caused them several minutes of disbelief, I'd say. But there was no question that the pigeons were making it work, and we could have large numbers of pigeons. The setup had already been setup so that 25-40 pigeons could be trained at a time, so that there would be no problem supplying lots of birds.

Q) How did you and Keller go from training pigeons to starting your own animal business?

Marian: During the time we were working with pigeons, what Skinner showed us in the way of shaping (which was never done in graduate school; he was running experiments then) was individual shaping of a response. We realized then how powerful the techniques were and decided right then and there, as soon as we could after the war, we'd go get into some kind of a business use. We decided that we weren't quite ready to tackle human problems, and we realized we weren't going to go on to finish our Ph.Ds. So then we began to think of animals. What could we do? They mentioned in several classes that they thought we should get into dog training. We bought a bunch of dogs. We knew there were so many dogs in the country and people always wanted to get them trained. So we thought this would be a cinch. We'd tell people about this new humane way of training, and they'd talking to us by the thousands. Nobody listened to us. The dog food companies, etc. They didn't think it was all that new. People had been training dogs for thousands of years. That's the kind of greeting we got.

Q) When the dog idea failed, what did you do?

Marian: We kept our dogs, but we abandoned the idea. We really cast around. We tried all kinds of animals. Well, maybe [other] pets. Hamsters and parakeets were coming in. We made a little hamster kit that had equipment the hamsters could play on, and a little tiny clicker feeder that the hamster could get pellets or a small piece of food from, and the same for a parakeet. We always used a bridging stimulus. We started using clickers with our first dogs.

Q) What was your first big break?

Marian: Our first big break was when we went to General Mills. Now, they had sponsored our army project during the war. They didn't have regular research grant systems then. The Navy contracted with civilian companies; in this case, they contracted with General Mills on this project and any products that might have come out of it. So after the war, we knew some people in General Mills, and we knew they were in the farm-feed business. So Keller dreamed up this little show — this chicken show — and went there for a demonstration. [General Mills] latched onto it as something they could use in their fairs to draw attention to their booths and in what they called dealer open houses. These are events where a dealer would open up a store to the surrounding countryside. We started out in the northern part of the Midwest and spread on down South. We shipped these acts around the country, meanwhile adding more animals and new behaviors. We didn't have to go along with any of them. We trained the salesmen. The public loved it.

Q) How long were you working with General Mills?

Marian: We were under contract with General Mills for 10 years.

Q) What other projects did ABE work on?

Marian: We began branching out in all directions even before our contract with General Mills was up. We couldn't advertise for any other feed companies, but we did a lot of behavior work for other convention-goers. For all sorts of business conventions, which had begun to become big business then, and still is. Attention-getters. A lot of miscellaneous companies were into the animal act for attention-getters. P.A. refinery company, Mobil oil, and just a large number of companies wanted acts for their convention. We also did research work for Quaker Oats on taste-preference research, and also some identification. They had gotten a challenge in court that cats couldn't tell one flavor cat food from another. But boy they sure can. They can not only tell one flavor of cat food from another, but they can tell different batches of the same flavor from each other. The cans were all stamped with [information] from when that batch was turned out and where. And they could tell the difference between two batches turned out in separate weeks from the same cannery.

Q) When did you get into dolphin training?

Marian: We started the very first of the scientifically-trained dolphin shows. It was called Marine studios at that time and [later] became Marineland of Florida. In 1955, we went down there. They did have trained dolphins prior [to that]. They had one dolphin that did the show and one partly-trained replacement. This trainer was an old sea lion trainer. He worked for two years training his first dolphin. The other he'd been working with 18 months and wasn't making much progress. He trained them the old-fashioned way, but no punishment. If you did that with a sea lion, it would roll you over and take you into the tank and drown you! He trained for fish. He didn't know anything about shaping. He taught a dolphin to turn and do a dance. The dolphin would come halfway out of the water and turn. That's how it finally looked in a show—not like a waltz. His way to get the animal to do this was to stand on the side of the pool, hold a fish over his head, spin in a circle and say, "Turn." Bob was the one who actually saw the training happening.

Bob: Originally animal training was considered black magic, because they thought that if you could control animals, you could control the human spirit. Adolph Frome was one of the European animal trainers, and no one was allowed to watch him train. He was one of the old guild system where secrets were passed on from father to son. Only the senior animal trainers could watch him train; the regular trainers couldn't. They didn't want to spread these secrets around. I was Navy, I wasn't commercial; therefore I was permitted to be there and watch him train. I had watched this turn training and was dying, trying to squelch a laugh inside. I was watched this very nice gentleman say, "Tuuuuurn," with a beautiful teutonic inflection as he held this fish over his own head and he turned around. This was what he was teaching his students. That was part of his secret. I watched a number of sessions of him teaching like that. It was even funnier watching him teaching a dolphin how to bowl. He'd put the ball on his own nose and toss it.

Frome was in his very late 60s, early 70s, and getting close to retirement. I felt privileged to talk to him, because he was one of the old trainers. He was part of history. He was the first person to really train a dolphin in performance in the US, so he a was a pioneer in his own way. But I never did anything other than the Breland way.

The Brelands got into dolphin training when Frome quit and a dolphin died. The one trained dolphin died, and Marineland in St. Augustine, Florida hired Keller to train the young dolphin. Adolph spent two hard years training one dolphin to do a few things. Keller went down, and in six weeks, had two dolphins doing all the behaviors that Adolph Frome had spent two years getting the dolphins to do

Q) Marian, you and Keller published a several well-known scientific articles based on the data collected at ABE. What were they and how were they received by the scientific community?

Marian: The initial article about what we had accomplished was in 1951 in the business. Back in 1961 is when we published the misbehavior of organisms. That was when my first husband was still alive. The first one didn't cause much of a splash. People, I think most of the people in the field read it, and we did get some enthusiastic queries from some young people in psychology, mostly to the effect of, "Can I come work with you?"

Q) Your paper "Misbehavior of Organisms" covered a number of cases with different species where strong species-specific behaviors interfered with the learning process and caused delays in performance and delays in reinforcements. What was the response to this paper?

Marian: The reaction was dramatic. It spread not only to the behavior analysts but also to the biologists, anthropologists, and all sorts of people seized on that one. They had been very turned off by modern psychology and the idea that it seemed so mechanical to them. They hadn't been acquainted with Skinner's work, of course. So we got two kinds of reactions: One from the psychologists who had been waiting for people to find species differences, because that at one time had been a great thing in this country. We had a comparative psychology area, but it had been completely lost. The rats and the pigeons were the only things that they were using. And so the psychologists at that time didn't know anything about species differences. A number of psychologists and biologists who were waiting for this development really seized on it. The behavior analysis, a lot of them took it the wrong way. I think my first husband, he was very outspoken and probably said some things that some people took the wrong way. It didn't mean that we were abandoning operant conditioning or behavior analysis at all; it just meant that people needed to look at these other animals and see what they're doing, because they had forgotten how to do that. But anyway, so we got this very positive reaction from other psychologists, biologists, and anthropologists, and other groups like that, who were interested in species differences and general biological differences. And so that part was very gratifying. And then we got all these critical behavior analysts who thought we were abandoning behavior analysis. But we kept earning our living. Skinner took it that way himself at first. But we made up with him.

Q) How has your work helped human programs?

Marian: Oh, well, actually, I didn't do much of this. I was involved in developing training of ward attendants at institutions for the severely mentally handicapped or the developmentally disabled (mentally retarded, as they were known as in those days). But they had just been warehoused prior to that program. They weren't toilet trained. They couldn't feed themselves. They couldn't dress themselves or undress themselves. They were just piled in a big room, and drove the ward attendants crazy all day. And that was essentially what it was. So my husband and I, and Ken Burgess, developed a training program so the ward attendants could develop operant techniques to use on these children. And they worked beautifully. In fact, they're the standard techniques used in the institutions now. Now, I didn't start all of that. There were three our four of us in different places who were working with retarded children and teaching methods for teaching them. So it's been a great move for the children and the ward attendants. They still use these techniques in the institution there. It's taken the children out of the wards. Some of them are adults now; put them in cottages. It's really a terrific change.

Q) Do you finally get your Ph.D.?

Marian: After many years, we realized, while my first husband was alive, that one of us needed to get a Ph.D. to get back into the academic hold, into the sanction of the academic world. My husband as much as told me that I was going to be the one to do it. "It's not going to be me!" he said. He didn't agree with the academic world a lot. But I didn't do anything about it for a long time because I was just too plain busy and I had three kids by then. That put a few strains on my time. It was 1967 that I started back at the University of Arkansas, 200 miles away. What I did was went down there two to three days a week and took classes. And I had to review everything, I was so rusty. I found they'd changed quite a bit, so I had to get re-acquainted with the field. Because I was only part time, I dragged on and I didn't get my Ph.D. until 1978 (11 years from start to finish). That was kind of a record from the time I left my PH.D. work in 1942 (36 years from leaving the first time). They were getting a little sick of me, I think.

Q) Bob, how did you get into animal training?

Bob: I was at UCLA. I was an Ich and Herps man while I was an undergraduate. I'd always been interested in behavior and watching animals. I was particularly interested in what they do to survive. So much of their survival depends on their behavior. They don't just go out and suck their food in by osmosis; they go out and get it. And that involves very intricate behavior. I've always been interested in evolution and the fact that behavior seldom leaves footprints. All we can do is speculate what behavior was like before based on what we know of the circumstances and the survival of the animal. Anyway, I started thinking up ways of conducting experiments. What could I do in the way of shaping this particular behavior? Can these animals do these things? I'd had a few psychology courses, and I'd heard of Skinner, and I had enough information where I could find books that I needed.

Q) What types of experiments did you devise?

Bob: I was feeding Congo Eels in the lab and tested the effect of putting baby mice in different sections. Could I condition the eels to go to different places in this aquarium? By jove, I could. They learned very quickly. When I'd walk in, the animal would anticipate and go to a particular corner. Well, I started to get more sophisticated, and I'd move the plant around and always feed where the plant was. Pretty soon they'd go to wherever the plant was. That's where I started really getting hooked. The first real experiment I did was working with a few of the tidepool fishes. I chose two varieties of one species that came in different colors: one was a reddish brown, and one was a green with silver on it. I started studying first in the tide pools to see what kind of sea grass did you find them in. It turned out statistically significant, relative to the color of the plant. I found that the fish would be found in plant of its color. So I asked what would happen if I created an environment with a matrix. I made four matrixes: clear, black, green, and brown. I had eight aquaria, and I studied the distribution in the eight tanks. I made the matrix out of clothes hangers and some plastic material like cellophane, where the plastic was in the material, but that the color didn't leach out. The coloring was cut into strips that hung vertically like plants. There were hundreds of strips per area. Each day I'd walk in and observe, using mirrors to see where the fish were and note what time. I let it sit that way for two days and then just rotates them 90 or 180 degrees according to a plan. The fish hung out in the plant of the same color. Now, I didn't know about controlling for light. I should have had yellow lighting or sunlight instead of fluorescent. So there were a lot of things I didn't know about and didn't care about. But I thought that was pretty neat because I could get them to move around very easily.

Q) Bob, how did you become involved with the Brelands?

Bob: In about 1962, I was chosen to be the Navy's director of training. I really hadn't had much formal training in animal training; however, one of the few smart things [the Navy] did was hire Keller and Marian Breland of ABE. So they came out with some chickens, and we spent a fair amount of time learning to train chickens. And I thought that was neat, and I started applying that to training dolphins. Then our two dolphins died. When we captured them, they were parasite-infested, and while we were getting new dolphins, I went to Hot Springs, Arkansas and spent a number of weeks there. There I was introduced to what animal behavior was all about. That is, changing behavior. At ABE, they changed behavior, and a lot of behavior. They changed lots of behavior in a short amount of time. Behavior analysis was the name of the game, and that's what they were calling it...behavior analysis. And that's what they taught me to do.

I spent a little while with Keller to begin with. Keller was expansive, articulate. He could really articulate this stuff. Then I spent the rest of the time in an automatic trainer room. I got introduced to the monster—a bank of chickens in a box arranged four across and three down, and you had to train all of them. You were shaping behavior of 12 chickens all at once. I found out what training was all about. You start out with one chicken. That's not so bad. Two chickens gets interesting. Three chickens gets more interesting. At four chickens, the perspiration drips. Pretty soon you start being able to look and see pieces of behavior coming out. I got to about six. I was reasonable at six. That is the way to learn training. And I loved it. To see your first few chickens coming out of the box and replacing them with new ones is great. I spent many months over the next three years in Hot Springs.

Q) When the Navy finally got healthy dolphins, what sort of missions did they train?

Bob: For sea missions, normally the dolphin was launched from a helicopter or from a sea pen (they didn't have special boats back then). Sometimes we used a high speed boat if we were in a hurry, but it was in the 1960s. It's different today and work has changed, but that's how we started.

We'd have a large sea-pen which housed the dolphin, a boat which we'd monitor from, and a target. The pen and boat are about one to two miles away, and the target could be over six miles away. The dolphin would be guided in an erratic way instead of straight on, and get to a target at the very end. So to go six miles, the dolphin had to go much farther, which meant that missions could last up to 12 hours. They would go through some terminal maneuver once they hit the target. Then they would guide the dolphin back to another pen. They used tracking systems, most of which are still classified. If the animals or humans screwed up, they had an alternative sites and jobs to do. They didn't want to lose the animal or abort the mission. There were other dolphins and schools of fish, but the trained dolphins tended not to get distracted. Although, once when we were working in Key West once and a dolphin disappeared. It caught a grouper and came back and dumped it in the boat.

Q) After the Navy, you went to work as a research assistant for ABE and later, a number of years after Keller passed away, became general manager. Can you tell me what made ABE different from other animal business?

Bob: It's right in the charter of Animal Behavior Enterprises that the company was to demonstrate that there's a better way, a scientific, technologic way of training animals, and it need not use punishment. The real effort was to train animals in a humane way with less aversives. And to use the information that comes out of the laboratory. That was right in the charter. So the Brelands did that. When they began this in 1943, they believed that this technology was much more powerful that the scientists at the time thought it was. And not only that, within six months of the time they'd started their business, they realized that the key to high productivity was the use of the secondary reinforcer. Now they call it clicker training and the like. Regardless of what the secondary reinforcer was, they realized that precision training demanded a precision secondary reinforcer. So of all the people alive at the time, Skinner, not with standing, the Brelands were the ones to realize the technological impact of that one tool, the secondary reinforcer. And they really built their business on the secondary reinforcer.

Q) Since you've found that the secondary reinforcer is such a powerful tool, are you clicker purists?

Marian: We're not pure clicker trainers. We use the clicker when it's advantageous, and appropriate and when it will do the most good. If you don't know exactly what you want and you're just waiting for the dog to do some behavior, you'd do a lot better to just chuck food. Just reinforce the dog. But if you want to establish precision, if you have a delicate point in the behavior that you want to emphasize, there's nothing like the clicker. If you're good on your timing, you can click the precise moment in the behavior that you want. There's nothing like it.

Bob: We deal in operant conditioning. I use positive reinforcement, I use negative reinforcement, I use positive punishment, and I use negative punishment. And the vast majority of all our training has been positive reinforcement. Between Marian and myself, we probably have about 103 years of training experience. In the course of that, we've used positive punishment maybe a dozen times. So we stand pretty well on the side of, you don't have to use positive punishment except under the really extreme, unusual situations. And certainly in pet training, there's no reason I could see that you'd need to use an aversive for pet training, or, for that matter, obedience training in the ring.

Q) How did you get started with chicken training camps for the public?

Bob: We started in 1997, largely because of Terry Ryan and Karen Pryor and the like, who nudged us out of retirement, back into training life. We had a lot of requests for chicken-training seminars and workshops.

Q) In these workshops, what do you notice as the most frequently training errors?

Bob: The number one error is that trainers are late on reinforcements, or their reinforcement is ill-timed. The next is the criteria—what you're going to reinforce. One time they reinforce one thing and the next time they reinforce something else. Sometimes this is just poor decision-making, and sometimes it's just that people don't recognize the behavior. They haven't analyzed the behavior, so they really don't know what it is they want to reinforce. They just know what they want the final behavior to be. Thirdly, so many people are stingy with their rate of reinforcement. Also, trainers often don't control the environment, and the animal becomes distracted or afraid.

Q) What encouragement would you offer to someone who wants to improve his or her training skills?

Bob: Training is a mechanical skill. If you're applying the proper techniques and your mechanical skill is good, and you are following your timing, criteria, and rate of reinforcement, you'll get what you're after.

First landmark paper by Keller and Marian Breland

"A Field of Applied Animal Psychology"
Keller and Marian Breland
Lonsdale, Arkansas
First published in *American Psychologist*, 1951, 6, 202-204.

Recent developments in behavior theory have made possible a new field of applied psychology. This new field has yet to be finally christened. It might be called the field of applied animal psychology, or the field of behavioral engineering. We consider it an excellent example of how the findings of "pure" research can be put to practical use.

The core of the field is the work of the neobehaviorists, which has so ordered the facts of behavior that many of their experimental data and those of earlier workers have become immediately applicable to the engineering of animal behavior. We have found most useful the systematic formulation presented by B. F. Skinner in The Behavior of Organisms. This body of theory has made it possible for us, since the spring of 1947, to develop a flourishing and expanding business concerned with the mass production of conditioned operant behavior in animals.

Applied animal psychology brings together the two formerly unrelated fields of professional animal training and modern behavioral science. The field is new in that it represents, we believe, the first application of systematic behavior theory to the control of animal behavior. We are now in a position to outstrip old-time professional animal trainers in speed and economy of training. In many instances, we can use automatic training methods. We can apply to our training the data of comparative psychology, utilizing new tricks, new animals. We can turn out multiple units – 200 "Clever Hans"es instead of one. Furthermore, the systematic nature of the theory puts us in a position to advance to new and more elaborate behavior patterns, to predict results and forestall difficulties.

So far, all our applications have been made for the purpose of advertising exhibits for General Mills, Inc. We developed first a series of trained chicken acts, which were used for county fair booth exhibits in the Midwest, for the purpose of advertising farm feeds. These acts were performed by a group of two-year-old hens, which had been culled from a neighbor's flock and were destined for the stew pot. We used a hen-sized stage, some specially constructed props, and a solenoid-driven automatic feed hopper for dispensing reinforcements in the form of scratch grain.

One hen played a 5-note tune on a small piano, another performed a "tap dance" in costume and shoes, while a third "laid" wooden eggs from a nest box; the eggs rolled down a trough into a basket—the audience could call out any number of eggs desired, up to eight, and the hen would lay that number, non-stop.

The basic operation in all these acts was reinforcement at the proper moment in the behavior sequence, by presenting the chicken with a small amount of scratch grain from the solenoid-operated hopper. During the training period, successive approximations to the desired behavior, and component parts of the final pattern, were reinforced. During performances, longer ratios or more elaborate completed patterns were reinforced to keep the behavior at a high level of strength.

During the ensuing year, three sets of these acts were prepared and shipped all over the United States in the hands of men who had had only once or two days' training. The birds played thousands of performances without a single failure, except for an occasional sluggish performance due to ill health or overfeeding. The acts proved to be unprecedented crowd-stoppers at the fairs and feed-store "Open house" events where they played, showing to as many as 5,000 people in a day.

The success of these acts led to the development of a trained pig show, "Priscilla the Fastidious Pig," whose routine included turning on the radio, eating breakfast at a table, picking up the dirty clothes and putting them in a hamper, running the vacuum cleaner around, picking out her favorite feed from those of her competitors, and taking part in a quiz program, and answering "Yes" and "No" to the questions put by the audience by lighting up the appropriate signs.

Priscilla was likewise shown at fairs and special feed-store events and conventions throughout the country. She also appeared on television. She was even more successful than the chicken acts at jamming fair booths and feed-stores with spectators. The pig act was in use almost steadily from the fall of 1948 to the summer of 1950. It was necessary to train a replacement about every three to five months, since the pigs rapidly became too large for easy shipping. After training, the pigs were turned over to their handler, usually a General Mills' feed salesman, who had had one or two days' instruction at our farm, or in the field under our supervision.

In addition to teaching handlers to manage the animals on the road, we have twice taught instructors to do the basic training of the animals and assist with the instruction of the handlers. Both experiences in training instructors were successful and demonstrated clearly that people with no special psychological background can learn the methods and theory behind our animal training procedures. One instructor was a woman college graduate who had taken her degree in statistics and sociology. The other was an average male high school graduate, whose only specialty had been radio repair work. Both acquired, in a few weeks, most of the techniques of training the existing acts, and enough of the theory and nature of the process to train new acts on their own.

Our next development was a baby chick act. Sixty to 100 chicks are trained for one show. Beginning at about one week of age, they are trained for about 10 days. The show is run with about 10 or 12 chicks on stage. Each runs up a ramp or inclined plane to a platform from which he can reach a feed hopper. He "roots" the top chick off, grabs a bite of feed, then in turn gets pushed off by the next in line. As he goes, he falls onto a tilting pan and is deposited onto the stage floor, accompanied by the sounding of a chime and flashing of a trade name sign. This sequence of behavior results in an endless chain of baby chicks running up the ramp and sliding off. When the group becomes sleepy, they are replaced by a fresh batch, and the show can thus go on indefinitely; it has actually been used about 12 hours a day in most cases.

This act is our first "packaged act." It is designed to run virtually automatically. It requires only the attendant to keep the feed hopper full and change the group of chicks on stage when they become sleepy. No special training is required for the attendant; mimeographed directions are shipped out with the chicks and provide the only necessary instruction. This act has been a perennial favorite, and we have trained more than 2,500 chicks to fill our orders for this display.

We have developed two variations on the baby chick act. One uses a projector to present advertising copy, which an endless chain of baby chicks in motion around it. The other variation substitutes for the ramp a series of steps onto which the chicks must jump.

A calf was trained for the General Mills' booth at the International Dairy Exposition at Indianapolis. "Larro Larry" took part in a quiz program by lighting up "Yes" and "No" signs, as did Priscilla the Pig, and played "Bull in the China Shop" by systematically upsetting an elaborate display of dishes, to the great alarm of the passing crowd.

A turkey act has been developed in which members of the audience play a game with the turkey. This bird is placed in a display case and has access through an opening to part of the miniature playing field. The turkey is trained to rake a steel ball off this field into his goal. The audience player is given a long pole with a magnet on the end and tries to guide the ball along the playing field into his goal before the turkey wins. Various barriers are placed along the playing field to make the game more difficult for both players.

Additional acts using grown chickens have been designed and used, two involving discrimination problems: the Card Sharp, who picks out a better poker hand than a member of the audience; and the Old Shell Game, in which the chicken picks out the shell with the bean under it; and two contests between two birds, a High Jump contest, and a Strength of Pull test. Another automatic act was created by training a hen, on a very high fixed ratio, to beat a toy drum for hours at a time. We also trained a hen in some bizarre contortions; the hen twisted her neck to one side an over her back so that she appeared to be looking frantically in all directions at once. This was billed as "The Civilian Aircraft Spotter" or "The Atom Bomb Neurosis." We have done a few experiments and some developmental work on rats, hamsters, guinea pigs, ducks, pigeons, rabbits, cats, dogs, and crows.

There are, obviously, innumerable other possibilities in the field of advertising exhibits. One is the perfection of the "packaged act," the fully automatic unit which can be shipped anywhere, set up in a store window or convention booth, an operated day in and day out with no more instructions than are necessary for the operation of any machine designed for such use. One adaptation of the automatic act is the animated display – show window advertising in which live animals take the place of puppets and robots.

However, probably the biggest applications exist in the entertainment world. Here we can take over the formal animal training involved in the standard animal act for stage, circus, and movies, and do it faster, cheaper, better, and in multiple units. It is possible to create new acts, and in fact whole new circuses, using unusual animals and unusual acts, and again do it cheaply, quickly, and in numbers limited only by time and production facilities. Television offers unusual opportunities. We can invade the field of night-club entertainment with novel small animals. We can sell or rent trained animal units to hospitals, doctors' offices, waiting rooms of various sorts, or even to private individuals, supplying instructions on care and maintenance.

Another important application of animal psychology is the training of farm animals. Farm dogs and horses could be rendered much more useful to the average farmer if they were given appropriate training. Farmers could themselves be instructed in training and handling their own animals.

The training of dogs for the blind could probably be done on a larger scale, more rapidly and efficiently. One of the big problems of the Seeing Eye institution was obtaining instructions. The difficulty was, apparently, that the first masters of the art did not have a sufficiently precise theoretical formulation in training the dogs and hence could not pass the information on to new instructors. They then encountered another problem in instructing the blind to handle the dogs and met numerous failures here in adapting client to dog. Many of these failures could now doubtless be avoided.

Dogs, of course, can be trained more readily with the new methods in all the traditional fields of canine service to mankind: hunting, guarding children and property, and detective work. Military use of dogs in such tasks as guard duty and carrying messages can also be made more effective.

This, then, seems to be the general outline of a promising new field which we have only begun to explore. It is so vast, we feel, that we cannot begin to develop one-tenth of the projects we have thought of. More psychologists, grounded in the theory, are needed to advance the technology and explore the undeveloped portions of this program. Furthermore, once the technology gets underway and the business develops, there will be active need for academic psychologists to do the background research necessary for full development of the program. And, of course, as psychologists continue to do basic research using animals as subjects, one by-product will be new and better methods of applied animal psychology.

Two types of problems have cropped up repeatedly in our efforts. (1) Apparatus problems have consumed much more time than problems connected with the behavior. The apparatus must be durable enough to stand up under cross-country shipment, and must be foolproof enough to be operated by relatively untrained personnel. (2) We need to know the answers to various "academic" problems, such as "What sort of fixed ratio will an animal sustain on a response made to a disappearing manipulandum, a key available, for example, only every three minutes?" "What would constitute an adequate reinforcement for a hamster, to sustain performances over several hours without satiation?" "What are the emotional characteristics of rabbits and guinea pigs – to what sort and magnitude of stimuli will they adapt, and what is the nature of the curve of recovery from such an adaptation?"

The study of these and related questions – in short, the re-examination of the whole field of comparative psychology in this new light – by psychologists who have available the facilities of an animal laboratory, would greatly speed up the development of the applied field.

In conclusion, we feel that here is a genuine field of applied psychology, old as "group living" and "parenthood" in its subject matter, but new in method and approach, which psychologists can enter with promise of financial reward and a sense of accomplishment and ultimate benefit to the science. For we all know that there is nothing as convincing to the layman of the worth of a discipline as achievement, and the present field offers the psychologist a fine opportunity to demonstrate control of his subject matter.

Second landmark paper by Keller and Marian Breland

"The Misbehavior of Organisms"
Keller Breland and Marian Breland (1961)
Animal Behavior Enterprises, Hot Springs, Arkansas
First published in *American Psychologist*, 16, 681-684.

There seems to be a continuing realization by psychologists that perhaps the white rat cannot reveal everything there is to know about behavior. Among the voices raised on this topic, Beach (1950) has emphasized the necessity of widening the range of species subjected to experimental techniques and conditions. However, psychologists as a whole do not seem to be heeding these admonitions, as Whalen (1961) has pointed out.

Perhaps this reluctance is due in part to some dark precognition of what they might find in such investigations, for the ethologists Lorenz (1950, p. 233) and Tinbergen (1951, p. 6) have warned that if psychologists are to understand and predict the behavior of organisms, it is essential that they become thoroughly familiar with the instinctive behavior patterns of each new species they essay to study. Of course, the Watsonian or neobehavioristically oriented experimenter is apt to consider "instinct" an ugly word. He tends to class it with Hebb's (1960) other "seditious notions" which were discarded in the behavioristic revolution, and he may have some premonition that he will encounter this bete noir in extending the range of species and situations studied.

We can assure him that his apprehensions are well grounded. In our attempt to extend a behavioristically oriented approach to the engineering control of animal behavior by operant conditioning techniques, we have fought a running battle with the seditious notion of instinct. It might be of some interest to the psychologist to know how the battle is going and to learn something about the nature of the adversary he is likely to meet if and when he tackles new species in new learning situations.

Our first report (Breland & Breland, 1951) in the American Psychologist, concerning our experiences in controlling animal behavior, was wholly affirmative and optimistic, saying in essence that the principles derived from the laboratory could be applied to the extensive control of behavior under nonlaboratory conditions throughout a considerable segment of the phylogenetic scale.

When we began this work, it was our aim to see if the science would work beyond the laboratory, to determine if animal psychology could stand on its own feet as an engineering discipline. These aims have been realized. We have controlled a wide range of animal behavior and have made use of the great popular appeal of animals to make it an economically feasible project. Conditioned behavior has been exhibited at various municipal zoos and museums of natural history and has been used for department store displays, for fair and trade convention exhibits, for entertainment at tourist attractions, on television shows, and in the production of television commercials. Thirty-eight species, totaling over 6,000 individual animals, have been conditioned, and we have dared to tackle such unlikely subjects as reindeer, cockatoos, raccoons, porpoises, and whales.

Emboldened by this consistent reinforcement, we have ventured further and further from the security of the Skinner box. However, in this cavalier extrapolation, we have run afoul of a persistent pattern of discomforting failures. These failures, although disconcertingly frequent and seemingly diverse, fall into a very interesting pattern. They all represent breakdowns of conditioned operant behavior. From a great number of such experiences, we have selected, more or less at random, the following examples.

The first instance of our discomfiture might be entitled, What Makes Sammy Dance? In the exhibit in which this occurred, the casual observer sees a grown bantam chicken emerge from a retaining compartment when the door automatically opens. The chicken walks over about 3 feet, pulls a rubber loop on a small box which starts a repeated auditory stimulus pattern (a four-note tune). The chicken then steps up onto an 18-inch, slightly raised disc, thereby closing a timer switch, and scratches vigorously, round and round, over the disc for 15 seconds, at the rate of about two scratches per second until the automatic feeder fires in the retaining compartment. The chicken goes into the compartment to eat, thereby auto-matically shutting the door. The popular interpretation of this behavior pattern is that the chicken has turned on the "juke box" and "dances."

The development of this behavioral exhibit was wholly unplanned. In the attempt to create quite another type of demonstration, which required a chicken simply to stand on a platform for 12-15 seconds, we found that over 50% developed a very strong and pronounced scratch pattern, which tended to increase in persistence as the time interval was lengthened. (Another 25% or so developed other behaviors—pecking at spots, etc.) However, we were able to change our plans so as to make use of the scratch pattern, and the result was the "dancing chicken" exhibit described above.

In this exhibit, the only real contingency for reinforcement is that the chicken must depress the platform for 15 seconds. In the course of a performing day (about three hours for each chicken) a chicken may turn out over 10,000 unnecessary, virtually identical responses. Operant behaviorists would probably have little hesitancy in labeling this an example of Skinnerian "superstition" (Skinner, 1948) or "mediating" behavior, and we list it first to whet their explanatory appetite.

However, a second instance involving a raccoon does not fit so neatly into this paradigm. The response concerned the manipulation of money by the raccoon (who has "hands" rather similar to those of the primates). The contingency for reinforcement was picking up the coins and depositing them in a 5-inch metal box.

Raccoons condition readily, have good appetites, and this one was quite tame and an eager subject. We anticipated no trouble. Conditioning him to pick up the first coin was simple.

We started out by reinforcing him for picking up a single coin. Then the metal container was introduced, with the requirement that he drop the coin into the container. Here we ran into the first bit of difficulty: he seemed to have a great deal of trouble letting go of the coin. He would rub it up against the inside of the container, pull it back out, and clutch it firmly for several seconds. However, he would finally turn it loose and receive his food reinforcement. Then the final contingency: we put him on a ratio of two, requiring that he pick up both coins and put them in the container.

Now the raccoon really had problems (and so did we). Not only could he not let go of the coins, but he spent seconds, even minutes, rubbing them together (in a most miserly fashion), and dipping them into the container. He carried on this behavior to such an extent that the practical application we had in mind—a display featuring a raccoon putting money in a piggy bank—simply was not feasible. The rubbing behavior became worse and worse as time went on, in spite of nonreinforcement.

For the third instance, we return to the gallinaceous birds. The observer sees a hopper full of oval plastic capsules which contain small toys, charms, and the like. When the SD (a light) is presented to the chicken, she pulls a rubber loop which releases one of these capsules onto a slide, about 16 inches long, inclined at about 30 degrees. The capsule rolls down the slide and comes to rest near the end. Here one or two sharp, straight pecks by the chicken will knock it forward off the slide and out to the observer, and the chicken is then reinforced by an automatic feeder. This is all very well—most chickens are able to master these contingencies in short order. The loop pulling presents no problems; she then has only to peck the capsule off the slide to get her reinforcement.

However, a good 20% of all chickens tried on this set of contingencies fail to make the grade. After they have pecked a few capsules off the slide, they begin to grab at the capsules and drag them backwards into the cage. Here they pound them up and down on the floor of the cage. Of course, this results in no reinforcement for the chicken, and yet some chickens will pull in over half of all the capsules presented to them.

Almost always this problem behavior does not appear until after the capsules begin to move down the slide. Conditioning is begun with stationary capsules placed by the experimenter. When the pecking behavior becomes strong enough, so that the chicken is knocking them off the slide and getting reinforced consistently, the loop pulling is conditioned to the light. The capsules then come rolling down the slide to the chicken. Here most chickens, who before did not have this tendency, will start grabbing and shaking.

The fourth incident also concerns a chicken. Here the observer sees a chicken in a cage about four feet long which is placed alongside a miniature baseball field. The reason for the cage is the interesting part. At one end of the cage is an automatic electric feed hopper. At the other is an opening through which the chicken can reach and pull a loop on a bat. If she pulls the loop hard enough the bat (solenoid operated) will swing, knocking a small baseball up the playing field. If it gets past the miniature toy players on the field and hits the back fence, the chicken is automatically reinforced with food at the other end of the cage. If it does not go far enough, or hits one of the players, she tries again. This results in behavior on an irregular ratio. When the feeder sounds, she then runs down the length of the cage and eats.

Our problems began when we tried to remove the cage for photography. Chickens that had been well conditioned in this behavior became wildly excited when the ball started to move. They would jump up on the playing field, chase the ball all over the field, even knock it off on the floor and chase it around, pecking it in every direction, although they had never had access to the ball before. This behavior was so persistent and so disruptive, in spite of the fact that it was never reinforced, that we had to reinstate the cage.

The last instance we shall relate in detail is one of the most annoying and baffling for a good behaviorist. Here a pig was conditioned to pick up large wooden coins and deposit them in a large "piggy bank." The coins were placed several feet from the bank and the pig required to carry them to the bank and deposit them, usually four or five coins for one reinforcement. (Of course, we started out with one coin, near the bank.)

Pigs condition very rapidly, they have no trouble taking ratios, they have ravenous appetites (naturally), and in many ways are among the most tractable animals we have worked with. However, this particular problem behavior developed in pig after pig, usually after a period of weeks or months, getting worse every day. At first the pig would eagerly pick up one dollar, carry it to the bank, run back, get another; carry it rapidly and neatly, and so on, until the ratio was complete. Thereafter, over a period of weeks the behavior would become slower and slower. He might run over eagerly for each dollar, but on the way back, instead of carrying the dollar and depositing it simply and cleanly, he would repeatedly drop it, root it, drop it again, root it along the way, pick it up, toss it up in the air, drop it, root it some more, and so on.

We thought this behavior might simply be the dilly-dallying of an animal on a low drive. However, the behavior persisted and gained in strength in spite of a severely increased drive—he finally went through the ratios so slowly that he did not get enough to eat in the course of a day. Finally it would take the pig about 10 minutes to transport four coins a distance of about 6 feet. This problem behavior developed repeatedly in successive pigs.

There have also been other instances: hamsters that stopped working in a glass case after four or five reinforcements, porpoises and whales that swallow their manipulanda (balls and inner tubes), cats that will not leave the area of the feeder, rabbits that will not go to the feeder, the great difficulty in many species of conditioning vocalization with food reinforcement, problems in conditioning a kick in a cow, the failure to get appreciably increased effort out of the ungulates with increased drive, and so on. These we shall not dwell on in detail, nor shall we discuss how they might be overcome.

These egregious failures came as a rather considerable shock to us, for there was nothing in our background in behaviorism to prepare us for such gross inabilities to predict and control the behavior of animals with which we had been working for years.

The examples listed we feel represent a clear and utter failure of conditioning theory. They are far from what one would normally expect on the basis of the theory alone. Furthermore, they are definite, observable; the diagnosis of theory failure does not depend on subtle statistical interpretations or on semantic legerdemain—the animal simply does not do what he has been conditioned to do.

It seems perfectly clear that, with the possible exception of the dancing chicken, which could conceivably, as we have said, be explained in terms of Skinner's superstition paradigm, the other instances do not fit the behavioristic way of thinking. Here we have animals, after having been conditioned to a specific learned response, gradually drifting into behaviors that are entirely different from those which were conditioned. Moreover, it can easily be seen that these particular behaviors to which the animals drift are clear-cut examples of instinctive behaviors having to do with the natural food getting behaviors of the particular species.

The dancing chicken is exhibiting the gallinaceous birds' scratch pattern that in nature often precedes ingestion. The chicken that hammers capsules is obviously exhibiting instinctive behavior having to do with breaking open of seed pods or the killing of insects, grubs, etc. The raccoon is demonstrating so-called "washing behavior." The rubbing and washing response may result, for example, in the removal of the exoskeleton of a crayfish. The pig is rooting or shaking—behaviors which are strongly built into this species and are connected with the food getting repertoire.

These patterns to which the animals drift require greater physical output and therefore are a violation of the so-called "law of least effort." And most damaging of all, they stretch out the time required for reinforcement when nothing in the experimental setup requires them to do so. They have only to do the little tidbit of behavior to which they were conditioned—for example, pick up the coin and put it in the container—to get reinforced immediately. Instead, they drag the process out for a matter of minutes when there is nothing in the contingency which forces them to do this. Moreover, increasing the drive merely intensifies this effect.

It seems obvious that these animals are trapped by strong instinctive behaviors, and clearly we have here a demonstration of the prepotency of such behavior patterns over those which have been conditioned.

We have termed this phenomenon "instinctive drift." The general principle seems to be that wherever an animal has strong instinctive behaviors in the area of the conditioned response, after continued running the organism will drift toward the instinctive behavior to the detriment of the conditioned behavior and even to the delay or preclusion of the reinforcement. In a very boiled-down, simplified form, it might be stated as "learned behavior drifts toward instinctive behavior."

All this, of course, is not to disparage the use of conditioning techniques, but is intended as a demonstration that there are definite weaknesses in the philosophy underlying these techniques. The pointing out of such weaknesses should make possible a worthwhile revision in behavior theory.

The notion of instinct has now become one of our basic concepts in an effort to make sense of the welter of observations which confront us. When behaviorism tossed out instinct, it is our feeling that some of its power of prediction and control were lost with it. From the foregoing examples, it appears that although it was easy to banish the Instinctivists from the science during the Behavioristic Revolution, it was not possible to banish instinct so easily.

And if, as Hebb suggests, it is advisable to reconsider those things that behaviorism explicitly threw out, perhaps it might likewise be advisable to examine what they tacitly brought in—the hidden assumptions which led most disastrously to these breakdowns in the theory.

Three of the most important of these tacit assumptions seem to us to be: that the animal comes to the laboratory as a virtual tabula rasa, that species differences are insignificant, and that all responses are about equally conditionable to all stimuli.

It is obvious, we feel, from the foregoing account, that these assumptions are no longer tenable. After 14 years of continuous conditioning and observation of thousands of animals, it is our reluctant conclusion that the behavior of any species cannot be adequately understood, predicted, or controlled without knowledge of its instinctive patterns, evolutionary history, and ecological niche.

In spite of our early successes with the application of behavioristically oriented conditioning theory, we readily admit now that ethological facts and attitudes in recent years have done more to advance our practical control of animal behavior than recent reports from American "learning labs."

Moreover, as we have recently discovered, if one begins with evolution and instinct as the basic format for the science, a very illuminating viewpoint can be developed which leads naturally to a drastically revised and simplified conceptual framework of startling explanatory power (to be reported elsewhere).

It is hoped that this playback on the theory will be behavioral technology's partial repayment to the academic science whose impeccable empiricism we have used so extensively.

Beach, F. A. "The snark was a boojum." American Psychologist, 1950, 5, 115-124.

Breland, K., & Breland, M. "A field of applied animal psychology." American Psychologist, 1951, 6, 202-204.

Hebb, D. O. "The American revolution." American Psychologist, 1960, 15, 735-745.

Lorenz, K. "Innate behaviour patterns." Symposia of the Society for Experimental Biology. No. 4. Physiological Mechanisms in Animal Behaviour. New York: Academic Press, 1950.

Skinner, B. F. "Superstition in the Pigeon." J. exp. Psychol., 1948, 38, 168-172.

Tinbergen, N. "The study of Instinct." Oxford: Clarendon, 1951.

Whalen, R. E. "Comparative psychology." American Psychologist, 1961, 16, 84.

INDEX

Note: **Boldface** numbers indicate illustrations.

C

calm down, rewarding, **162**, 163, 193, 194

car, getting out of, 119, **119**

chaining, 64–65, 98, 236

chasing or lunging, heeling for, 151

chewing, 184–187, 192

chicken training camp, 6–8

children and dog safety, 29, 208–213

choke chains, 92, 93, 135

citronella collars, 92, 93

clarity in training, 67, 69, 70

classical conditioning, 39, 40–45, 236

bridging stimulus in, 68

changing behaviors with, 55

instinctive drift in, 74

operant conditioning and, 47, 53, 85

Pavlov's experiments in, 41–42, **42**

Q&A for, 43–45

real-life occurrences of, 42–43, 43

classical counter-conditioning, 81, 83, **85**

definition of, 82, 236

using, 85–87

clicker training, 6–7, 236

bridging stimulus in, 68, 110, **110**

timing in, **68**, 68–69

cloning, 233–234

collars, 92, 93, 113, 135

"come," 115, 152–157

distractions for, 155, **155**

for fighting, 224

importance of, 153

longer leash for, 155–156, **156**

off-leash practice of, 156–157

teaching, **154**, 154–155

tip for, 156

troubleshooting, 100

variable reinforcement for, 71

when to use, 157

communication, 24–29

approaching dogs and, **26**, 26–28, **27, 28**

body postures in, **20**, 20–22, **21, 22**

exercises for, 34–37

fixing gap in, **108**, 108–113

interpreting message in, 78–79

Q&A for, 29

recording behavior for, 31–32, **32**–34

secondary message in, 25–26

troubleshooting, 99, 100, 101

conditioned response, 42, **42**, 236

conditioned stimulus, 42, **42**, 236

conditioning. *See* classical conditioning; operant conditioning

consistency

of punishment, 91

of training, 67, 69, 140, **141**

continuous reinforcement, 70, 236

Coppinger, Ray and Lorna, 15

Copy Cat, 233–234

corticosteroids, 16

counter-conditioning, 42–43, 81, 236

classical, 82, 83, **85**, 236

operant, 82, 83, 85, **86**, 237

using, 44, 45, 85–87

crates, 177, 181

crate training, 176–179

for housetraining, 180

procedure for, 178–179

for separation anxiety, 195

criteria

defining, 67, 69

troubleshooting, 97, 99, 100, 101

cue words, 103

for barking, 228–229

for crate training, 178–179

exercise for, 113

for heeling, 148

for housetraining, 180

for leave it, 125–126

for lying down, 159, 161

for nipping, 188

pairing behavior with, **109**, 109–110

for sitting, 118

testing understanding of, 162, 172

D

desensitization, 43, 81, 83, **84**

definition of, 82, 236

systematic, 43, 238

using, 85–87

distractions

for "come," 155, 155, 156, 157

for down-stay, 169, 193–194

for heeling, 150

for "place," 173

for sit-stay, 166–167

dog trainers, 199, 206, 219, 224, 240

domestication, 11, 12–17

definition of, 13–14, 236

individual traits and, 16–17

process of, 14–15

tameness and, 15–16

dominance, 197

dominance aggression, 14, 17, 196–199

dominant posture, 32

doorway, waiting to go through, 122

"down," 158–163

adding cue for, 161

games for, 162–163

methods of teaching, 159–160, **161**

reinforcement for, 161

testing understanding of, 162

down-stay, 164–169

games for, 168–169

MannersMinder training system

Dedication

To my parents Raymond and Jackie Yin, who gave me the dog that sparked my interest in dog behavior—a problem Boxer named Max. I thank them for their patience in letting me find my own career path. They are still trying to figure out what I do for a living but they keep their worries to themselves.

Acknowledgments

I would like to thank Alan Bauman, who first introduced me, through a demonstration at a dog training conference, to the power of waiting for the behavior; Trish King, who taught me a number of these exercises, which I've modified for my own use; Marian and Bob Bailey, who helped me understand the unbounded potentials for operant conditioning; Dennis Reis, who expanded my knowledge to horses; Bud Williams, who showed me how to apply the principles to animal herding and movement; Ray Coppinger and Erich Klinghammer, who inspired my interest in ethology; Dr. Don Owings, who encouraged my study of vocal communication in dogs; the Sharper Image for hiring me to perform operant conditioning research that forced me to learn in greater detail how subtle differences in dog-owner interactions have huge impacts on training outcomes; and my Master's advisor, Dr. Ed Price, who allowed me to study dog behavior for my thesis, even though he wanted me to study cattle.

I would also like to thank Jill Pindar, Nancy Abplanalp, and Elaine Last for reviewing sections of this book.

About the Author

Dr. Sophia Yin is a graduate of the UC Davis School of Veterinary Medicine and is the author of three books: *How To Behave So Your Dog Behaves*, *The Small Animal Veterinary Nerdbook*®, a best-selling textbook for veterinarians, and her newest textbook *Low Stress Handling, Restraint, and Behavior Modification of Cats and Dogs*.

Dr. Yin earned her Master's in Animal Science from UC Davis, where she studied vocal communication in dogs and worked on behavior modification in horses, giraffes, ostriches, and chickens. During this time she was also the award-winning pet columnist for the San Francisco Chronicle. Upon receiving her degree focused on animal behavior, Dr. Yin served for five years as a lecturer in the UC Davis Animal Science Department. She taught three upper division undergraduate courses in domestic animal behavior and supervised students in various animal training and behavior research projects. She also developed the Manners Minder positive reinforcement dog training system which can be found at www.MannersMinder.net.

Dr. Yin currently sees behavior house calls, works at San Francisco Veterinary Specialists (www.SFVS.net), writes for several veterinary and popular magazines, has consulted for several zoos, lectures internationally on animal behavior, and has served as a behavior expert for shows such as Dogs 101 on Animal Planet. She is also on the executive board for the American Veterinary Society of Animal Behavior. For more information on animal behavior or to take some of her online animal behavior courses, visit www.DrSophiaYin.com.